COWBOY*S*, ARMAGEDDON,

AND THE TRUTH

Scott Terry's stirring memoir about a boy growing up in the American West illustrates the maiming pain that families can inflict on their members, especially the young and powerless, and the many ways that orthodox religion can isolate and warp its believers. It's also an inspiring depiction of human endurance and the heart-healing balms of generosity and kindness.

—Jeff Mann, author of *Purgatory*

COWBOYS,
ARMAGEDDON,
AND THE TRUTH

How a Gay Child was Saved From Religion

Scott M. Terry

Lethe Press
Maple Shade, NJ

Published in 2012 by Lethe Press, Inc.
118 Heritage Avenue • Maple Shade, NJ 08052-3018

Cover design: Ben Baldwin
Book Design: Toby Johnson

ISBN-13: 978-1-59021-366-7

I wrote this book using the name Scott Terry. That is my real name. Many other names in this story are also real, but I invented a few others, for obvious reasons. Some names have been changed and a few events have been condensed or slightly modified, but that dishonesty aside, this is a memoir of the usual sort —a memoir where I tell things in the way I remember them.

For everyone who didn't know why.

ABOUT THE AUTHOR

A freelance writer, Terry has written warm and fuzzy gardening stories for the San Francisco Chronicle Home & Garden section. In Cowboys, Armageddon, and The Truth, he has produced a gritty and poignant autobiography of an innocent boy escaping an abusive and fanatical childhood.

Scott Terry was raised as a devout Jehovah's Witness. He spent his childhood praying for Armageddon to come and asking God to heal him of his homosexual thoughts. By adulthood, he had escaped the Witness religion and no longer believed in an upcoming apocalypse. Indeed, as a gay man, he had become a real cowboy and was riding bulls in the rodeo. He then attended college to develop into the successful man he is now.

Scott Terry is an urban farmer, a watercolorist, an installation artist and a successful businessman. He lives in Northern California. His website is scottterryprojects.com.

INTRODUCTION

My best grandma died today. In the usual way. Not tragically. Not unexpectedly. Not too soon.

Grams spent her final three years in a storage facility for elderly folks who need assistance with medications and don't remember who they are. In between crossword puzzles, not knowing anyone anymore, and waiting out the boredom of life at Beverly Healthcare in the Bible-thumping Okie town of Anderson, Missouri.

Anderson's a hick town. An easy-to-miss map dot that's so close to the Oklahoma and Arkansas borders that a little shove one way or the other would likely push it into a neighboring state. Not that there's any point to that because in the end, it would still reside in the Bible Belt where people worship The Lord, white bread, the American flag, and Wal-Mart. It's a neglected community buried thick under the weight of religion where the bulk of the population surreptitiously divide themselves into two groups: those who wouldn't dream of missing Sunday church services, and those who always do. The righteous and unrighteous. A town full of folks who genuinely believe they're nice people, and generally are, unless just maybe you turn out to be different.

The religious people in town can be fairly self-righteous but don't always recognize themselves as such. Some get all hot and bothered over the fear of going to hell, which isn't where they think they're headed because they claim to control the only path to salvation and enjoy telling you so. It's a shame when people do that, soaking themselves in superiority and thinking they know where your grandma goes when she isn't alive no more. Believing they own the rights to God and claiming to know your destination after fulfilling your ashes to ashes and dust to dust requirement. Talkin' all about how Grams has gone to heaven to hang out with Jesus, which is where she thought she was headed, too.

They talk about this, even over breakfast. I know these things, because I've been in the middle of such discussion over bacon and eggs in the only restaurant in town. As diners go, the place is a bit of a has-been. Decades ago, it was probably packed with people on its opening day, but since then, the neighborhood has collapsed under community disinterest. The restaurant is situated in the middle of town, along what is now a barren nine-block section from the early part of the last century and on the main street that's naturally called Main Street because it used to be the main street through town... until the Wal-Mart showed up. Main Street is a neglected shell of rural America with countless empty lots and vacant storefronts. The primary problem with Main Street today, other than being pretty much abandoned and somewhat useless, is that it's only paved in the middle, with mud and gravel and potholes along the parts where you park your car. Everything's quiet as hell—not peacefully but disappointingly—cause all the shopping abandoned Anderson for the frontage road outside of town next to the Wal-Mart.

If people from out of town accidentally find themselves in Anderson and wander into the Main Street restaurant looking for eggs Benedict or blueberry coffee cake on the morning menu, they will leave hungry or disappointed. The menu is sparse and the interior's a bit run down, but it's the only choice in town for a morning meal—unless you count the little doughnut shop on the other side of the railroad tracks, or the new Shoney's chain restaurant out by the Wal-Mart.

On my last visit, Grams asked to go to there for breakfast, just to introduce me to the fifty-something blonde woman who owns the place. I don't remember her name, but she was nice and fried eggs well and drove Grams to church every weekend for prayer services to The Lord. She was gracious and kind to my grandmother, and that makes it too bad to have forgotten her name. Grams and I drove to the café for breakfast that morning and parked in the dirt up against the curb, right outside the café front window where you could look through and get a sense of what you were in for. It's not your regular kind of restaurant, in spite of the fact that it smells like bacon and looks fairly ordinary when you walk through the door. It's cozy and greasy with a dozen or so tables, but people don't act normal when they get there. Grams led me in when there wasn't hardly anybody in the place, mostly just empty tables and little conversation, to a big family-style table in back that would logically seat a single party of eight and close to the kitchen where you can talk to the blonde lady who owns the whole deal. She has no employees, so you can watch her do all the cooking and clean up from that particular table…and that's where Grams chose to sit. Alongside three other people who were already occupying that table and were the only other customers and were unrelated and didn't arrive together and were at different stages of working through their own breakfast. They didn't mind when we joined them; in fact, they acted like it was ordinary.

It was pretty damn weird, if you ask me. To crowd around one table with folks you don't know, while surrounded by empty tables that yearn to be filled. There's some weird vibe going on in that diner, but only an out-of-towner would recognize it.

Grams acted like she was best-friends with everyone, but not in a way to make them think she was putting her nose in their business. She couldn't tell me their names or addresses or what anyone did or who they were related to, but the whole table chatted about living just a piece up the road, or two miles around the corner next to the egg farm, or halfway to the neighboring town of Lanagan where all the Anderson old people travel to the Senior Center for two-dollar dinner and dominoes.

Grams introduced me as her favorite grandson from California that morning. Everyone "oooed" and "ahhhd" like it was a really big deal to have traveled all the way out to the Ozarks, but only because they didn't know much about my history with Grams. I never told them, and it wouldn't have made any sense to do so, given that they were strangers to me.

Everyone at that table knew someone who had recently died. That's mostly what they talk about in Anderson over breakfast, people who died, and everyone says the dead people went to be with The Lord. And they hold prayer meetings in that place, too. Right in the middle of breakfast, when folks are getting acquainted and reminiscing about dead people and spreading inexpensive store-bought grape jam on white toast washed down with coffee so weak you might mistake it for tea, 'cause they don't serve any other kinds in that part of the country…at another big round table where six later-arriving men held hands and bowed their heads and prayed to The Lord and took turns reading the Bible out loud for an hour in public while carving off mouthfuls of cold cherry pie in between scriptures for breakfast. Swear to God.

I stood up to leave, paying the bill that was about ten bucks, and unfolded a couple of dollars from my wallet and left it on the table in plain view.

Grams said, "Oh you don't need to do that!" The entire table looked at me with the pity bestowed upon outsiders, and when I protested, the blonde lady laughed and said, "I don't want your money! Take that back!" Apparently, it's abnormal to leave a tip in Anderson.

Anderson is a town of early twentieth-century cottages on big lots, buried behind trees, some in good shape and more on the verge of crumbling to the ground. And trailers. They've got plenty of those. An extraordinarily large part of the population in that corner of the planet gets their mail delivered to disposable single-wide trailers, parked up alongside abandoned buildings that used to be family homes. They live in a part of the country where churches and burger joints inform everyone that "Jesus is Lord" on enormous billboards out front, and I'm glad Grams died there. That's a nice way to end things, in a peaceful town where you feel at home, just before moving above to take up residence with The Lord. Grams loved The Lord. She was a front row Baptist and they generally love The Lord, but the fact is she effectively died a couple of years past when she couldn't remember anyone. The last time we spoke, she asked, "Whose son are you?" Our final phone calls were mostly hollow conversations, my sharing reminders and memories, gently nudging her through a cloud of Alzheimer's, hoping she would remember me.

Now that Grams is dead, I've become overwhelmed by thoughts of things that happened so long ago. Her death has caused me to contemplate The Truth that I knew as a child—a religion that I did not choose—and the truth as I know it today. I've been reflecting on these memories, the bulk of which are mine, a few of which were given to me later by the people who were there. My childhood and that of my sister Sissy was controlled by a religion that prided itself on not being "part of this world," and by people who weren't our intentional parents. The individuals who found themselves in the position of being parents did not do so intentionally or with pleasure, and all of them would have undone that circumstance if given the opportunity. Our world was barren at best, painful at worst...except for the six years in our childhood when we were sent to live with Grams and Gramps for a few long weeks during summer. Those precious few visits were never encumbered by tears or conflicting messages of self-worth. Only the usual pleasures of youth…laughing, singing, berry picking, cake eating, rabbit hunting, and wading through the irrigation ditch on hot afternoons, free from beatings, bruises, and hunger. Even today, those visits give me the greatest memories of my life and I think of them often, a frequent romp through old times, and that has prompted the writing of this story.

This is the truth about what happened then.

HORSE TRADING

My real mother traded me away for a horse. My stepmother, Fluffy, wanted me to have that information when I was seven.

Her name was not, in fact, Fluffy. Not in public. My father referred to her as Fluffy in intimate and private moments, but she would have beaten the living daylights out of me if I had ever called her Fluffy.

I was doing chores in the kitchen that morning, clearing the breakfast dishes from Fluffy's dinette set with her mother, Granny M, while the two of them unexpectedly went off on some tangential and bitter conversation about my mother. I stacked plates from the table, eavesdropping on their complaints, not daring to join but craving information about the woman who had given birth to me. I did not know my mother. People did not say nice things about my mother.

Fluffy griped about the state of things, the non-existence of my mother in particular.

She turned slightly over her shoulder to me and stated, "Your mother traded you to your dad for his horse."

I watched her exit the kitchen, wondering why she had brought that story up again. She'd said it before.

Five steps into the living room carpet, Fluffy found herself overcome with laughter at the epiphany of an unexpected joke. She stopped to throw it in my direction.

"Yeah, and your dad got the short end of the stick." She laughed some more.

I emptied the plates in the sink, not daring to argue. The mere hint of wanting to argue with Fluffy was a sure way to get slapped hard upside the head and besides, I did not know my mother.

Fluffy disappeared into the privacy of her bedroom, a room that was verboten to me. I filled her kitchen sink with soapy water and washed the dirty dishes, trying to recall something meaningful about my mother. Discussions of my mother didn't exist in Fluffy's house, unless you count the snide remarks from Fluffy that showed up once every few years. There were no phone calls with my mother. No visits, of any kind. My memories of her had faded. She was a memory so distant that I wondered if she was simply a figment of my imagination. It seemed so long ago, maybe four years earlier, when I had last seen her. I vaguely remembered our last visit when I was three, in the front seat of her car, when she spit on her fingers and smeared it across my face to erase the dirt I didn't know I had. I remembered squirming around to evade her spit.

And I thought about another day, also when I was three, when Dad drove us over to visit her new apartment after she divorced him, and the thousands of round pebbles embedded in the concrete stairs that led up to her second-floor unit. At the age of seven, I washed dishes in Fluffy's sink, wondering what my mother looked like. I couldn't remember her. I couldn't remember her apartment. I couldn't remember anything about her, except for pebbles and spit.

My sister, Sissy, remembered our mother, and she remembered the divorce. In the privacy of our childhood discussions, she often went on tangents when she claimed that our real mother would eventually reappear and rescue us from Fluffy's house. I never believed her.

—∞—

Here is what I know to be true about my family history, and the circumstances of how my mother met my father. Over the last few decades, people who were right in the middle of things at that time have told me that shortly after my mother entered high school in Los Angeles, her parents each had a midlife crisis. In the year when Mom turned fourteen, her mother, Millie, discovered the Jehovah's Witnesses and embraced all their promises of salvation and near arrival of the end of the world. Two years later, my grandfather, Bob, who was rumored to be an atheist, abandoned his career at the Northrop Aviation Company and then moved his wife and two daughters up to the northern end of the state to breed earthworms on a worm farm in the rural town of Orland.

My mother met my father at the Orland high school where he was fighting like hell to fend off accusations of being an Okie. He was a year older than her, a junior, but he wasn't popular. He wasn't a jock, wasn't the star pupil, or the star of anything. Virgil was born out in the boondocks of a dairy farm in rural Missouri, but raised on a cattle ranch in the mountains west of Orland in the California soon-to-be ghost town of Newville. In those days, the residents of Newville, half of which were my family, could be counted on two hands. My father escaped from their lowest rung of poverty when my grandparents abandoned their one-bedroom cabin in Newville and moved their horses and five children to the neighboring town of Willows, then Orland—rising one rung higher.

At that time, in California, there was a clear distinction between cowboys and Okies. Today, it would be considered an imperceptible difference, but when my father was growing up, there was an enormous chasm between the two. Cowboys of the day were tolerable. They could be wealthy landowners. Movie stars, even. Okies weren't. Not tolerable, never wealthy. Okies were just a tidal wave of poverty that swept into California in the 1930s and '40s, and my father was part of that immigration.

Virgil drove my mother all the way to the neighboring town of Chico to have dinner at the Peking Chinese restaurant on Main Street for their very first date, and they later conceived their first child, my older sister Sissy, in the front seat of his truck. In 1961, circumstances such as that required a hasty wedding.

Grandma Millie pulled my mother aside and told her that she didn't have to marry Virgil. Not if she didn't love him. "Do you love him?" she asked.

"Yes," replied my mother, but only from the fear that her father's sense of pride wouldn't have it any other way. My mother would marry Virgil, by God. They were escorted to Reno for a dishonorable wedding on a cold December morning in a miserable caravan of two cars—no one said boo until halfway through the drive when growling stomachs forced them to stop for a late breakfast.

Breakfast was lengthy and heavy, I've been told. My father ordered trout off of the dinner menu at a time of day when roadside diners aren't generally prepared to serve trout. Grandpa Bob grew increasingly impatient. He drank coffee at the table, pissed at the marriage, pissed at having to drive to Reno, and pissed at having to wait for trout.

Virgil consumed his breakfast fish while everyone else had the normal fare of pancakes or eggs, then the wedding party continued on to Reno. They parked in front of a downtown chapel—one of the nicer ones in town, my mother was told. She wore a cheap grey suit because Grandma Terry informed her that she couldn't wear white. The ceremony was short and sterile, no photos were taken, then everyone loaded into the cars out front and drove back to Orland.

My mother dropped out of school, her parents sold the worm farm and moved back to Los Angeles, and my married parents, still teenagers, followed them. They moved into a little apartment in Inglewood, then Grandpa Bob reclaimed his job at Northrop and talked his boss into giving Virgil an entry level position. A few months after accepting it, Virgil complained about being cooped up in an office building and quit. He then took the grocery store position in El Segundo, only to discover that he didn't want to be a long-term grocery store man. He came home from work each day to sit on the couch and stare at the TV, and that's when my mother saw where her life was headed and divorced him.

He took the two kids as part of the divorce agreement—a horse trade, Fluffy called it, but her assertion was untrue. My mother did not ask for the horse. Dad sent his horse back up to his father in Orland, and he then joined the Jehovah's Witnesses. No one seems to know why.

Virgil was now a single father with two children, at his age of twenty-two.

We were cute kids, but no more so than other children. I was a perfectly average looking little boy with a potbelly. My brown hair tended to be unruly. My mother picked us up for visits every now and then. Each time she delivered us back to Dad, Sissy threw angry screaming fits that lasted for weeks. Her separation anxiety was visceral and devastating. I was amiable and even-tempered, absorbing the chaos of life easily, but Sissy was a train wreck after our parents split. She didn't handle the divorce well.

Dad struggled with affording our care, so he sent us to Orland for a few months.

I went to Orland to live with Grams and Gramps, and Sissy went to the neighboring town of Chico to live with Aunt Donnis, Dad's oldest sister.

Aunt Donnis cuddled Sissy in bed and referred to her as "Chocolate Eyes" in affectionate moments, trying to soften the fact that Sissy's four-year-old vocabulary was dominated by "Goddamn It" and "Fuck" and "I want some Goddamn cookies!"

Virgil retrieved us from his parents in Orland, and then moved us into a little brown house in Los Angeles. I remember it. It is my oldest memory from childhood. For a short time, we lived in a little brown house with one bedroom. One bed for three people in a little brown house.

My earliest memory is of me sitting in bed amidst a tangle of blankets in that little brown house, early in the morning, watching my father walk to the bathroom in his underwear. Sissy played on the floor with her horn-rimmed glasses that she was supposed to be wearing. They were supposed to fix her eyes, but didn't. People knew she was fixin' to break them.

I watched my father stand at the sink and shave for work. A year had passed since the divorce. I no longer remembered it. I had just turned three.

Virgil dressed, then smoked a cigarette.

An old lady in a sacky but flowery dress that hung well down below her knees knocked on the front door. She had been to our house before. Babysitters showed up often. Old ladies, mostly.

She poured cereal for our breakfast in the kitchen.

Dad walked out the front, leaving for work at the El Segundo Grocery where he bagged groceries.

A few months later, we got a new babysitter who wasn't so old and who let me eat the crumbs from the bottom of her cookie jar after her children finished the cookies. She turned the cookie jar upside down to shake the crumbs in a bowl, and I ate the veritable gumbo of cookie dust with a spoon. I bent down and peaked under the folds of her dress, partially wanting to see what was under there, mostly wanting to be naughty. I giggled. She got in a fuss, but didn't hit me.

We had a string of babysitters over the next year, each of whom disappeared. My mother had done likewise.

Virgil got a new wife to replace them. He referred to her as "Fluffy" during intimate moments. It was a compliment, he presumed, to privately refer to his soft and fluffy wife by that term. She was our new mother, Virgil said.

----&oooo----

Virgil was introduced to Fluffy in the Jehovah's Witness Kingdom Hall. She was a tall but soft woman who was unaccustomed to physical activity. Fluffy's hair was generally a version of red, often revealing the darker roots beneath. She was plagued by health problems, and she officially became my new mother two weeks after my fourth birthday, at her age of 23.

Their wedding ceremony was solely a Witness affair—an inexpensive but formal occasion where people from our new religion dressed up. Men wrapped skinny black ties around their necks for the event, Fluffy had bridesmaids, and the entire procedure was recorded in the pages of a thick photo album that was displayed on Fluffy's coffee table throughout my childhood. I paged through it more than once, but I wasn't in it. My father's parents didn't attend the function. My father's four sisters, Aunt Donnis, Aunt Dot, Aunt Jan, and Aunt Susan, didn't know about it.

On the morning of Fluffy's wedding, her bridesmaids swamped our rental house and barricaded themselves behind bedroom doors, dressing up and fussing over each other. I hung out in the kitchen corner, backed up against the fridge, watching them prance around, struggling to stay out of their way, wondering who they were and what they were so excited about, and not having a clue as to why everyone vanished shortly after they dressed in their very best clothes. En masse, they left for the ceremony, and Sissy and I sat home with a babysitter.

Fluffy's mother became our new grandmother that day. Granny M, we called her. She gave us Danish pastries and hot cups of Lipton tea with sugar for breakfast the next morning while Virgil and Fluffy consummated their marriage in Las Vegas. For months after, a gold wedding ring adorned Virgil's left hand, until it got caught on the edge of a chain link fence as he was climbing over top and about yanked his finger off. From there on out, if asked, he would point to the scar and rub it in memories of pain and swear that rings were too dangerous for him to ever wear again.

Virgil was a very thin man when he married Fluffy. A year later, he was no longer considered trim and handsome. Grandma Terry walked into our El Segundo house for a visit at that time and greeted him with, "Hello Fatty." That hurt his feelings.

When introducing himself to strangers, he had a tendency to stick his hand out for a shake and say, "Hi. Clyde Kadiddlehopper." When they grasped his hand in greeting, pondering the humor of Clyde Kadiddlehopper, they undoubtedly noticed that his hands were exceptionally small. And they perhaps glanced at his narrow shoulders, which he passed on to me. If he had removed his cowboy hat, which he wouldn't have, they would have been confronted by a pale and sweaty scalp, strings of hair plastered over top. They wouldn't have known he was bald unless they ran into him at the Jehovah's Witness Kingdom Hall where he couldn't cover everything over with a hat, because you can't just walk into a Kingdom Hall and stand at the podium and preach to the congregation about Jehovah while wearing a cowboy hat. You just can't.

So I now find myself as an adult, unfolding memories and reassembling the whole mess on paper with a little boy stumbling around in the middle of things, interrupting my concentration, begging for his version to be heard, too. I've been carrying that kid around my entire life, listening to his fears and frustrations, memories and tears...but he's suddenly become urgently vocal, wanting a piece of this. Insisting it won't be fair if I don't let him talk, too. Demanding equal time in this unexpected opportunity to share his story. Wanting something he craved as a child, but was denied. To be heard.

I wrestled with him at first, because how does one choose? Who could best write this story—the grown man who found a need to share his memories, or the little boy who would change them if he could? Do I give that kid an opportunity to speak? That's generally the point of a memoir, isn't it? So I will share it with him, my inner child, with young impressions and vivid memories, demanding to be heard. Such as his following description of my father:

He likes to cuss about 'Sam Hell' a lot. Especially when he's mad at you for tryin' to get somethin' to eat when no one's lookin'. He yells, "What in the Sam Hell are you doin'?"...but he can't admit to saying 'Hell' 'cause Jehovah wouldn't like that.

Dad gets really mad if you tell him he said 'hell.' We don't believe in hell, there ain't no such thing as hell...but Dad says 'Sam Hell' when he gets mad. If you ask him about that, he'll yell and say he wasn't cussin' at all and was only talkin' about some guy named Sam Hill that nobody's ever met...but it isn't true. He says "hell." All the time. I've heard him.

Virgil wouldn't have been caught dead in a pair of shorts on a hot summer day in Los Angeles. His wardrobe was 100% cowboy. There were three western style dress suits hanging in his closet, and he wore them with cowboy boots to the Kingdom Hall for three religious meetings each week. Several guns were stacked upright in the closet, next to his boots, and I was an unwilling spectator to many arguments between him and Fluffy over the cost of dog food, horse hay, ammunition, and vet bills.

He first took me hunting when I was five.

I climbed into the front seat of his creaky old step-side pickup, mindful to keep my legs from getting tangled around the shotgun that rested between us, unloaded, while we drove to the barren hills on the outskirts of Los Angeles. He parked the rusty truck at the dead end of an unpaved road.

We exited into the dust and he pulled the shotgun out of the cab, loaded several shells into the magazine, then leaned it over his shoulder, muzzle pointed upwards.

He warned, "You stay behind me, you hear?"

I would tote the portable victims, he promised. Dead quail destined for our dinner table.

We climbed the first hill, not a pretty hill, weaving our way through cactus and scrub brush of the southern California desert. Halfway up, Virgil said, "Scott…you go that way and walk around the hill. I'll meet you back on this side."

"Go what way?" I asked, horrified.

"Just walk around to the other side of the hill. If there's any quail over there, you'll scare them over to me. I'll stay here and shoot them when they fly over. And I'll stay right here and wait for you."

I didn't want to go. I didn't trust his intentions. I could get lost. He might go back to Fluffy's without me. I didn't know. I wouldn't go. I was about to cry.

Virgil gave in to my visible fear, and we traipsed around for several hours after that. I followed him up and down the hills, ten steps behind on account of the fact that he was carrying a gun, lugging quail carcasses in silence, happy to do so, unsure I was doing it right, discovering that dead quail are warm and limp, with heads that flop around lifelessly until rigor mortis sets in, swinging them around by their dead little heads. Swinging them by their dead little feet. I poked at their feathers. Poked at their glazed eyeballs. Happy to spend time with my dad.

After Virgil's marriage to Fluffy had survived a full year, Grandpa Terry sent him another horse to replace the one he had lost during the divorce. The new horse was young and unbroken, and it put Virgil in the hospital with a white bandage over a bloodied nose.

Fluffy drove us over to see him after visiting hours had ended. Sissy and I stood out on the sidewalk in the dark and stretched our arms upwards to wave at him as he stuck his bandaged nose through the second floor window to say hello and attest to the fact that he was still alive. Not long after, Virgil traded Grandpa's gift for a new and better horse named Misty. That hurt Grandpa's feelings because, let's face it, a gift of a horse isn't comparable to receiving a pink sweater. No one will be offended if you politely explain that pink isn't your best color and you intend to exchange it for, say, a blue one, but a gift of a horse is a different set of circumstances. When someone gives you a horse, you shouldn't run right out and trade it for a different one.

I'M A BAD KID AND
SO ARE YOU

"In case a man happens to have a son who is stubborn and rebellious, he not listening to the voice of his father or the voice of his mother, and they have corrected him but he will not listen to them, his father and his mother must also take hold of him and bring him out to the older men of his city and to the gate of his place, and they must say to the older men of his city, 'This son of ours is stubborn and rebellious; he is not listening to our voice, being a glutton and a drunkard.' Then all the men of his city must stone him with stones, and he must die." Deuteronomy 21:18-21 - The New World Translation of the Holy Scriptures.

Fluffy was a pale, tall, and hefty woman who mostly wore cheap stretchy polyester pants from Kmart. Her father had died years earlier in Pittsburgh, but I don't know how. Her family moved to California shortly after, but I don't know why. They could just as well have gone to Toledo. It would have been an easier and shorter drive from Pittsburgh if they had packed up their stuff and traveled to Toledo. Things would have been better if Fluffy had found herself in Toledo. Or Winnemucca. But she moved to Los Angeles while in high school—Hawthorne, to be specific—

and hadn't the slightest interest in hunting, horses, stepkids, or any details defining my dad's life.

Before meeting my father, Fluffy had only known one encounter with a horse—a short carnival ride in Pittsburgh when an unruly pony bucked her off, hung her up in the stirrup by her tennis shoe, and dragged her down the road, fracturing her spine. My dad sometimes lectured her on the fact that she only got hung up because she wasn't wearing cowboy boots, a detail that wasn't particularly helpful because Fluffy didn't own any of those.

Fluffy was born and raised as a Jehovah's Witness, and she decided I was defective when Virgil began dating her and made the mistake of taking me to her house to have dinner with her mother for the first time. During our visit, I discovered an open tube of toothpaste in their bathroom and emptied the contents over their rug. I don't remember committing that crime, but it sounds like fun. Fluffy and her mother didn't find it fun and reminded me of my terrible toothpaste mishap many times while I was growing up. It appeared frequently over the years, an incessant and monotonous reminder of their discovery that I was a bad kid...on my first visit to their house at the age of three.

In the first few months of Fluffy's marriage to Virgil, she went to some big office building every morning to perform secretary duties and her Uncle Clarence and Aunt Mabel played the reluctant role of our babysitter. Uncle Clarence had a small 1940s house, a no-character single-story box for a home, stucco, on a busy street with flowers along the driveway and a dinky little square of lawn masquerading as a front yard. We weren't allowed to play in it because it was too close to the street. He grew flowers under his front window and along the driveway.

I underestimated the value of those flowers and waded right through the middle of them, fascinated by the path of destruction left behind in my wake.

Fluffy dragged me into the house and put me in the corner behind Uncle Clarence's favorite chair as punishment.

"You can just stand in the corner," she said. "And put your arms up above your head! I want to see your arms above your head!"

I stretched my arms upwards and held them in place while staring at the emptiness of a blank wall.

Fluffy walked across the room to occupy the couch.

"I will spank your butt if you let your arms down," she threatened.

She parked herself on Uncle Clarence's old furniture and turned her focus to his TV. She could monitor my punishment easily from there, without turning her head, even.

I felt her occasional gaze on my back. My arms soon tired. They drooped lower.

"Scott! Put your arms back up! I'm gonna spank you if you don't keep your arms up!"

My arms grew heavy…I couldn't hold them up much longer…a spanking was inevitable…then Granny M walked in the front door. She had words with Fluffy, and I spent the rest of my punishment with my arms down at my sides.

Uncle Clarence's house burned down a few weeks later. It was my fault. Sissy's, too. Apparently, it blew up because our toys were too close to the heater and they caught on fire and that was the end of Uncle Clarence's home. For years after, Fluffy and her mother distributed occasional reminders that we were responsible for the fiery demise of Clarence's house, just another example of how they knew we were terrible stepkids.

I never knew why I was bad. If I had been a better kid, Fluffy might have liked me. That's what I thought, then. In my eyes, she was an overweight and angry redhead with foul-tempered hair ranging from auburn to orange and all the shades in between, impossible to please. And big puffy lips that got lipstick smears on her coffee cups. Sissy often whispered to me, "Fluffy looks like a fish."

And phlebitis. She had phlebitis. When you have phlebitis, you have to lay on your back a lot. On the couch, with your feet elevated, which means they have to be higher than your head. And you have to wear thick white stockings that go all the way up to your crotch. Fluffy spent most days griping about how ugly they were. Every once in awhile she got up off the couch and stomped around the house all grouchy in her stockings, complaining about phlebitis.

—∞—

Fluffy had a passion for snacking on Planter's dry roasted peanuts, and Chinese egg rolls on the rare occasions when we went out for Chinese food. She would share neither. She intentionally chewed gum in a manner that popped and crackled, and her most favorite activity in the whole wide world was stacking Elvis records on her stereo, her entire collection, playing him over and over for hours, for years, while occasionally interrupting with a breathy sigh and the announcement, "That's my man!" She had just about every Elvis album there ever was, except for the Christmas records, of course. That would be a sin. Jehovah's Witnesses don't do Christmas, or birthdays, or any other celebrations that they consider "worldly." Marriages, wedding anniversaries, and baby showers are the only occasions that aren't tainted by the worldly definition.

Fluffy's house often swayed to the sounds of Elvis, except for the single unusual summer afternoon when Virgil showed up with a John Denver album. *Rocky Mountain High* briefly pushed Elvis aside, until we heard the horrible rumor that John Denver had a severe dislike for Jehovah's Witnesses. I don't know if that piece of gossip had any truth to it and he's now dead, purportedly spending eternity in the presence of The Lord, but Mr. Denver was rumored to have opened one of his concerts by demanding that all Witnesses in attendance get the hell out, just because he was pissed that we had the gall to invade his doorstep with a *Watchtower* magazine one too many times. So that was the end of enjoying John Denver. He got shoved into the depths of the stereo cabinet, never again to see the light of day.

Other than dreaming of a passionate rendezvous with Elvis, Fluffy had no hobbies. She didn't learn things. She didn't collect stuff. Her house was spotlessly empty. Her outlook on life was the antithesis of a hoarder, and she wrapped her new vinyl couch and dining room chairs in plastic for protection. She didn't have much for friends, unless you count the divorced lady who Fluffy converted to the Jehovah's Witness religion in 1968. She didn't read books for fun, unless you count *Coma* in 1978. She had a minimalist life, composed of nothing other than sitting on the couch sick, watching TV, and caring for her son, Grant, and later, her daughter Amber (who I'll tell you about soon), plus the two stepchildren she didn't ask for. And inventing chores. That was about the closest thing to a hobby that Fluffy had…inventing chores.

My first chore was cashing empty Pepsi bottles at the grocery store with Sissy and struggling to haul full bottles back home for Fluffy, at my age of five.

It wasn't terribly far, not a long walk, only a few blocks to the nearest market.

Sissy and I headed down the street, through our Los Angeles neighborhood, sharing the weight of the bottles.

A block from home, they became heavy for me. I passed them to Sissy.

When they were tiresome for her, she gave them back to me.

I stumbled at the curb and slammed the six-pack of empties on the pavement, breaking the bottoms of two bottles.

We wallowed in debate and consternation, thinking we should walk back home and confess, hoping Fluffy wouldn't spank us hard.

Sissy would share my punishment for carelessness that wasn't her fault, so I left it in her hands to devise a plan.

We continued our slow walk to the store while Sissy mulled in thought. Outside the store entrance, she announced her plan to separate the Pepsi buyer from the shattered glass. Sissy disappeared into the aisles and pulled a new six-pack of Pepsi off the grocery store shelf, then she walked it to the checkout stand, that was her role in the plan, while I remained up front, waiting for her. I stood a safe distance away, displaying our empty bottles to the cashier, cheerfully offering to place them inside a wire bin holding those returned by other people, just to be helpful, feeling very clever, while Sissy distracted the gentleman cashier who said, "Thank you," and I gently lowered our broken bottles into the wire cage, fearing he would inspect them first.

In addition to those occasional Pepsi runs, my daily chores included a search for dog dirt. Everyone else considered it "poop," but we called it "dirt" 'cause "poop" is obviously a bad word. I was never proficient at collecting dog dirt and frequently went to bed hungry as punishment.

My dad couldn't live without a dog. Sometimes two, sometimes ten. Bird dogs and cattle dogs. Purebreds. Dogs and horses of pedigreed bloodlines were proof that he had escaped from Okie poverty. He wouldn't stand for a mutt. Most were chained up in our backyard and I loved every one of them, they were my friends, except perhaps for Fluffy's toy poodle Princess because she was Fluffy's property and wasn't a real dog, anyway.

Our first dog was Princess, but she doesn't count. The second was Petey. Petey arrived when I was in kindergarten during the six months we spent in a two-bedroom rental with a little one-room playhouse built up against the backyard fence. Sissy and I used the neglected space behind that playhouse as a bathroom dump when Dad wasn't home…hidden from view and squatting over a two foot hole dug by Petey…being reluctant to enter Fluffy's house for a potty break…knowing Petey would eat the evidence we deposited in the dirt…until the day when Dad returned empty-handed from a day of hunting and simply stated that Petey got bit by a rattlesnake, so Dad had shot him dead and left his carcass out in the hills. I cried. My dad might have cried too, but I didn't guess so at the time, given his nonchalant explanation for how we lost Petey.

Sissy's first and primary household task was washing the dinner dishes. She was instructed to wash, I was instructed to dry. They didn't trust me to wash at my age of five. Shortly after taking on dishwashing duty, Sissy ruined Fluffy's new electric skillet by submerging it in water. Fluffy never forgave her.

Our Sunday evenings in particular, were reserved for three things in a specific and mandatory order—washing dishes, taking a bath, then enjoying *Mutual of Omaha's Wild Kingdom* with Marlin Perkins, followed by *The Wonderful World of Disney*.

Sissy stood on a brown vinyl dinette chair with gold trim in front of the sink, the dirty dishes piled inside.

I stood next to her, on a matching chair.

Sissy washed the cups first. Plates were next, then silverware from the bottom.

She passed each piece into the next sink, full of rinse water.

I stacked them into the drainer, wiped them dry, then nudged Sissy to speed things along. Washing and drying did not have similar timeframes.

"Hurry up!" I whispered. "Mutual of Omaha just started."

Sissy moved on to the skillets. She couldn't hurry up on skillets. Pots and skillets had their own timeframes. Hurry up got us nowhere. Hurry up got us in trouble. *Mutual of Omaha* was almost over. We frantically tried to get the dishes done and take our turns in the bathtub before *Disney* started, risking the chance of Fluffy finding a dirty item the next day, something we hadn't washed properly. A bowl with a bit of dried food caked inside. Perhaps traces of Fluffy's lipstick from the previous day, still smeared red across the edge of a cup.

When Fluffy found dirty dishes, something we hadn't washed properly, she added an additional chore as punishment—washing every single dish and pot and skillet from every cupboard in her kitchen, dishes that were already clean, silverware included, just to hammer home the importance of cleaning dishes properly the first time.

Nothing that came out of her head made sense to me. Fluffy was haunted by visions of automobile doors abruptly flying open down the freeway—ejecting occupants all over the road. I'm sure of it. Back then, no one believed in seat belts, they weren't mandatory, but Fluffy was convinced that car doors could burst open at the slightest provocation and she would reach over to the back seat and pinch the hell out of the nearest body part on any sleeping stepkid who committed the unforgivable sin of leaning against the door… just to ease her terrible visionary seizures of your tragically flying out into the path of other vehicles…cause there you'd be, splattered all over the road. She'd have to pay someone to clean up the bloody mess out there on the freeway. She'd be really pissed that you cost her money, to clean up the mess and everything, it would probably cost millions, but wouldn't matter, 'cause you'd just be squished all over the road and that's why you're never ever supposed to lean against a car door. It was a rule.

—∞—

A year after Virgil married Fluffy, on a night when he was away stocking shelves at El Segundo Grocery, Sissy suggested that we should go live with my mom's parents, Grandma Millie and Grandpa Bob. She thought things would work out better that way, she said.

Fluffy was reclining on the couch with her mother, watching TV. She was pregnant. She took great offense at Sissy's recommendation.

"You're ungrateful for what I've done for you? Fine! Then go pack your stuff and get out. You think your grandmother wants you? Then get out! Go live with her."

We stalled in confusion, not knowing how to comply.

Fluffy rose up partway from the couch. "Hurry up! Go pack your clothes and get out!"

We ran to the back porch to shove our belongings into two child-sized paisley suitcases—gifts from Grandma Millie, overnight cases, really. Mine was blue. Sissy's was pink. Boys get blue and girls get pink.

I pulled clothes out of the brown four-drawer dresser that I shared with Sissy, then stuffed the small pile into my luggage.

From the living room, Fluffy screamed, "You can't take anything you didn't pay for!" She lifted herself off of the couch to stomp over and inspect the contents of my suitcase.

She pulled a shirt from inside and waved it at me. "You didn't pay for this! What did I tell you? You can't take anything you didn't pay for!"

Under her glare, I removed most of the clothes from my suitcase. Gifts from grandparents were allowed to stay, given the definition of gift.

Light suitcases in hand, Fluffy then escorted us out the front door with a good riddance comment of, "Good luck with finding someone who wants you."

Sissy stepped off of Fluffy's front porch.

I followed, wishing she would learn to keep her mouth shut. I didn't want to get kicked out of Fluffy's house, it wasn't my argument, but Sissy had opened her mouth again and we were a packaged deal.

Four steps down to the driveway, a few more steps to the curb, we rounded the chain link fence along the sidewalk...Fluffy closed the door behind her...tropical jungle plants typical of southern California neighborhoods, hiding hordes of snails in her front yard...a short and spiky palm tree in the backyard...a few dried-up paint cans stacked on an otherwise empty garage shelf by a previous resident...Granny M still sitting on the couch, watching TV.

Several steps ahead, Sissy was on a mission to arrive somewhere I didn't know, in the dark, little brother in tow. She stopped at a house where the children shared her second grade class—not enough reason to show up on their doorstep, I thought.

She rang their doorbell.

Their father leaned out the door.

"We don't have a place to live anymore," she told him. "But if you call my Grandma Millie, she'll come get us."

The stunned man called for his wife, then let us in. His children ran around frenzied, unsure how to react to our invasion. They said hello to Sissy, but didn't know me.

From the outside, their house was like ours, a cheap box of post-war 1940's construction, but their interior was decidedly unlike Fluffy's. Their home was packed with furniture...stuff strewn everywhere...a stark contrast to the emptiness of Fluffy's. I escaped to the children's bedroom and staked out a small corner of their bed, feeling terribly guilty for delivering chaos to their home, surrounded by their toys and belongings, wondering if their mom and dad would be angry at having two new mouths to feed... hoping we would live with them until Grandma Millie could rescue us...wondering if they might feed us dinner before sending us to bed...watching the unfamiliar children frantically run in and out of the room while their parents debated what to do, and I wondered how it would be to live with a family who I imagined thought we were horrible for not having any place to live.

But that didn't happen. They called the police, and a few uniformed officers escorted us back to Fluffy's.

To this day, I imagine my father knows nothing of that incident. Neither Sissy nor I ever told him. There was no solace to be found in our father. Fluffy wielded her parental authority with amazing vengeance, and we didn't dare tell him what had transpired that night. Our fear of her had only begun to grow.

———— ∞ ————

Fluffy's first child, her son, Grant, came along a few months later. I learned of his conception late at night in a liquor store parking lot.

Virgil pulled up to the rear wall of a liquor store and left his vehicle running in the pitch blackness of the evening. He ran around to the front entrance of the brick building. He wouldn't be gone long, he said. Our headlights reflected off the wall, illuminating the car interior. I was alone with Fluffy, she in front, me in back, and she used the empty moment to inform me of Grant's existence inside of her.

She seemed happy to share the news, smiling even, but I found it slightly traumatic. Up to that point, I had thought of my family arrangement as a fairly fluid environment where people came and went, houses and babysitters changed, and Sissy and I were temporarily shuffled off to various relatives, but learning of Grant's upcoming arrival was the moment when I realized that Fluffy was going to be around for awhile.

Grant entered the world as a fussy and sickly child, a problem inherited from his mother, so she and Virgil once found themselves discussing the possibility that a glass of wine might quiet him down. A little bit of wine wouldn't hurt him that night, they agreed. Somehow, the specifics of which parent would dole out the wine got mixed up, and both unknowingly gave him a short glass of white Tyrolia wine from a screw cap bottle. He wasn't yet two, but after giggling and rolling around on the couch for an hour, he fell asleep drunk.

You can't tell people that Grant's mother is really your stepmother, 'cause Dad says that's disrespectful. If you tell anyone that she isn't your real mother, he'll get all mad and make a speech about how you're being disobedient and then he'll spank you with his belt and yell about how your new mom's getting tired of putting up with you, except you know she doesn't want to be your new mom and he knows it, too. But everyone pretends like she does, 'cause it would be disrespectful if you don't.

He calls her Fluffy when they're hugging and kissing in the kitchen. She giggles and acts embarrassed and pretends she doesn't like it when he calls her "Fluffy," but she really does, 'cause that's how she knows Dad likes her. She would kill him if he ever called her Fluffy in public.

ON THE MOVE

"Pow! Pow!" Blood-thirsty Indians were massacring cowboys in our front yard.

I killed the next-door neighbor boy several times in a mock gunfight, stretched out behind a mound of dirt in the front yard of our rental house, one of our many rental houses—never more than six months in each.

"Pow!"

This particular rental was a duplex with a concrete wall for a backyard and a big, empty and neglected square of front yard filled with devil-grass patches and dirt piles. Virgil bought dog biscuits for his new bird dog Britty at that house, but Sissy and I thought they tasted just fine and consumed half the box when he wasn't looking. That's the same rental where I threw a rock through the neighbor's garage window, just to see if it would break. It did.

But on this particular day, I stretched out behind a soft hump of soil in the front yard, feeling protected and firing make-believe bullets at the next-door-neighbor kid who pretended to be a cowboy.

"Pow! Pow!"

I was a gun-toting Indian. Sissy was a squaw, or a beautiful Indian princess, depending on whose fantasy you entered. Sissy didn't look much like a princess. Or a squaw. She did not have a pretend-gun, nor did she crawl around in the dirt. An Indian princess would not crawl around in the dirt.

"Pow pow pow!"

Fluffy stuck her head out the front door and screamed, "Scott! Get over here! You cannot pretend to kill people! Jehovah doesn't like that. Now get in the house until your father gets home!"

We moved to another two-bedroom rental a few months later, directly across from a public laundromat...a bedroom down the hall that I shared with Sissy...walls painted baby blue...watching *Flipper* on Fluffy's TV in the living room...popping zits on Dad's back at his insistence while he stretched out face down on Fluffy's bed when she wasn't home, assuring us it didn't hurt to have his pimples pinched hard, and then asking if we got the white stuff out.

My bed looked directly into the kitchen of that rental. I lay under the blankets each morning after our father had left for work, Sissy in another bed across the room, waiting for Fluffy's permission to get up. Lying in bed for what felt like eternity, waiting for the back door to swing wide open when Granny M came over to rescue us and pour Post Toasties cereal for our breakfast.

Fluffy had a worn-out gray Formica and chrome kitchen table with four chairs in that house, squeezed up against a kitchen wall across from the sink so we had to pull it away from the wall at dinner time if we wanted to make room for two adults and two stepkids. She slapped my hands at that table and got really angry if I held my fork wrong. Or if I chewed with my mouth open. She'd reach across the table and pinch me hard for that.

There was an evening in that very rental when Sissy wasn't home for dinner, but I can't remember why. I must have known then, but I don't know now. But we didn't have to pull the table out that night, on account of only needing to seat two people and one stepkid, and I sat next to Dad, across from Fluffy, knowing she was miserable on account of being forced to sit at an itty bitty table in a dumpy rental house with a clueless stepchild who didn't know how to hold his fork right.

After dinner, I lay in bed sideways and squinted my eyes halfway tight, blurring the view of the clothes hamper in the hallway, making it jiggly and distorted, easy to imagine it was a boogey man, right outside my bedroom door, ready to invade my blue bedroom at any moment, but all I had to do was make my eyes go back to normal and the hamper magically returned to its previous state, easily identifiable as a receptacle for dirty clothes and not a boogey man at all.

The next morning, Fluffy sent me to my blue bedroom with an order to get dressed in meeting clothes for the Sunday meeting at the Kingdom Hall. For the first time, I stood on Sissy's bed and leaned in to pull my clothes down from the top rack in the closet—Sissy's clothes occupied the bottom—and dressed myself without grown-up assistance in a pair of pants and a short-sleeved buttoned-down shirt, then ran back to the living room to model my clothing choices, imagining Fluffy might like me better, now that I could dress myself.

⸻

In the first three years of Virgil's marriage to Fluffy, we lived in El Segundo, Redondo Beach, Hawthorne, and Inglewood, and we even moved to Seattle for a few months where Fluffy had a serious hate relationship with the damp and cold weather.

After leaving El Segundo, we moved to a two-story house in Redondo Beach that shook like crazy in the San Fernando earthquake on February 9, 1971. I slept on a white vinyl foldout couch in the den on the first floor and was solidly asleep when the shaking erupted at 6 am. I never understood why our Redondo Beach rental had a den, or why it was called a "den," or why the den was my room but we couldn't call it "my room" because it was a den, after all, but that's where I slept through the trembler until

Fluffy staggered downstairs all worked up, traumatized, claiming to have ridden her rolling bed all over the second floor. Sissy and I walked to school that morning, searching for cracks in the sidewalk from the huge quake that killed 65 people—a quake that I never felt.

In those early years of living with Fluffy, stealing from her was my greatest sin. I had a tendency to get up in the middle of the night, hungry…waiting until everyone had gone to bed…thinking it was safe to steal when I heard my father's snore…Fluffy didn't snore…creeping into the kitchen under the cover of darkness to steal a banana or slice of Fluffy's raisin bread. Darkness did not, as I believed, make me quieter…an instant spanking when Fluffy caught me, sometimes a spanking the next day when Fluffy's morning banana count came up one short.

If there was a banana in Fluffy's kitchen, chances were good I would steal it. After quietly consuming the sweet fruit in the blackness of the den, I stuffed the bruised peel under my fold-out couch, resulting in a delayed spanking every time she went looking for proof of my thievery. It was a sure bet on their part. If I was in need of a spanking, they only had to investigate the depths of my couch to find justification.

Granny M once suggested, in front of me, that a little snack before bedtime might reduce my tendency to steal…a suggestion that I turned into a fantasy, believing they would heed her advice and give me a banana at night. Or maybe a Twinkie.

Fluffy buried a hoard of silver Mercury dimes in a glass jar in the bottom drawer of her desk in the den of the Redondo Beach rental, and over the course of several weeks in first grade, I stole them. For several weeks after first discovering the dimes, a single and collectible coin resided in my front pocket on my morning walk to school. At lunchtime, I retrieved it in the cafeteria to buy milk for five cents or Fudgesicles for ten cents. The lady who gave out the Fudgesicles eventually asked Fluffy why I was spending what was obviously a coin collection. Fluffy removed the remaining dimes from the den before I could spend them all.

We left Redondo Beach for a new rental, and I joined a new school. My new first grade class rode the bus to Olvera Street in Los Angeles to visit the Mexicans. Olvera Street was the only remaining block of original California history in the antique section of Los Angeles, and we traveled there for a long afternoon of immersion in the Mexican lifestyle. We invaded the abnormally long block on a school fieldtrip, poking our heads in trinket shops and drenched in the intense cacophony of Mexican flavors. Mexican colors screamed from Olvera Street. Green. Red. Yellow. Piñatas draped from overhangs and mariachi music blared from doorways, filling the afternoon air. Everything Mexican was loud, vibrant, and colorful. Olvera Street was fully alive. My classmates bought Mexican food for lunch and Mexican souvenirs to carry home on the bus.

A female chaperone took up a collection from all the other ladies who rode our bus to Olvera Street, convincing them to donate a quarter or two to the only kid who didn't have money for lunch.

"Open your hands," she said.

I folded my hands into a cup, and that kind lady poured a whole handful of change into them.

"Now you can buy lunch."

I stared at her in disbelief, basking in the unexpected wealth and wondering if it would cause trouble at home. I bought a Mexican lunch and a hollowed-out chicken egg souvenir stuffed with paper confetti, and then avoided her for the rest of the day, fearing she would ask for her money back. On our bus ride home, I cradled my egg souvenir in my lap, and a block from Fluffy's, I threw it at a parked car, disposing of the evidence. Confetti cascaded over the hood.

I had money left over when I got home, but I didn't tell Fluffy about that. I buried it in a hole alongside the driveway and covered it up with a clump of grass. Several days later, I bought Hershey bars for ten cents apiece for me and Sissy from the liquor store around the corner where we more than once had stolen Twinkies.

A few weeks later on the walk home from school, several blocks from Fluffy's, I ran out into traffic, chasing a classmate across the street, and collided with a car that wasn't speeding. I crashed into the driver's side of a slow moving sedan, scaring the hell out of the driver.

I thought my foot got run over. It probably didn't.

I hobbled to the curb and cried, thinking I had just escaped a violent death...the panicked driver and the lady from the nearest house tried to comfort me. Bystanders gathered.

They asked if I was okay. They poked at my foot. I was sure it had been run over. I wondered if I might be kidnapped. I cried, and pleaded, "Please don't tell my mom" while surrounded by strangers and refusing to disclose where I lived. Fluffy would be so angry.

"Please don't tell my mom," I begged.

Virgil checked out from work at the grocery store in El Segundo and drove over to rescue me. He put me on Fluffy's couch and stacked ice on my foot, then turned the TV volume up loud.

I stretched out across Fluffy's couch, my leg propped on the armrest, an icepack balanced on top, feeling terribly special. The TV did little to distract me. The pain of getting hit by a car had banished the certainty of getting spanked for daring to put my feet up on Fluffy's couch. The icepack made my foot cold. I wondered how that could possibly make things better. Thinking a frozen foot wasn't much of an improvement on the damage from being run over. Remembering the adults who surrounded me on the sidewalk and listened to my fears of punishment. Knowing they told my father. Thinking that's why he was talking to Fluffy in the kitchen, in hushed voices.

I laid there quietly, straining to eavesdrop on the low volume conversation behind me, wondering if he would make Fluffy like me, now that my foot had gotten run over and all. I listened to the soft but serious whispers leak out from the kitchen, wishing they were louder, and wondered if he knew that Sissy and I were often hungry. I wondered what they were whispering about. I wondered if he knew that I was afraid of her. He must have known, I thought. The strangers who rescued me after the car accident had told him so.

—⚭—

At that time, Sissy and I had three grandmothers—Minnie, Minnie, and Millie. My father's mother was Minnie Mae. She's the one who got Alzheimer's and just died. Then there was Fluffy's mother, Minnie Idela. She wasn't technically our grandmother, but most times she acted like one.

The third was my mother's mother, Grandma Millie. She and my grandfather Bob had moved back to Southern California after dumping the Orland worm farm, and Sissy and I saw them often. They first met my stepmother when Virgil drove her over for an introductory dinner at their house.

Grandma Millie washed the dirty dinner dishes with Fluffy.

"So, how does it feel to marry a man with a ready-made family of two kids?" she asked. A bonding question, she thought.

"I don't know," Fluffy answered. "I don't like kids."

Grandpa Bob sometimes drove his Volkswagen Bug to Fluffy's rental house and drove us back to his home for once-in-a-while weekend visits.

He was somewhat regal. Grouchy, even. Stern and serious, a square jaw, blocky forehead, handsome hair that grayed at the temples, a former boxer for the Navy. He commanded respect. I was afraid of him. Loved him, but was afraid. Grandpa Bob was not a warm and fuzzy individual.

When he showed up on Fluffy's driveway to get us, Sissy and I argued over who got to sit in the front seat. To kill the argument, Grandpa made us both sit in back while our traveling clothes went to the front, folded inside paper grocery store bags, until Grandma Millie purchased two child-sized suitcases for us...boys get blue, girls get pink.

A few miles before arriving at his house, Grandpa cut the anticipatory air of the Volkswagen by asking, "What did the monkey say when his tail got run over by the lawnmower?"

In unison, Sissy and I answered, "I don't know. What did the monkey say?"

Grandpa Bob laughed. "It won't be long now..."

I never understood that joke. It was our ritual on every visit with my grandfather, but it hardly seemed believable that monkeys would roam around our front lawn to have encounters with lawnmowers. It wasn't until I got older that I finally figured out that the point of the joke was to answer a child's incessant question of, "How much longer 'til we get there?"...and the answer was, "It won't be long now."

My mother's parents weren't poor. Their home was situated in the newly developed southern California town of Cerritos, on a curved street in a stark subdivision of brand-new two-story houses with cow pastures and a dairy behind it...wide stairs leading to several bedrooms on the second floor and more room than I thought necessary. They had a double front door, one side of which was stationary and never opened and seemed unneeded to me.

Grandpa Bob built a swing set in his backyard with a slide for me and Sissy to climb up or go down, but I only know this from looking at old photos. I have no memories of that play structure or their yard, but I do remember my grandparents as always having nice sheets. The double kind, where you sleep between a top and bottom sheet, crisp and starchy, in an oversized bed with lots of blankets, and in a room you don't have to share with anyone else. And I remember those oddities interfering with my being able to fall asleep at night. And I remember my grandparents insisting that we weren't supposed to wear underwear when we went to bed because they said pajamas negated the need for underwear and I thought they were seriously weird for that.

And Pop Tarts. They always had Pop Tarts. Sissy and I sat on stools at the end of my grandmother's kitchen counter...sorting a bag of M&M's into colors...trading a red one for two brown ones and pondering the inequity of that exchange...pulling hot, dry-as-dust Pop Tart pastries out of the toaster and luxuriating in the scent as it bathed the kitchen, feeling special, knowing my grandmother spent money on treats for the simple reason that she thought we liked them. I never really cared much for Pop Tarts.

My grandmother often took us to Disneyland, Knott's Berry Farm, or the beach while Grandpa went to work or stayed home. Sissy's preference was always Disneyland...damn Disneyland where we stood in line for hours at the Matterhorn and waited for a two-minute ride on a fake mountain.

In my head, a hot and salty southern California beach was the most magical place on earth, easily worth a dozen trips to Disneyland. I buried myself in powder-fine sand, hunted for sea treasures, and wore brand new rubber flip-flops 'cause if you didn't have flip-flops, your feet burned on the hot sand as you ran from the parking lot to the water.

I never understood why we didn't just wear our regular shoes instead. The flip-flops hurt my toes, but I wore them anyway, because hot sand was worse than sore toes.

When those weekend getaways came to an end, Grandpa Bob drove us back to Fluffy's house. A day or two later, she sometimes sent notes back that read, "Please don't send the kids home with junk. If I want them to have toys, I will buy them."

Or, "Please don't take Scott to get a haircut. If I want him to have a haircut, I will give it to him."

In preparation for an upcoming visit to Grandma Millie's, I desired to take a few small toys with me. I spotted a new shirt that Fluffy had recently purchased for me and imagined that the empty plastic wrapper would be an ideal carrying case for toys. I filled it with small belongings and carelessly discarded the shirt on the floor.

Fluffy found it.

Sissy cringed in the corner, squeezed up against a wall, one leg crooked into the other, head tucked, an uncertain and shy countenance sweeping her face, looking as if she would be swallowed up by the safety of the wall, if only she wished for it harder, while Fluffy beat me.

Grandpa Bob picked us up the next morning. We recited the ritual Monkey-Meeting-Lawnmower conversation in his Volkswagen, and at the end of the day, my mom's younger sister, teenage Aunt Victoria, walked us upstairs to a second floor where there was more than one bathroom. She stripped us down in front of the tub for a bath and screamed for Grandma to "Come quick!" at the sight of my bruises from Fluffy's beating the day before.

Grandma Millie ran upstairs, then turned me around in front of the mirror to show me why they were going into hysterics. A few days later, she called our Kingdom Hall.

Grandma was a Jehovah's Witness, but Grandpa was not. When we visited them, she took us to the Kingdom Hall for meetings while he stayed home.

Jehovah's Witnesses are adamant about self-regulation and discipline. Reporting another Witness to the police can be grounds for disfellowshipping, so Grandma Millie reported my bruises to the elders in our congregation. The elders probably had a meeting about that, but Sissy and I knew nothing of it when we were children. We were completely unaware of what was going on behind the scenes of our childhood.

Several months later, Virgil moved us out of town. It was a secret.

"You keep your mouth shut," Fluffy warned me. "It's no one's business where we're moving."

We left Los Angeles a month before I finished second grade, just before the Easter holiday. On my last day of school in Los Angeles, my teacher, Mrs. Yamanaka, laid out dozens of hardboiled eggs across the school tables, bowls of food coloring nearby, in preparation for the Easter weekend.

I told her I was a Jehovah's Witness and wasn't allowed to decorate Easter eggs, but she got mad and dunked my hands in a bowl of food coloring, insisting that I decorate eggs like everyone else. I was wracked with guilt all day, certain I would be in an enormous amount of trouble if my parents found out. Mrs. Yamanaka couldn't understand that, and I couldn't find the strength to stand up for my religious instruction and refuse her demand that I participate in the celebration of Easter.

After months of searching, my mother's parents eventually located our new home in Fillmore, Ventura County, southern California. They called and asked to visit.

"You're not gonna see your grandchildren again," Virgil told them.

So that was it. Those grandparents disappeared, and Sissy and I spent the rest of our childhood wondering why.

THE TRUTH

I n the spring of 1971, a week after I turned seven, we moved to a new three-bedroom, two bath, single-story ranch-style brown stucco house in the town of Fillmore. It was a secret.

Fillmore had previously been crowded by orange groves, but each orchard was successively plowed under, finding new life as a housing development, and Fluffy picked out the model that she liked most.

I haven't a clue where the money came from to buy that house.

Fluffy was no longer employed. Virgil had recently taken over a pool cleaning business and was driving his old stepside pickup around the nicer neighborhoods of Hollywood and Beverly Hills, cleaning swimming pools, which wasn't going to make us rich.

While the house was being built, Fluffy drove us over to sweep sawdust off the plywood subfloors, then she picked out special some brown Spanish tile counters and a rust-orange ceramic sink to match the twisted-wrought-iron-painted-orange-coffee-cup-holder that sat on the kitchen counter so people who came to visit could see all our cups. She ordered orange shag carpet for the interior, knowing it needed to be raked once a week. The rake came free with the purchase of the house.

Months after we moved in, the rake broke into two pieces, so Fluffy decided that carpet maintenance wasn't really necessary and threw both parts away. She then painted the single dining room wall bright orange, just to match the sink and coffee cup holder.

Or maybe just to shock the hell out of Dad, 'cause it did. Fluffy glued mirrors to the backs of the bathroom doors and hung long strands of orange beads in the windows, just to make everything pretty, and then ordered a truckload of crushed red rock to be delivered. We scattered it along the entire length of the driveway, and after she discovered that such adornment was not the beautiful no-maintenance landscaping technique that she had imagined, she assigned an everyday task to me of sweeping rocks off the concrete.

My chores expanded in Fillmore. Fluffy bought a new station wagon, and I occasionally scrubbed its interior with aerosol foam from a can of Tannery while she watched *General Hospital* and *Let's Make a Deal* with Monte Hall. I watered the yard when we had stuff to keep alive. And eventually mowed the lawn when we had one.

And dusted baseboards, 'cause that was really important. Fluffy wanted the baseboards in her house cleaned every day, and if I didn't spend enough time dusting them, she would send me back to do it over. I crawled around the floor on my hands and knees each day, a kitchen rag in my hand, dusting baseboards, unless we had company. She wouldn't yell at me to dust baseboards in front of company.

For school, Sissy walked six blocks to Sespe Elementary for fourth grade and I rode the bus to San Cayetano Elementary on the far side of town for second grade.

The school bus to San Cayetano Elementary stopped around the corner from Fluffy's new house, on the backside of our block, just seven houses away. On the morning of my first day of school, Fluffy told me about it.

"You have to ride the bus to school," she said.

I looked at her blankly.

"You have to take the bus every day," she repeated. "Just walk around the corner to the bus stop."

Incomprehension still registered on my face.

"What bus?" I asked, confused.

"It's a school bus. A bus will take you to school every day. Just walk around the corner to the bus stop and wait for it."

"Where? What's a bus stop?" I was about to cry.

"Just walk around the corner! You'll see other kids waiting. Just get on the bus when it arrives. It will take you to school!"

I left the house, choking back tears and distress, not understanding the concept of a school bus. San Cayetano Elementary was my fifth school—the previous four had all been within walking distance of whichever rental house we were in at the time.

I rounded the corner to Sespe Avenue and discovered that Fluffy was wrong. There was not a line of kids waiting for the bus. One kid, older than me, was standing by a newly installed street sign. I assumed he was possibly waiting for the illusory bus to take him to school. Perhaps things would be alright if I tagged along to wherever he was going.

A yellow school bus arrived, and I boarded it, hoping it would deliver me to where I was supposed to go. Fortunately, it did.

A week later, I arrived at the bus stop too late.

I'd never missed a bus before. I still didn't know much about buses. We hadn't been long in Fillmore. I walked back home, all seven houses away.

Fluffy stood at the stove, fixing tea for her breakfast. I confessed.

"Well, then just walk!" she hollered. "It's not that far. You can walk to school. That will teach you to not miss the bus!"

I couldn't venture all the way across town by myself. I might get kidnapped.

Mid-morning, the school called to inquire into my whereabouts.

Fluffy went looking for me.

She found me sitting in the dirt, behind the garage.

"What are you doing? I told you to get to school! You can just stay there until your father gets home!"

I heard his truck pull into the driveway late that night. His door slammed. The kitchen door shut behind him. Time passed. He was eating dinner, I presumed. More time passed before he retrieved me from behind the garage and gave me a lecture for being disobedient and causing trouble for Fluffy. He threatened to send me to bed without dinner, but gave me a plate of leftovers anyway.

———— ∞ ————

We got new neighbors in Fillmore that live two doors away on the corner, except no one's ever seen them and their house is mostly empty and they have an olive tree and a red maple tree in their front yard. Everyone says it's a maple tree, so I dug a hole in the side of it and tipped an empty green bean can underneath to catch all the syrup that shoulda come pourin' out, except nothin' happened. There wasn't even a drop. It must not have been a real maple tree.

People who told me it was a maple tree were wrong. You shouldn't believe everything people tell you, 'cause sometimes they don't know what they're talkin' about. Sometimes people tell you things that don't make sense but it doesn't bother them, 'cause sometimes they get these ideas in their head and after a lot of time goes by they don't wonder anymore where they got them from. And that's a fine mess to be in, when you can't wonder where you got your ideas from or remember why you think they're true.

It's like when your parents think you're a bad kid, a stupid boy, but you don't want them to. So you try to be good, but they can't think of you that way. They just can't. So when they get mad, they spank you with a belt and make you read the Bible scriptures about stubborn and rebellious children who were stoned to death with rocks. So you stand in the living room and read the Bible out loud for everyone to hear and then you close your Bible 'cause you think you're done, but Fluffy says, "No. Read it again," 'cause she doesn't think you meant it. So you read it again and tell her you understand what it means and promise you won't be bad anymore.

━━━━

Our religion was known as "The Truth." The phrase "The Truth" was never used in public, or around people of other faiths. It only appeared in the Kingdom Hall, like a secret decoder ring, amongst people who shared a belief that the Jehovah's Witnesses had "the truth."

In the Kingdom Hall, someone might have asked Fluffy, "Is your sister still in The Truth?"

Fluffy would have answered, "No. Jackie left The Truth several years ago."

The primary philosophy of The Truth was that of separation. The Truth expected social isolation from mainstream society. In compliance, Virgil reduced contact with family members who weren't fans of The Truth. He especially reduced contact with anyone who caused conflict with his new wife Fluffy.

Members of The Truth generally prohibited their children from joining clubs or playing sports in school. Those who didn't were admonished about the dangers of associating with worldly people. Extra-curricular school activities were discouraged and social gatherings were rarely thrown for friends because there were enormous restrictions on both of those. People outside of our religion were considered "bad association," so the bulk of my childhood was spent on TV and weekend naps. Hours of sedentary waste in Fluffy's house, interrupted only by evening and weekend Bible studies and once in a while afternoons going door to door to push religion and *Watchtower* magazines into the hands of non-believers for a nickel.

Members of The Truth are obligated to bring new sheep into the fold. To find those sheep, we devoted occasional weekends to the preaching work, going door to door, searching for converts. We purchased *The Watchtower* and *Awake!* magazines for five cents apiece at our local Kingdom Hall, and then recouped our nickels when we sold them for an identical amount on the streets. There was no profit motive for placing literature, other than trying to break even. If we didn't sell what we had purchased, those lost nickels were considered a donation to The Truth.

I was in love with going door to door as a Jehovah's Witness. Immensely. It was a fantastic escape from Fluffy's house, weekend afternoons in service to our beliefs, hunting for people to convert to our church, keeping tally of the hours spent and magazines sold, reporting the results at the end of each month on the Field Service Report, racking up points to report to Jehovah, I thought. We deposited thousands of leftover back issues of *The Watchtower* on empty doorsteps, those where no one answered our knocks, hoping Jehovah would open people's hearts when they found our left-behind religious tracts and miraculously discovered the true path to righteousness.

That never happened to my knowledge, not from any random magazines I left behind, but one could always hope and I was eager and passionate to spend my life in service to the Kingdom Hall...regularly walking through neighborhoods under constant admonition to "Slow down! We're not running a race!" as I sometimes ran ahead, leaving others behind, eager to share The Truth. I can explain today, just as it was repeatedly described to me then, that door-to-door work is meant to be done slowly. A gentle and lethargic meandering down the street, sharing the good news of the kingdom. It wasn't a race. It was a patient, restrained approach...which I found maddening and illogical as a child.

In preparation for our Saturday mornings in service to Jehovah, I memorized the introductory lines of a sales pitch.

"Good morning," I said. "We're out in the neighborhood sharing some words of encouragement from the Bible. Did you know that God has a plan for your future? A day when people won't get sick and no one will die?"

I thrust the latest issues of *The Watchtower* and *Awake!* towards whoever answered my knocks, fanned out so the front covers were visible, a friendly and hopeful smile on my face.

"We are offering *The Watchtower* and *Awake!* for a contribution of ten cents!"

I knocked on hundreds of doors, perhaps thousands, delivering that pitch, knowing that if I ever found myself in the circumstances where someone wanted to engage in meaningful discussion beyond my introduction, they would do so with the adult who accompanied me. I knocked on doors and rang countless doorbells and learned that some people would not answer their doors. They'd seen us before.

It wasn't unusual to introduce ourselves to concerned homeowners who were incredibly offended at the appearance of proselytizing children on their doorsteps. When they gave my dad grief and suggested that he take me home to play with friends, I wished he would tell them to mind their own damn business. "Shut the heck up!"

Denial of the opportunity to walk the streets and share my knowledge of Jehovah, forcing instead a long and boring weekend to languish in Fluffy's home, was horrifying. There was nothing to do in Fluffy's house other than watch TV and do chores and learn about Jehovah and prepare to live forever in a new paradise on earth. The New Order, the Witnesses called it. We prepared for the New Order. The New Order would follow Armageddon and was promised to be a new world where God's true followers would enjoy everlasting life. Pain and sickness would disappear in the New Order. The New Order would restore the earth to God's original plan. Jehovah's Witnesses would live forever in the New Order.

Fluffy's house was devoted to preparing to live forever in the New Order. It was a vacuous world of simplicity. You wouldn't have heard a lick of discussion of hopes for retirement. Or dreams of children graduating from college. Or dentist appointments, Hawaiian vacations, the possibility of grandkids, or anything else that requires one to believe in a future…because there's no point in getting too wrapped up in modern life when you believe "Armageddon is coming and this wicked system is about to be destroyed." Or when your religion assures you that you're in "the last days" and the New Order will be here soon. Maybe even tomorrow. So when Armageddon failed to show up tomorrow, we added a request to our daily prayers, begging God to "Please bring this wicked system to an end."

Granny M was a Pioneer for Jehovah that summer—devoting full-time hours to preaching work in Fillmore. She took me to the San Cayetano neighborhood one Saturday, hoping to convert people to our religion in the nice but older part of town where carob and macadamia trees littered the sidewalks with dropped nuts. Elm, carob, and macadamia trees graced the sidewalks, shading pedestrians below.

We strolled through their neighborhood under the cool shade of their trees, chatting about Jehovah and the New Order with people who answered our knocks. Those who were receptive to our solicitation gave us a contribution of ten cents in exchange for a pair of *Watchtower* and *Awake!* magazines. Where people did not answer our knocks, we deposited out-of-date issues on their front steps.

In between doorsteps, I filled my pockets with dropped macadamia nuts and scuffed carob pods across the sidewalks.

Granny M said, "People can eat the carob pods if they want to."

"Really?" I asked. "What do they taste like?"

"I don't know," she answered. "Why don't you try one and find out."

I picked a long carob pod off the concrete and smeared away the street germs with sweat from my fingers. Later that day, I gnawed the edges off of it and learned that carob pods are harder than rocks but taste vaguely like coconut with sweet chocolate and honey mixed in, once I thought about it hard and told myself so.

Virgil was still cleaning swimming pools in Beverly Hills and Hollywood, and I often went with him that summer. We drove down to Hollywood with one overriding rule for my behavior— when cleaning pools for private residences, I had to sit in the truck. An escape from incarceration in the truck was only permitted at apartment buildings.

We once walked into an apartment courtyard where a lady had spread herself out across the grass, on a towel, front down, half naked, baking in the afternoon sun.

Her back was bare. Tanned brown.

She raised her head as we walked by. "Hello," she said.

The edges of her boobs peeked out, pale and pancaked, slightly exposed by the weight of her chest on the grass. I stared.

Virgil answered, "Hello," then walked me back to the truck while explaining in very generic terms that some women liked to sit in the sun with their tops off. I sat in the cab and thought she should have been embarrassed, and wondered why she wasn't. And I thought someone should have told her to put her top back on, but they didn't.

We drove over to our next pool job and some kids, older than me, who had the money to live in a big house up on the hill with pretty landscaping in front and a swimming pool in back, came out the front door of their house and stood on the sidewalk and talked to me through the open truck window.

"Do you want to come over to play?" they asked.

"No, I'm not allowed out of the truck while my dad's cleaning pools."

"Really? Don't you get bored?"

"I don't know. What does bored mean?"

"It means you don't have anything to do. It's not fun."

"Oh. No, it isn't boring, but thanks for asking." That's what I told them.

It wasn't the truth. It really was boring.

When Virgil needed a half bottle of chlorine and a little bit of acid for pools at the apartment complexes, I ran back to the truck to haul it for him, knowing he was about to give me a lecture about how I shouldn't ever mix the two together, 'cause some other kid did that once and the fumes killed him. Chlorine apparently does terrible things when mixed with acid, and Virgil constantly reminded me that I should never ever pour one bottle into another or else I might get killed, too.

An older male resident on the second floor of an apartment complex often smiled and leaned halfway out from the second floor to say hello. He acted friendly and threw a few coins into the pool for my dad to scoop off the bottom with a net. I never understood why he threw money out the window instead of walking downstairs to give it to me. My dad said he was probably a homo. Apparently, homos and fruits were everywhere, especially in Hollywood. Hollywood was saturated with homos, Virgil said.

And vegetarians. And Jews. They were everywhere too, and we didn't like them, either.

There's one pool in this big brown stucco house in a subdivision full of identical big brown stucco houses, and it's one of the pools where I have to sit in the truck until Dad's done, 'cause they have a dog and they're Jews who wouldn't want the pool cleaning guy's kid walking through their yard. My dad says Jews have lots of money and they probably stole some of it, but how they got it doesn't really matter. They have somethin' we don't.

In spite of my massive hours of boredom, I enjoyed driving around in an old truck with my dad, peanut butter and jelly sandwiches thrown in a brown paper bag for lunch and deposited on the truck seat between us. And every-once-in-a-while visits to the Taco Bell drive-through for a bean burrito on days when we scooped enough pocket change out of pool bottoms.

We shopped the same store for pool supplies every week, parking in the alley to pick up cases of chlorine through the back door. They had two toilets—one for retail customers up front, and one in back for the rougher male blue-collar trade that was described as off limits to me. There was no explanation as to why, so I snuck in once, on purpose.

That back bathroom was plastered with *Playboy* centerfolds. All four walls were consumed by nudity.

I sat on the toilet and scanned every wall and every picture. All of them. In detail. There were all sorts of women, different colors, different poses, different sizes...I was truly perplexed and curious as to why there were no pictures of my gender. Disappointed, even.

Sometimes we ran into Dad's new friend Walt at the pool supply store. Not Walter, just Walt. He was in the pool cleaning business too, and he was tan. Handsome tan. Short and stocky. Bald and sweaty, like my dad, except Walt didn't wear a hat and his bare scalp had seen the sun which made him very cool, to wear baldness that way.

Walt drove a little brown Datsun pickup and every time we bumped into him, I thought about how much I liked him, and about how handsome he was, and about the fact that "Walt" seemed a great name for a guy and "Datsun" a strange name for a truck. I would have liked being named Walt, except that couldn't really happen because I was named after my dad's best friend from high school and his name isn't Walt.

His name is Scotty Michael Watts and I was named Scott Michael Terry. After my dad's best friend. Scotty's family owned the Watt's Ranch in the town of Willows, not far from Orland, and I met him at my grandparents' 50th wedding anniversary. He was a skinny blond guy who said he hadn't really talked to my dad since high school, ever since we moved to southern California and became Jehovah's Witnesses. That's outright sad. If they were such tight friends that Dad chose to name his first son after him, you'd think they'd still be friends today. But they aren't, and that makes it decidedly un-special and doesn't sound like much to tell people I was named after my dad's best friend, because they haven't been friends since my dad got married to Fluffy and found The Truth.

—∞—

In late July of 1971, Dad drove us down to the LAX airport and sent us up to Orland on one-way PSA airline tickets, just as he had done the two summers before.

Grams picked us up at the air-conditioned airport in Sacramento and then walked us outside into the heavy summer air to her brown four-door car with plastic seats that fried our bare legs in the hot sun. Sissy and I had a love-hate relationship with the Sacramento airport. A single cavernous terminal…a tiny gift shop tucked into a far corner, conveniently and intentionally located at the landing spot for the single escalator leading down from the gates…the gateway to our summer fantasies…a jumping off spot where Grams met us with hugs and kisses and led us out to a world where dreams became reality…a parking lot for shedding tears when Grams sent us home.

Orland was an earthly heaven. We flew to Sacramento every summer on an airborne journey to replenish affection, surrounded by adult passengers who constantly offered reminders of how brave it was to fly alone and under the care of flight attendants who were called "stewardesses" and were restricted to members of the female gender with 1970s miniskirts. They looked out for us while acting friendly and squeezing up and down the aisle with plastic cups of fruit punch and a bowl of pink and yellow butter mints that passengers scooped out with their bare fingers, 'cause that's how things were on PSA airlines.

I never once went pee on a plane. Fluffy had flown to Portugal with a group of Witnesses a few years earlier to smuggle copies of *The Watchtower* to the Portuguese brothers and sisters who were being persecuted and banned from going to their local Kingdom Halls—that was before she entered my life—and she said some stupid fat lady ignored the warnings about when she could go pee and when she was supposed to hold it and got her ass stuck in the toilet and found herself screaming bloody murder for help. The fire department got called to come get her off. It was the highlight of Fluffy's trip to Europe. Apparently, according to Fluffy, there was some widely unknown but highly pertinent information floating around about how sitting on the airplane commode at precisely the wrong moment could put you at risk for some unexplainable aeronautical suction gluing your ass solidly to the toilet seat. That screaming fat woman found the precise moment, or so Fluffy said, and I wasn't about to put myself in danger of the same embarrassment by daring to pee on a plane.

—∞—

My father's parents were Okies. Cowboys, if we're looking for a more respectable term. My grandfather was born Isaac Willie Terry. Not Isaac William, but Isaac Willie, and everyone called him "Ike." He was born on a large piece of farmland in Oklahoma, but his father died from diabetes at the age of 29 and Gramps ended up with a stepfather who beat on him. His stepfather sold the property and spent the proceeds fueling an alcohol addiction, or so they say, and Gramps abandoned school and home at the age of 13. After long stints of sleeping in barns and a neighbor's chicken coop, he ended up in Bushy Head Hollow, Missouri, and that's where he bumped into Grandma who had arrived to pick strawberries with her older sister Letha. They married shortly after Grams graduated from high school in La Harpe, Kansas.

Grams was born Minnie Mae Roush. She didn't originally come from poor—she was smothered by poor after marrying Grandpa. She was born in Iola, Kansas, and raised in a pretty little two-story white Victorian in La Harpe—fairly middle class by early twentieth century standards.

In the 1930s, Grams and Gramps were forced out of what they called "Bushy Head Holler, Missoora." You can tell real Missouri people by how they pronounce it…"Missoora." You cain't get any more Okie than claiming to come from Bushy Head Holler, Missoora.

Grams' sister Letha and her husband Uncle Earl were the first to flee the poverty of the Dust Bowl and depression. They moved out of Bushy Head Holler, and that began the exodus of the Roush and Terry families to California, where most settled around Orland.

Grams' parents, Louis and Anna Roush, built a tiny one-bedroom cottage on Road FF with an irrigation ditch in front. It was a residence for poor people...surrounded by acres of weeds, horse corrals, and a small fruit orchard. That side of town was referred to as "Okie Land" and so named for obvious reasons.

Gramps worked as a cow puncher for several ranches in the area, and he bought wild horses from the Bureau of Land Management roundups in Nevada to break into saddle horses for resale. He cleaned ditches for the county irrigation system, rode the mountains on horseback for the Forest Service, worked for the Orland auction yard, and then went into the cattle business with a shady character named J. Tilley. After purchasing calves and grazing them on leased land during the summer, they sold the fattened beef at the Orland auction yard and J. Tilley ran off with the proceeds, leaving my grandparents destitute.

They moved into the Roush's little house on Road FF and Gram's ailing mother moved into a tiny little shack in back. When she died, Grams inherited the property and remained there with Gramps for more than twenty years. They never found their way out of poverty.

For me and my sister, that little house on Road FF was awash in love and affection, outside the town of Orland. Orland was nothing more than an ugly rural pit stop along the freeway, about 100 miles north of Sacramento. There were no monuments, museums, or famous dead people to visit. Orland was slowly drowning in poverty.

Life was so slow downtown that people were allowed to park parallel in the middle of the street, between opposing lanes of traffic, and children could wander back and forth between the movie theatre and library without fear of being run over. Sissy and I watched many double *Disney* features at the theatre, checked out library books for lazy summer day reading, and spent long afternoons in the high school swimming pool for thirty-five cents, then a barefoot walk to the snack bar for a sticky sack of Abba Zabba taffy and sour apple suckers afterwards.

Bucke's feed store on Sixth Street was the highlight of town. They had the best selection of western clothes, and the stuffed carcasses of pheasants and rabbits and other critters that people had killed for dinner were nailed to the walls and suspended from the ceiling for decoration.

Other than allowing a maze of irrigation canals to lace their way through town, the Orland founders had an unfortunate lack of imagination. They laid out streets and mostly straight roads through square tracts of farmland in a tiresome grid-pattern typical of flat rural communities in the rice fields and orchards of the Central Valley, but over the years, miscellaneous shortcuts haphazardly appeared and ran diagonals over what originally had been laid out in neat blocks. Streets in Orland didn't get beautiful descriptions like "Shady Grove Lane" or "Happy Valley Road." They weren't named after famous people or interesting places. They mostly just got letters and numbers.

Like A Street and B Street. And Road L. And Road H. And Road HH. And County Road 10. And County Road 10 ½, which is honest-to-God true but must have originally been a joke. And First Street and Second Street. And South Street. And East Street. And South-East Street. And East-South Street. And Road FF.

It was generally 105 degrees on the dusty gravel of Road FF in the middle of August, so I often cooled off in the irrigation ditch in front of my grandparents' house, stumbling barefoot through the mud and knee-deep water, dodging bugs and other unidentified critters that I feared might be hiding in the soupy mess. Sissy wouldn't set foot in there. She thought the irrigation ditch was gross.

On those warm and worry-free summer days, we had once-in-a-while drives with Grams to the Frosty Cone restaurant under the railroad overpass for chocolate and vanilla twisty cones, and then back up and over the tracks as we peered at cows grazing below and laughed and licked at our ice cream before it melted in the heat.

Grams' sister, Aunt Letha, lived in Orland. I visited her often. She and Uncle Earl were remarkably poor but had somehow avoided the embarrassment of Okie Land by owning an old house right in the middle of town, a massive gnarled elm tree shading the front. A clothesline occupied the side, grape vines and a potato patch out back.

Uncle Earl rolled his own cigarettes. Slow and patient, he was. A shiny, pocket-sized, brass case occupied his front pocket, holding smoking paper. He poured tobacco out of a little draw sack, careful not to spill, then licked the paper edges. Tobacco smoke wafted in slow curls over his haggard head.

Aunt Letha wore her long gray hair in braids that she curled up on her head, and she attired her body in a daily costume of long handmade dresses with longer sleeves. She took care of her laundry in an old open-mouthed washtub that I recognized as an antique. It was missing a lid, which might have been on purpose or by accident. I didn't know. Her ancient washer was essentially a large metal tub with a motor attached to one side, lacking a spin or drain cycle, and more than once I watched her fish the soggy clothes out of the bottom and then mindlessly run each piece through an electric wringer mounted over top the tub five feet away. I feared, sure as anything, that her fingers were on the verge of getting sucked into the rollers. She'd scream and I'd scream, and my favorite great aunt would then be limbless.

Aunt Letha taught me to plant potatoes one afternoon after she finished "hangin' out the warsh" on the clothesline between her back porch and the potato patch. For those who don't know, you grow potatoes by cutting a perfectly good one into pieces and burying the parts in the ground, an impossible concept to imagine; that bits of old potato buried in the dirt would result in brand new ones to dig up later. I speculated that she was probably full of it as we plodded through the furrows, burying potato parts six inches into the soil, thinking it was just a lame joke. It didn't seem believable until the end of that summer when Grams asked my help in digging 'taters from her potato patch. We unearthed a bucketful of baby red potatoes with a shovel that looked like a giant fork, but we referred to it as a shovel because everyone knows it wouldn't sound right to say you dug potatoes out of your backyard with a fork.

Aunt Letha and Uncle Earl took turns driving me out to the larger irrigation canals in Orland on hot afternoons to stand on an overpass to catch fish, except they called them "feesh," 'cause that's how you say it if you're from Bushy Head Holler. Uncle Earl could lean over at the edge of the canal to unhook a fish from my line and accidentally get himself stuck in the thumb by a catfish barb and not cry while watching his own blood drip thick off his fingers. That was impressive. It hurts like hell to get stuck by a catfish. We pulled lots of them out of the irrigation canals running through Orland and hauled them back to Grandma on a stringer in a plastic bucket. She cut their heads off on her front porch, and then rolled them in cornmeal and fried them up for dinner in her cast iron skillet.

Grandma Terry was intensely creative. More so than anyone I've ever known. She canned everything, could sew and bake anything, made gifts no one ever imagined, and once designed purses for her granddaughters out of discarded Clorox bleach bottles. She cut the empty plastic jugs into small squares, punched holes along the perimeters, and then stitched them together with blue and pink yarn until a unique purse creation was complete. They even came with lids and handles. I didn't get a purse that summer and didn't really feel neglected by that, but I've never forgotten my realization on that hot August afternoon that my grandmother was the only person I knew who could look at an empty Clorox bottle and envision the creation of a purse.

Grams baked cakes for part-time money—Cinderella cakes and cowboy cakes and graduation cakes and wedding cakes and any color or shape that people were willing to pay for, and all baked from scratch. She would bake you a purple cake, if you were willing to pay for it. In the process of a two-layer creation, she cut the rounded dome off the bottom layer so the cake would be level when she stacked the second one on top—that's important if you expect people to pay good money for a cake. Sissy and I always got the "cut off" piece, smeared with leftover frosting. That was a big deal.

Grandpa ran cattle in the mountains west of Orland during summer, but earned most of his living hauling other folk's livestock back and forth to the auction yard. People thought I liked to ride around in the stock truck with him, but they were wrong. Given a choice, I would have opted to stay home with Grams and eat cake.

Grams bought me a genuine bow and arrow from the Green Stamp catalog. We drove to the Orland Green Stamp office in her little brown car to get it. Sissy went, too, but she didn't get anything. She'd already gotten a Clorox purse. The Green Stamp store was surprisingly desolate, not having anything to buy. They didn't sell stuff inside…the catalog did the selling.

We unwrapped my new bow and arrow on Grams' kitchen table, and I spent every summer thereafter chasing rabbits and shooting arrows straight up in the sky, a seriously stupid idea, running like hell as they fell back to earth and bounced off rocks in the road.

I roamed the neighbor's fields with my bow, shirtless, out in the blazing sun, optimistically stalking jackrabbits in the yellow star thistles across the road, hoping to kill one and check it for tularemia disease, after which Grams might turn it into dinner.

The closest I ever came to killing a wild rabbit was the time behind the barn in the back corral with the horses when I shot at a neighbor's chicken. It ran off cackling and screaming like I was trying to murder it, which I was, but other than that single attempt, I generally missed the concept that the point of a bow and arrow is to allow you to kill from a distance. I stalked rabbits in the weeds, thinking I must be close enough to practically touch one before letting an arrow fly, only to watch my quarry bounce off to safety before I ever loosed an arrow from my bowstring.

When I got back to Fillmore, Dad said "You need a bow and arrow like you need a hole in the head."

My grandfather had a body odor that strongly whiffed of cologne, cows, hay, sweat, dusty barns, and manure. I didn't go to work with him often and didn't find his job to be very interesting, unless we had a stopover at the Orland auction yard. The auction was an absurdly chaotic place where I strained to decipher the hyper-fast sing-song language that poured out of the auctioneer's mouth, unable to fathom why it was necessary to talk that way when selling farm animals. We sprawled out over a tier of wooden benches inside, amidst the music of the auctioneer's voice, amongst old men and cowboy boots, evaluating bellowing livestock through clouds of dust and the aroma of fresh green manure. You can taste it, ever so slightly, the flavor of auction yard dust, if you breathe with your mouth open and think about it while sitting there…but that would be a mistake. You don't want to think about that.

The back of the auction property was a tangled mess of livestock corrals—squealing hogs and rowdy animals imprisoned inside, waiting to enter the ring. Baby calves were separated into small pens where they bawled for their mothers and begged to suck on people's fingers, optimistically hoping to suck out a bit of warm milk. Grandpa said it would give me "the runs" if I let the calves suck on my finger.

The main building of the auction house enclosed a beat up and crowded café with old men lingering over afternoon coffee and slow stories and dreams of the old days with good cattle and better horses. Gramps occasionally bought a bologna sandwich for me at the counter, and a can of Dr. Pepper that I couldn't finish until I burped.

He swapped cowboy stories with all the old guys who found enormous interest in watching me eat.

"Are you gonna grow up to be a truck drivin' man like your grandpa?" they asked.

Gramps had a beautiful two-story barn out behind the house, and he stacked it full of hay each summer. He hung an old wind-up antique telephone on the tack room wall downstairs and connected it to a matching antique phone in the kitchen. Sissy and I used that phone often, calling each other from the house or the barn to laugh about Dolly Parton music or to share a ripe and juicy peach picked off the tree in the garden.

Nailed up over the barn loading chute, out of my reach, were a couple of Gramps' deer hunting trophies, scraps of hide hanging off the antlers. To my wannabe-Indian eyes, the shriveled skin had the potential to be turned into a genuine Indian armband. I would decorate it with beads pilfered from Grandma's sewing cabinet and wrap it around my skinny bicep to publicly display my work of art, in front of strangers even, just to inform them of my miraculous conversion into a red man.

Gramps patiently listened to my young dreams of Indian desires, then he climbed a ladder to pull bits of hide off the antlers. He showed me how it was all dried up and brittle and wouldn't make a very good armband, after all, but his indulgence in my fantasy meant the world to me. I don't know if he ever knew that.

A highlight of our Orland vacations was a trip to an ancient Indian village up in the mountains where Grandpa ran cattle on Forest Service land that he leased for almost nothing each summer. Squaw Camp served triple duty: an inexpensive family camping vacation while investigating the health and well-being of Gramps' cattle, all timed around the opening of deer season.

We drove out of my grandparents' house on Road FF early on a morning late in the month of August, guns and horses loaded in the stock truck, then turned left at Newville Road and drove forever until we were about halfway into the Mendocino National Forest. It was a long and hot drive on a dusty, treacherous, single-lane, unpaved logging road where Grandpa occasionally went crazy and pretended he was about to lose control at hairpin curves.

Our drive back and forth to Squaw Camp each summer took us through the town of Newville, except the whole place had disappeared and there was no town there at all. Nothin. Just some trees, a creek, and dry California hills, but nothing recognizable as a town. Newville was an agricultural community in the 1800s with a school, a hotel and Masonic Hall, but by the 1940s it had dried up into nothing that resembled a town.

Only five occupied homes remained in Newville in 1946, and Grams and Gramps bought one for $1,000 after their second move from Missouri. It was a single story shack on three acres of land, built prior to indoor plumbing, with electricity to power a single bulb in the living room and an outhouse out back that had to be moved whenever the hole underneath was about to overflow with sewage. The only running water wasn't technically running. Water was provided by a manual hand pump out back by Heifer Camp Creek. Water for indoor use was stored in a galvanized milk can, and the bedroom was lit by lanterns at night. My grandparents raised their five children in that cabin in the late 1940s and early '50s, but when we passed through Newville in the 1970s, there were no homes remaining. The whole place was gone.

I never understood how an entire town could just up and disappear, but every time we drove through, my grandparents pointed out the barren location of their home at the confluence of North Fork Stony Creek and Heifer Camp Creek, and shared stories of shoveling snow off the roof in winter to keep it from caving in. And they explained how they fed their family on the occasional deer or bear that Gramps killed while riding the hills of the Drew ranch or working for the Forest Service. Grams said the only part of the bear worth eating was the ham.

Grandpa hauled two small travel trailers up the crooked road to Squaw Camp to keep us safe from bears. We shared the trailers with some cowboy friends…Leo Dado, George and Edith Ferry… some of whom slept in the second trailer, and some of whom slept on a tarp in back of the stock truck.

My memories of Squaw Camp are dominated by roasting marshmallows over huge campfires at night…angry yellow jackets that threatened to sting me during the day…the shock of arriving one summer and viewing the devastation of our mountain after it had been logged…three foot tall stalks of skunk cabbage that blanketed the hills except Grams said "you cain't eat it and it doesn't taste like cabbage, anyhow" which meant whoever decided to call it cabbage didn't know what they were talking about…nighttime campfire tales of old bear hunts and generations before me when everyone slept in back of the cattle truck to escape the bears except Aunt Jan was too scared to go to the outhouse in the dark when she was little, so she peed in her sleeping bag and it ran downhill into my dad's bed…cans of soda fished out of an old bathtub collecting icy spring water trickling out of a pipe in the ground…chasing chipmunks through trees and water skeeter bugs in the creek.

On those lazy Squaw Camp vacations, the men left camp each morning with rifles and fishing poles slung over their backs to round up stray cattle, fish for brook trout in the creek, and kill deer.

Just past the town of Newville was an Indian burial ground where, twenty years earlier, my father had unearthed a collection of beads and arrowheads and an Indian jawbone. It didn't look like much as we drove by. It was just a hill like any other hill except for being surrounded by a chain link fence to keep out little kids like my dad who spent hours of his childhood digging for things he shouldn't. And to keep out little kids like me who pretended himself to be an Indian and fantasized of my own quiet invasion into the burial ground to hunt for arrowheads.

More than once, I asked to stop and explore the graveyard, certain that a real Indian arrowhead would result in my laying a dead rabbit on the kitchen table, but my grandparents insisted that "people shouldn't be digging up things that don't belong to them," which was precisely why a fence had been put around it years after my adolescent father had been there.

About that time, Sissy and I acquired the belief that we were of very remote Indian descent—Cherokee, of course, 'cause just about everyone who claims to have minute amounts of Indian blood running through their veins is convinced it must be Cherokee. I don't know how the Cherokees feel about that. Don't know why we believed it, either. Or who said it. But we acquired that idea from some unremembered and unsubstantiated hearsay, along with the belief that our great-great-great-not-really-sure-how-many-greats grandfather was General Custer's commanding officer during the Indian wars of Montana. General Alfred E. Terry. We latched onto that rumor and attached it to our belief that we were partial

Indians, one-sixteenth we hoped, which is the minimum needed to be considered part-Indian by people who believe that infinitesimal bits of Indian blood will enhance their otherwise humdrum lives. Neither of us ever recognized the absurdity of hoping to have descended from a mixture of an unknown batch of Indians and the commanding officer of one of the country's most notorious Indian killers.

When the month of August came to an end, my grandparents bought the return tickets for $16 apiece to ship us back to Fillmore on PSA. After arriving home, I questioned Dad about our family history and expressed an interest in substantiating the General Custer link, just to learn more about where we came from…a desire he quickly declared to be "a sin"…something about "the Mormons do that kind of thing." He said Jehovah wouldn't like it if we traced our family history, because the Mormons did it.

Fred and Wilma Hooper live on Road FF in Orland, too. They live at the very end next to Newville Road, right up alongside the Stony Creek irrigation canal that the neighbor kids drowned in.

Fred and Wilma are really old, and they're the poorest people we know. They don't have a couch or a TV, and they grow their own food 'cause they can't afford to buy it.

Fred stinks like liquor. Everyone says Fred drinks like a fish and steals water out of the irrigation ditch for his garden, and then he gives fruit and vegetables to the ditch rider who comes around to bust him for stealing.

Fred and Wilma are in The Truth too, and they take us to the Orland Kingdom Hall for meetings when we go visit Grams and Gramps. That's important, 'cause Dad won't let us go to Orland if we don't promise to go to meetings with Fred and Wilma. Grandma doesn't like it and she doesn't like Jehovah's Witnesses, either. She's a Baptist. That means she has to believe in hell and she said, "Fluffy's gonna end up there someday."

Witnesses don't believe in hell. We know that people don't go to heaven or hell when they die. They just die. But after Armageddon arrives, all the good ones will get resurrected and we'll all live on earth in The New Order and no one will die and people will be perfect.

Grandma Terry doesn't really say much about what she thinks of Jehovah's Witnesses, but you know she doesn't like them. She says Fred and Wilma are always preaching and trying to get her to join The Truth. Aunt Jan says Fred and Wilma are scary 'cause all they talk about is Armageddon and how the world's coming to an end, and Grandma especially doesn't like that...but she lets us go to the Kingdom Hall with Fred and Wilma anyway, 'cause she knows we won't get to visit her in the summer if she doesn't.

THE HOUSE OF FLUFFY

L ice invaded the Fillmore schools in 1972. A posse of nurses roamed the elementary campuses to search for bugs, and they sent me and Sissy home after finding lice crawling through our hair.

Fluffy was mad as hell, convinced that we had acquired lice by using another kid's comb. We should have known better than to use another kid's comb, she said. Stupid kids.

She bent us backwards over the kitchen sink for kerosene shampoos.

Kerosene was supposed to kill lice. It didn't.

"Close your eyes! This'll teach you to not use someone else's comb."

She quarantined us to our room to pick lice and nits out of each other's head.

I sat on the edge of my bed, Sissy on the floor in front of me, picking lice out of her hair, squishing them between my thumbnails—the nits, too, they "pop" when you squish 'em, that's how you know they're dead, by the "pop" noise—wondering how I got lice and thinking I would be more careful and never let such a thing happen again.

Aunt Jan and Uncle Marv came down from Chico with my cousins Trisha and Jason to go to Disneyland that weekend. I didn't have to dust baseboards during their visit, and we got Boo Berry cereal with real milk for breakfast each morning. During the night, Trisha acquired head lice while sleeping in our beds.

A few days after they drove home, we got a phone call from Uncle Marv who cussed and screamed and swore to never visit again. Fluffy then accepted the failure of kerosene shampoos to kill lice and took us to the Fillmore barbershop for haircuts. Sissy got a pixie cut and I had my head shaved bald—and that's how we got rid of head lice.

—∞—

Virgil gave up the pool business to become a foreman on a Grimes Canyon ranch in Ventura County. He worked and played there five and six days a week, doctoring cattle and gloating over the perk of having a private urban wilderness to hunt quail and board his horse.

He acquired a purebred Australian Kelpie cattle dog named Flo to help him herd cattle on the ranch. I let Flo in Fluffy's house, but she had never before been indoors. I thought it hysterical when Flo ran frantically from room to room, hoping to escape, until she saw daylight through the screen and crashed through, getting tangled in the mess. Fluffy was furious.

"You're going to pay for that!" she complained. "When you get your first job, you're going to pay me for a new screen!"

The ranch in Grimes Canyon was a fantasy world for me. I chased chickens on the backside of the barn and splashed around the horse trough with my bare hands, attempting to scoop out the mosquito fish. I ran after calves in the back pen with a rope, trying to catch one. Dad didn't think I'd snag anything, but I did, and he had to chase the calf down to get the rope off while we both laughed ourselves silly.

When Fluffy insisted, he took me to the ranch to work with him for the day.

He rode off into the hills, looking for stray cattle, leaving me to clean horse stalls by shoveling shit out the side window of the barn. He returned a couple of hours later, still astride his horse, and dismounted to inspect my progress. I wasn't yet finished.

"Good job," he said, after wandering through the stalls.

He stuck his head through the open window and looked at the pile of manure I had moved outside. "That's good," he repeated. "Why can't you be good like that when I leave you at home?"

He mounted to check cattle on another section of the ranch, and I finished shoveling clean the remaining stalls, wondering what the hell he would do with the massive pile of crap outside. With time on my hands to kill, I hiked a few yards up the hill and picked prickly pear cactus for lunch. Indians ate cactus, I'd read, and I wrestled with a couple of pale purple fruit, pretending I was an Indian, getting stuck by thorns in the process.

Virgil hunted quail in Grimes Canyon.

I followed him through the brush, carrying his kills, practicing my Indian skills.

Any minute now, I expected him to turn around, wondering if I had disappeared, on account of the fact that I was so quiet. And he'd tell me how good I was at missing all the sticks and dead, crunchy leaves, and I'd tell him I had been reading Indian books and was practicing for when all the Jehovah's Witnesses have to run to the hills to escape persecution and hunt rabbits before Armageddon.

Virgil blasted quail out of the air with his shotgun. He handed their bodies to me, then twisted their heads off with his bare hands at home and cooked them with bacon.

Rarely did he kill rabbits. Virgil wouldn't kill anything he didn't intend to eat.

"Rabbits have tularemia disease, which means you can't eat them," Virgil said. "Especially when it's hot, because that's when rabbits get tularemia. The best way to find out if your rabbits have tularemia is to pull their skin off and check for black marks underneath."

On the rare weekends when Virgil cared to stay home, rather than drive out to the ranch, my hopes always rose for a pleasant afternoon—praying that my stepmother wouldn't relay my sins from the previous week and him meting out overdue punishment for my transgressions—wishing for him to pull me out of her house and drive us away to some remote location where our lives would connect and I would follow in his footsteps. I was an idiot that way, never giving up my dreams for attention from my father and hoping he would rescue me from the home he often abandoned, but I think he was mostly tired. Or bored. Or brow beaten. I don't really know. Outside of the hours we spent in a Kingdom Hall or serving Jehovah, our infrequent weekends together were generally wasted on television—baseball games and Westerns. He wasn't the least bit of a sports fan, neither was I, and I struggled to understand why he spent his time at home glued to the La-Z-Boy, a victim of recliner paralysis.

In my adolescent mind, he allowed the whole world to ever-so-quietly pass us by…watching people we didn't know play games we didn't play. The passions of his life weren't found at home and I'm convinced he didn't know what to do when there, except watch TV, which seemed a terrible waste to me, imagining there were great discoveries to be found somewhere else. I wanted to discover them with my dad.

—∞—

While walking home from Safeway on a Pepsi run for Fluffy, I stopped in front of a newly-built but still vacant home. Our Fillmore subdivision was peppered with vacant lots. No fences. No trees. Construction crews roamed our neighborhood. With Fluffy's six-pack of Pepsi in my hands, I stopped to watch a sunburned and overweight blond guy pour concrete at one of the new houses. He knelt down to his knees in the hot summer sun, smoothing out freshly laid cement, his shirt discarded nearby. His pants hung halfway off of his butt. I stared for the longest time, inexplicably drawn to his nakedness. After delivering the Pepsi to Fluffy, I snuck out of the house and went back for a second titillating look, not knowing why I found him so fascinating but feeling the curious pull of an interest I didn't have a name for.

Months later, we got our own concrete patio poured in back—steel wire buried inside with an explanation that it would make the concrete stronger, which seemed ridiculously unnecessary since I couldn't imagine why concrete needed to be any stronger. Days later, the concrete patio set hard and Fluffy purchased two flimsy chaise lounge chairs to decorate it.

Sissy and I asked to sleep outdoors in the pretty new lounge chairs. Fluffy locked us outside for a long and adventurous night of backyard camping with two thin and fuzzy brown cowboy quilts that Grandma Terry had hand-stitched for each of us. We stretched out in the new recliners and about froze to death after it got dark. We were up most of the night, waiting for morning to come, too scared to bother anyone by asking to be let in, thinking Fluffy would be angry if we woke her up, praying for morning to come, tossing and turning from cold.

The dead-end nature of Dad's working on the Grimes Canyon ranch drove Fluffy up the wall, so he quit that job and found a grunt-level position on the southern California oil rigs. He returned home each night bathed in black sludge, with clothes so dirty they weren't allowed in our house. Fluffy parked her station wagon in the driveway most days because the garage was occupied by a stiff and greasy heap of Virgil's work clothes. Shortly after, she found a four inch scratch on its passenger door. She determined it was caused by me and added the unknown cost of repairing it to the unknown cost of a new screen door. I never knew what they would cost me. Hundreds, probably. Thousands, maybe.

She frequently argued with Virgil over his failure to get her out of the house for evenings of romance. With his new job, they could afford some romance, she argued. Movies. Dinner. An Elvis concert.

She wore her red wig on their dates. It sat on a white Styrofoam head in Fluffy's bedroom, decorating her dresser, out in plain view, waiting for dates with Virgil. I wondered why she didn't put it away in a drawer when not in use.

Granny M fell into babysitting duty when Fluffy went out with Virgil. Most times, she warmed up cans of pork and beans with sliced weenies for our dinner, then dressed in her favorite Hawaiian muumuu and stretched out in Dad's recliner to enjoy the upcoming performances on *The Lawrence Welk Show*. She'd never been to Hawaii, she was from Pittsburgh, but she lounged in her red muumuu when on babysitting duty and demanded silence for her favorite TV program of champagne music.

When the very handsome and blonde Tom Netherton sang, the earth stopped turning for Granny M. She got giddy, almost swooning at the sound of his velvet baritone voice. I would bet a million bucks that she had sexual fantasies about him.

"That man has such a beautiful voice, can you just imagine!" followed by, "Hush! I'm trying to listen to my program!"

Tom Netherton's performance would eventually come to an end and Granny M would come back to earth and the pretty little Mexican girl Anacani would then sing a pretty but boring little Mexican song which always launched Mr. Welk into a patronizing speech about how he miraculously discovered the pretty little Mexican girl. I couldn't quite put my finger on it, but he seemed unexplainably and ever so slightly derogatory to me. Even then, it was apparent to me that he would never have referred to the Semonski Sisters as his "pretty little Polish girls."

But Anacani would eventually find a conclusion to her Spanish musical performance and Mr. Welk would then introduce the dancing duo Bobby and Sissy.

I gazed in envy at the graceful couple waltzing across the TV screen. It was beautiful, those occasional evenings alone with Granny M, falling in love with Bobby and Sissy. I watched Bobby toss his head and flash his teeth and flit across the dance floor in his tight little polyester slacks and swing Sissy around 'til she must have been dizzy as a bat. Everyone on the planet suspected he might be gay, except for me because I didn't yet know what it meant to be gay. I only dreamed of being on a future *Lawrence Welk* episode where I would take Bobby's place and spin Sissy around a thousand times until she laughed and fell down.

We carried on and laughed ourselves silly when Granny M came to babysit. The oppression in our home would vanish for the evening and we'd get giggle attacks until she was besieged by migraines. Granny M was our savior. During daylight hours when she wasn't available to watch us, Sissy and I were locked outside and threatened with punishment if we were caught setting foot out of the backyard. If an adult wasn't home to supervise us, Fluffy's fenced-in backyard served as a quarantine facility.

The most forbidden zones in Fluffy's house were the kitchen and her bedroom. Simple indoor liberties such as turning on Fluffy's TV or opening the fridge were prohibited, because they weren't ours. Those rules did not apply to Fluffy's children.

Every now and then, for reasons we could never understand, there were rare occasions when Fluffy allowed us to stay indoors while she left home to run errands. Most of those times, she tucked a small and folded piece of paper at the top of her closed bedroom door, out of our reach, hoping to discover it on the floor when she returned—proof that we had entered her forbidden bedroom.

If Fluffy was too tired or ill to get out of bed to pour Post Toasties for our breakfast, Virgil dished it out before leaving for work. Post Toasties were like corn flakes, except cheaper. He scattered a spoonful of white sugar over top, then poured non-fat powdered milk over top and left it sitting on the counter for us to eat later. If Fluffy had not prepared non-fat powdered milk the night before, he left it for her to handle.

I watched her mix a pitcher of dried milk powder with tap water. We referred to it as "made-up milk." Foam floated on top of the room temperature milk.

"Grams keeps a jar of water in her fridge, just so it will be cold," I suggested.

"You don't need it to be cold!" Fluffy snapped. "Water from the sink is good enough."

A half-gallon of cold milk occupied Fluffy's fridge, but it was off limits to me or Sissy. Real milk was only for her and Dad's use.

One morning Dad left for work without having his usual breakfast. He did not pour our cereal that morning because we were out of Post Toasties.

Fluffy poured two bowls of Raisin Bran and set them on the table in front of us. Raisin Bran was Dad's cereal, but he didn't eat breakfast that morning because the box was swarming with ants.

"Just pick them out!" Fluffy said. "Ants aren't poisonous and people in Africa eat ants. If you don't like them, just pick them out. When Armageddon comes, you'll be wishing you weren't so picky."

If you don't eat your cereal, Fluffy will put it in the fridge and give it to you for dinner, 'cause she says there are starving people in Africa who would be happy to get Post Toasties with made-up milk. And she poured apple juice on our cereal once. She said it was an accident.

Sissy says you can usually tell when people don't like you, even if you don't hear them say so. You can just tell.

Typical punishment from an angry Fluffy was a hard spanking or the denial of meals, followed by banishment to our bedroom. When punished for my myriad of sins, I often laid in bed with pretend thoughts of turning invisible, thinking that an invisible me could steal food when hungry. Or I had repetitive and hopeful daydreams of a magical kitchen that was well stocked with food and located underneath our house, only accessible via a trapdoor in my bedroom closet—a secret trapdoor, under the shag carpet, with short stairs that led to an imaginary kitchen. A kitchen that wasn't controlled by my stepmother, and only available for my occasional needs. I lay in bed often as a child, dreaming of kitchen contents while surrounded by hunger and punishments. Interrupted by doses of reality and concerns of how an imaginary kitchen could possibly be replenished, a problem I couldn't solve, which made the whole idea disappointingly silly. I dreamed often of a day when I might run away from home and be adopted by an unknown Indian tribe. The Indians would protect me from being spanked with my own belt, the one with the buckle attached. Or the pancake spatula, except it broke while Fluffy was spanking me and that was too bad 'cause it didn't hurt all that bad to get spanked with a spatula. Then Fluffy salvaged a two foot piece of wood from a broken bookcase. She called it "The Brown Stick." The Brown Stick was unbreakable.

And she'll pinch you hard in the leg when you're sittin' next to her in the Kingdom Hall if she thinks you're not payin' attention to the lectures about Satan and Revelations and Armageddon when people's tongues will rot and fall out of their heads.

Or she'll make you read scriptures about people in the Bible who killed their disobedient kids by stoning them to death with rocks. Fluffy says I would have been killed with rocks in the olden days. Sissy too.

—∞—

"Scott! Sissy! Get outside!"

Fluffy was leaving for the grocery store. I ignored her and feigned interest in a book I had already read a million times, playing little fantasies in my head and wondering if she would forget to lock us out, just this once.

"Scott! Get outside!"

I followed Sissy out to the backyard. On that day, like so many others, she had unlatched the window over our bathtub, just a crack, enough to be unnoticeable. Still, a huge risk.

Less than a minute after Fluffy's station wagon pulled out of the driveway, Sissy boosted me up through our bathroom window. I squeezed through the curtain of orange beads and lowered myself down to the tub.

We ransacked the kitchen for something to eat, something that wouldn't be missed, then smeared mayonnaise across a slice of bread and split it.

Soon after, by accident, I realized that the locking mechanism on the patio sliding glass door could be switched into the lock position before pushing the door closed, and when closed that way, the door appeared to be locked...but wasn't. I tested it several times, stunned at my discovery.

"Click." Slide door closed.

"Click." Slide door closed.

It worked every time. The door looked locked, but wasn't.

A few days later, when Fluffy announced that she was kicking us out, I seized the opportunity to test my discovery when she went to retrieve her purse from her bedroom.

In her absence, I clicked the lever on the patio door into the lock position and quietly slid it closed. My heart pounded. I walked outdoors to join Sissy. My pulse accelerated, knowing Fluffy would check the slider and discover my deception.

I knew the risk I was taking. I knew Fluffy would check the door, because that's what people do when they don't want anyone in their house. They check doors.

I knew I would get caught, and I knew she would be so extraordinarily angry that she would fly into a rage and I would feign stupidity and deny what she surmised, but she wouldn't believe me. There would be hell to pay.

But Fluffy never checked the door. She simply took a sideways glance at the lever in the lock position, and then exited out to the driveway through the kitchen. Mere seconds later, I was inside, watching her station wagon disappear down Wileman Street from behind the cover of her living room curtains.

We jumped on Fluffy's king-sized bed to celebrate, unable to resist the allure of such an expansive mattress. We jumped so high we could touch the ceiling. We laughed and giggled and celebrated our newly discovered ease at getting into the house. The phone rang. We ignored it. We knocked popcorn spackle down onto Fluffy's bed. We laughed and played and straightened the blankets and cleaned the popcorn mess, then went back to the patio to wait for Fluffy's return.

Fluffy's sister, Aunt Jackie, called again, and then again, but her calls were met with a busy signal. Unknown to us, Sissy and I had knocked the bedroom phone off the hook. Aunt Jackie got so mad at being unable to reach Fluffy that she drove over to our house to ask what the hell Fluffy was doing on the phone, and that's how they figured out that we had been inside, and even worse, had gone into Fluffy's bedroom.

We denied it.

We didn't get dinner that night. Or breakfast, or lunch the next day, until Sissy confessed. I was so angry with her. We had promised to stick together and never tell. I was fully prepared to hold out forever and starve to death, but Sissy only lasted twenty-four hours before giving in and admitting that we had been in the house.

—∞—

We had Mexicans for neighbors. They had two kids, Ralph and Rudy Rodriquez, and they all seemed to like each other. Ralph went to school with Sissy, and Rudy was younger than me. They had freedoms. In my eyes, their house was an unincarcerated world of laughter and playtime and BB guns and beef tacos and weekend trips to the Fillmore swap meet.

The Rodriquez family played with fireworks on the Fourth of July. Mr. Rodriquez handed me a lit sparkler, and I waved it around the air in their front yard until Dad called me into the house and lectured me about the sin of celebrating the Fourth of July. Fireworks were a sin. I stood in the corner until bedtime as punishment.

A few weeks later, Sissy and I were home alone on a hot Saturday, locked out of Fluffy's house, peeking through the gate in our fence, watching Rudy play on his driveway next door with a skateboard.

Thinking he was also home alone, I left the isolation of my own backyard to talk to him, aware of the trouble I would be in if caught. Sissy stayed behind.

We rode his skateboard up and down the driveway. I chatted with Rudy like he was my friend.

"Is your mom home?" I asked.

"No. It's just me."

Rudy got bored. He went indoors, leaving his kitchen door wide open behind him.

I leaned inside, my feet planted firmly on his driveway, peering through the narrow galley kitchen.

"Can you get anything for us to eat?"

Mrs. Rodriquez stepped out around the corner from her living room and answered, "No. He can't."

I was mortified. Rudy had lied to me. He wasn't home alone.

Fluffy was due to come home soon. Not wanting to be caught out of the backyard, I left the skateboard on Rudy's driveway. Later in the day his mother ran over it with her car.

Rudy's brother, Ralph, sold candied peanuts to raise money for the Fillmore Boy's Club. He gave a can to Sissy as a present. We hid it in the garage and doled the contents out over a few days.

Fluffy found it. She was livid. She said we stole them.

She beat the hell out of us with my belt that Grandpa bought for me at the Cottonwood auction yard with my name engraved on the oversized chrome western buckle.

Sissy screamed.

I stood in the corner after the spanking, so close to Sissy I could reach out and touch her, waiting for Dad to come home, staring at the wall, poking gently at a fresh cut on my scalp, feeling the blood dry on my hair.

I whispered to Sissy, "Dad will see the blood and he'll fix everything and she won't be allowed to hit us anymore."

Hours later, Dad arrived home after a visit with his horse. He sent us to bed. Life went on.

—∞—

My best and only friend in Fillmore was George Ferry. George stuttered and had a perpetually runny nose that left green snot caked above his lip. He had no friends other than me, due to the stuttering problem and his issue with the runny nose. George had a buzz-cut and was kind of slow, but we sat next to each other for three years of elementary school where he let me copy his schoolwork when I couldn't read what was written on the chalkboard.

George really hated going home after school…much like me. I don't remember why. His mom was an alcoholic, I think. So, after lots of talk, I convinced him to run away to the hills with me. We would live like Indians, I told him, and in third grade, that's what we did.

I stole a sack of oranges from the orange grove and George brought plastic bags to carry water. Our classmate Gale Walker walked home after school to steal some chocolate Ding Dongs, and then met us back at San Cayetano Creek. George and I ate the Ding Dongs two minutes after Gale showed up, then drank water out of San Cayetano creek to wash them down. Gale thought we were idiots for not saving the Ding Dongs for dinner.

The three of us horsed around in the creek, chasing frogs, then we filled George's plastic bags with water. One leaked, so we left it behind and climbed the hill to camp for the night. Just like Indians.

Halfway up the slope, George snagged his pants in a barbed wire fence and was stranded out there in plain view. The school principal was driving around the neighborhood, searching for us, and he spotted George up on the hillside, flailing around in the dirt, trying to disentangle his leg from the barbed wire.

He yelled at us through his open window. "Get down here! Now!"

We hiked back down the hill and squeezed into the back seat of his blue Volkswagen. I was pissed at George for getting us caught.

George's mother was waiting for us at Fluffy's house.

She grabbed him by his ear and pushed him out the door to her car.

Fluffy screamed at me, "We should lock you up in prison and throw away the key so you can't ever get out!"

Virgil came home that night and spanked me, but it wasn't one of the bad ones. Not like George got. When his mom got him home, she cut a switch from their backyard peach tree and whipped him. He couldn't hardly sit down at school the next day.

A few months later, George and I ran away again—to the same hills across the creek from San Cayetano Elementary School. Fluffy didn't even bother to call the school. She just waited until Dad came home. He drove to the dead-end cul-de-sac behind school and found me and George hiding behind a section of fence on the other side of the creek.

I didn't get spanked that time. I didn't know why not.

———∞———

San Cayetano Elementary gave out free hearing and eye exams that year. When it was my turn to be tested, I walked to the cafeteria where some official looking people handed out a big plastic letter E and instructing me to rotate it in the same direction as the 'E' displayed on the screen up front. I sat on a stool for what could have been a mile away from the screen and told the official people that I didn't know which way to turn my E.

They moved my stool closer.

I completed my test, thought it was stupid to interrupt class for such a silly exercise, and didn't think anything of it.

The school nurse called Fluffy that same day to report the results.

I walked in the kitchen door, unaware that she had done so.

Fluffy knocked me to the floor.

"You're a liar!" she screamed. "You lied at school! There's nothin' wrong with your eyes!"

Granny M stood nearby. I looked up at her and cried out, "I told you so!"

She asked, "You told me what?"

I ignored her.

She asked again, "You told me what, Scott?"

I couldn't answer her. I didn't know what it meant or why I said it. I didn't know why something so stupid had come out of my mouth. So nonsensical. So useless. I lay on the kitchen floor and made up my mind to never again let anyone know that I couldn't see.

———

In the summer of 1973, Grams and Gramps drove down to Fillmore to take me and Sissy back to Orland. They brought presents for Fluffy—a case of home-canned peaches and a 50-pound burlap sack of English walnuts. Unfortunately, Sissy had fallen off her bike a few months earlier and broken her arm. She broke it twice that year…the first time when playing Crack-the-Whip at school, and then again when she got knocked off her bike by the older kid down the street whose name I don't remember. He didn't do it on purpose, it was an accident, but Fluffy was angry, on account of the medical expense and everything, so she said Sissy had an upcoming appointment with the doctor to get her cast cut off and couldn't go to Orland.

My grandparents argued with Dad and Fluffy, right in front of me, making them incredible heroes in my eyes—a view clouded by the certainty that Sissy was being punished.

We headed north for Orland the next morning, leaving Sissy behind. She cried. Grams said, "Thay ain't no reason why she cain't go, bless her heart," and "I never hearda such a thang in all my life," 'cause Grams said that a lot.

Halfway up the coast, we stopped for the night at some relatives' house. They were "shirttail relatives," the kind you have scattered all over the country and never really talk about. I'd never met them before, but their youngest son shared my name. He was another Scott Terry.

He had a swimming pool with a water slide in his backyard. I was afraid to go down that slide, but did anyway, because I wasn't gonna let the other kid with the same name as me know I was afraid.

The shirttail relatives drove us to the local Green Barn restaurant for dinner. We crowded into a small waiting room, surrounded by red carpet and Victorian velvet paisley wallpaper and not enough chairs, for what seemed like hours, while adults passed around drinks with miniature red plastic swords stuck in them, a candied cherry impaled in the center, and that's when I learned you aren't supposed to pronounce the W in sword.

That's a waste of a perfectly good letter, so I asked, "Why do you stick a W in the word if you don't pronounce it?"

The answer was, "You just do."

After a painfully long and hungry wait, everyone got grouchy until we were allowed to sit down to a dinner my grandparents couldn't possibly have afforded. It wasn't their usual way of dining, being a lengthy five-course meal with more silverware than necessary. There were two sizes of forks. And about triple the number of spoons needed at dinnertime.

A team of waiters cleared the dirty plates from our first course, then hauled in clean dishes for different food. It seemed magical to me, to eat in such an abundant manner. Food just kept arriving, like presents. Various parts of a long dinner were delivered in an endlessly long procession, and I sat next to Grams while she explained that some folks liked to serve dinner in bits and pieces instead of bringing everything out to the table at the same time.

On our way out of town the next morning, Grams spotted a patch of wild dill in a vacant lot around the corner. We trespassed on the property to pick handfuls, and cooked it with prickly cucumbers to put up quart jars of pickles in Orland.

Pickles were a big deal. Grams canned two kinds. Sweet pickles…I liked those…and dill pickles. I helped with those but didn't like them then and don't like them now.

We canned jam together that summer. On the outskirts of Orland, Grams flopped a board across some unintentionally planted blackberry thickets and we balanced on top, picking berries in sun because blackberries in shade aren't very sweet.

We stacked the pint jars of blackberry jam on a garage shelf amongst all the other flavors of Grams' home canned jam—peach, apricot, plum.

"You cain't open a new jar of jam until you finish that one you just opened," Grams warned.

Gramps asked me to mow his back lawn that year. To my eye it was a beautiful job, but he laughed and accused me of being drunk and unable to mow a straight line. I wasn't drunk. I was nine and nearsighted.

Each morning, I awoke to the twang of country music from the transistor radio on Grams kitchen windowsill, a dependable ritual, rising to the sounds of her radio while she stirred around making breakfast. My lazy afternoons were spent listening to eight-track tapes stacked up under the living room stereo, mostly old-time country tunes from Dolly Parton and Hank Snow.

My grandparents' music, old-time country and bluegrass with banjos and fiddles, rocked my world. I had favorites. There were songs that I listened to again and again.

"Pa fell asleep out under the tree, and the hogs ate him. The
    hogs ate him.
Pa fell asleep out under the tree, now Pa is gone forever.
Forever. Forever.
Pa is gone forever."

I parked myself in front of their stereo for hours, rehearsing songs and gazing upwards at a black and white formal family portrait hanging over top the eight-track player, a picture of the whole family, not long after Dad's wedding to my genuine mother. It was the only photo that documented her existence. When I stared at it, I looked into the eyes of a stranger. My mother had black hair piled up on top of her head like a lady from the 1960s, which she was. I wondered if Rocky Road was her favorite ice cream, too. And was she also in love with Dolly Parton and Glen Campbell?

I got lost often in the company of my grandparents' eight-track player, pressing "repeat" over and over, painstakingly scribbling notes and spelling out lyrics I didn't understand, dreaming I might grow up to be a fabulous country western singer like Hank Snow. Sissy would sing like Dolly Parton. We would grow up to be famous, and life would be good.

My solitary vacation in Orland without Sissy came to an end. I had never before been to Orland without her.

I flew back to Fillmore on PSA airlines, bringing presents for everyone but Grant and Amber. Grant was only three, a week away from turning four, and he was already the recipient of way too many gifts—every time he returned from a doctor's visit, which happened often. Fluffy's second child, her daughter Amber, was still a day or two away from being born. Grams sent a handmade baby blanket a few days later, but Fluffy didn't like it. Grams complained to everyone that "She was ungrateful and I'm not ever gonna send another quilt to her."

I brought a box of hand-me-down clothes for Sissy, and told her that Aunt Susan had purchased them at her church rummage sale as a present. Dad and Fluffy muttered about the sins of the worldly church they came from.

I brought some frozen catfish back to Fillmore too—fish that I had slung out of an Orland irrigation ditch with Aunt Letha, wrapped in thick layers of newspaper to get them south intact because Grams said, "Thay ain't no reason to let them feesh go to waste." The fish were thawed by the time I arrived home, but Dad cooked a few for dinner that evening, a perfectly normal thing, because personally killed critters were always cooked by him. Meals from Safeway were handled by Fluffy. Her family didn't kill things for dinner, being from Pittsburgh, so Dad cooked a few of my fish that night and Fluffy threw the rest in the garbage.

I had presents for Dad—old neckties salvaged from a pile of clothes from Grams' church rummage sale. They were beauties—leftovers from the 1950's, out of date, larger than Virgil's usual ties, the best being a garish peacock. I imagined him as the envy of the entire Kingdom Hall in his western suit and cowboy boots and such a gorgeous tie around his neck.

"I don't know why Grandma sends you home with junk," he complained. The ties went to the garbage.

But absolutely, the best present to fly back to Fillmore was my gift to Fluffy from the airport gift shop. They sold rocks in that shop. Honest to God. They sold plain old ordinary rocks with short and funny comments painted on them, and rocks with little indentations for people to rub their thumbs over. Grams said they were called "worry stones," and that if people had worries, they could buy one and hold it in their hands for the longest time and rub it to make their worries go away.

That was just plain stupid. No matter what you call it, a rock is still a rock, and I imagined that people who paid good money for a rock, believing it would solve their problems, surely had rocks in their head. I could have bought one for Fluffy, but she would have called me stupid for bringing home a rock, so I settled on a red ceramic toothpick holder in the shape of an apple with a hole punched through the top. I had a pocket full of change that day— money I had earned from trapping mice in my grandparents' home. They gave me a dime for every stiff mouse I pulled out of a trap, but what I had saved wasn't enough to buy the ceramic apple.

Grams offered to cover the shortfall.

"Her birthday's comin' up in a few days," she said. "If you want to buy somethin' for her, I'll help you pay for it. Just tell her it's a present from me."

I imagined Fluffy being completely overcome with joy at the sight of our gift. Her toothpicks were shelved out of sight in their plain original box, and I was so impressed by the idea that someone had the artistic talent to decorate an apple for displaying something as trivial as toothpicks that I proudly described selecting it special, just for her, and how pretty it would look sitting on her table, and buying it with money from trapping mice, and how Grandma had paid for the difference as a birthday gift.

It turns out, that was just plain wrong. Witnesses don't celebrate birthdays, so I was given a lengthy lecture about my sin. They said I should have known better than to accept Grams' money…and my little ceramic apple was deported to a kitchen cabinet where it sat empty, never holding a single toothpick.

But for months after, when Sissy and I were washing the dinner dishes, I often caught sight of it in the cupboard amongst the Tupperware and Fluffy's medications. It stared back at me every time I opened that cabinet—taunting me for being a fool. In frustration, I snuck it out to the garage and slammed it into the bottom of the trash can.

I shared stories of my Orland visit with Sissy, easing her hurt over missing out. In the privacy of our bedroom, I sang my favorite Hank Snow tune, *I've Been Everywhere*, feeling proud of what I had learned in my grandparents' living room, until a family of Fluffy's old friends from her Kingdom Hall in Pittsburgh came over to visit.

They drove all the way out to California on vacation and stopped to see us for dinner. They were "colored people." Apparently, all of Fluffy's old friends from Pittsburgh were in The Truth, and all were black, a detail that she'd never before mentioned and I'd never imagined. When they left, my dad said that there was a time, maybe just a generation earlier, when colored people weren't allowed in the Kingdom Hall at the same time as the white people. And he said that, back in those older days, Ozark Kingdom Halls had a spittoon in every corner for men to spit tobacco in, and all of that sounded strange to me. We'd never had colored people in our house before, but Fluffy was perfectly friendly with black folks and her old Pittsburgh friends had two teen-aged daughters with funny looking hair who belted out doo-wop songs in my bedroom with Sissy. We thought they were about the coolest kids we'd ever seen, until I let loose with my Hank Snow imitation and the colored lady who clearly didn't know a damn thing about bluegrass music pointed out it would sound much better once my voice deepened.

She was wrong. A deep voice isn't anything close to what you need to sound like Hank Snow.

Grandma's gifts to Fluffy were banished to the garage. Her case of peaches sat neglected on a table in the far corner, collecting dust. The burlap sack of walnuts leaned against a wall in the opposite corner. Sissy and I stole them when we were hungry.

We first stole the peaches, eleven jars of peaches, until we were left with one jar of pears that Grams had dyed green. We feared they wouldn't taste like pears at all, but when it was the only jar remaining in the box, we popped the lid off and discovered that green pears tasted just like regular pears.

When the preserved fruit was gone, we cracked walnuts until we were sick to death of walnuts.

I bagged them up in brown paper sacks and sold them to our neighbors for a quarter.

It seemed risky to solicit business from our immediate neighbors, fearing the news might get leaked back to Fluffy, so on a day when she wasn't home, I walked a block up the street and sold the first bag on my very first attempt. Afterwards, a quarter in hand, I ran to the Tipsy-Fox convenience store at the corner of C Street and bought a roll of Name Drop candies for fifteen cents. I shared them with Sissy, and we spent the next few quarters on potato chips at the café across the railroad tracks from school and bottles of Coke from the vending machine in the Laundromat next door.

Months later, while watching *The Love Boat* on Fluffy's TV, Virgil got an urge for peaches.

"Scott, go out to the garage and get a jar of Grandma's peaches," he said. "That sounds good right now."

I left the house, horrified. I dawdled in the garage, stalling for time, hoping a delayed return would cause Virgil to think I had ransacked the garage for peaches. Oh God. What would I tell him?

After a lengthy delay, I went back to face him.

"I can't find any peaches," I said. "I think they're all gone."

He turned to face me.

"What do you mean, they're gone?"

"There aren't any more peaches. I looked all over."

"Are you kidding me?"

A slow look of awareness settled over his face.

"You and your sister need to stay out of things!"

He went back to watching *The Love Boat*, and we never again talked about peaches.

A FINAL ESCAPE TO ORLAND

The following year I entered Sespe Elementary for fourth grade. Sissy was there also, she was in sixth, so we walked to school together and stole oranges from the orchards on our return home. Navel oranges ripened in winter and Valencias in summer.

George Ferry was also at Sespe. His mother sent him to school every day with a home-packed lunch, but she only knew how to make two kinds of sandwiches—thick peanut butter and jelly that she had spread out perfectly to all four corners of the bread, or tuna fish with sweet pickles and celery and black olives mixed in. In my mind, taking the time to be so elaborate with tuna fish meant that she liked him a lot.

I stole dozens of Grant's toy cars and traded them to George for sandwiches. Grant never missed what I took from his collection of toy Hot Wheels. He was a chunky kid, and he could spend hours, all day even, lying on the floor, doing nothing but lining up countless numbers of toy cars in imaginary traffic lanes while muttering, "Vroom Vroom Vroom"…happy as any boy could be with a car collection and dreams of staged vehicle collisions.

I was convinced that he was from Mars. Or insane. Or both. I wanted to climb trees, collect rocks, and chase rabbits. But Grant's imagination centered on lethargic hours of traffic noises. I watched him play with hot rods, day after day, for years, stretched out across the carpet while making strange noises, and tried to imagine what on earth, or Mars, could possibly be going on in his head to cause him to spend his day that way.

I didn't care one way or the other about cars and owned none. I was passionate about books and art supplies, none of which George would have traded a tuna fish sandwich for.

The lead in my afternoon class play about the California gold rush was given to me that year. I played the part of Sourdough John in a short performance about the forty-niners who arrived to seek their fortune. George wasn't given a part, but that didn't bother him. It wasn't an impressive production, only lasting a few minutes when we traveled around school with me in a floppy straw hat, enacting the life of a gold miner for students in lower grades. My performances went just fine, until we went to the second grade classroom that had Jesus. We walked in the door and there He was, in the front row—a little Mexican kid with a shaved head and a name tag that declared his name to be "Jesus."

I imagined that it was a mistake. No one should ever name their kid Jesus, should they? Jehovah would be so pissed when he found out.

———∞———

Fluffy hosted a few small parties to play cards with Vic and Sheila Percival. They were Dad and Fluffy's best friends, but we couldn't call them "Vic" and "Sheila" because it would be disrespectful to call them by their first names. They were "Brother and Sister Percival" to me.

Brother Percival went out with Dad and bought firecrackers and bottle rockets on Fourth of July. They shot them off in the hills outside of town and practiced telling fag jokes. The highlight of their time together was faggot jokes. They pretended to be homos and called each other "Sweets" while standing in line at Safeway to buy a watermelon for Fluffy's party, just to get a rise out of the clerk. And they always cheated when they played cards. Fluffy and Sheila got mad when they cheated, but not really, 'cause they kept playing and laughed about how Dad and Vic never played fair.

Fluffy hosted a Sunday party where a few other Witness families came over to play badminton in our front yard while the kids played in back. Halfway through the festivities, she peeked through the front door and saw me eating potato chips. After everyone went home, she surprised me with what she had seen.

"I saw you sneaking around behind my back! You're gonna eat an entire bag of chips as punishment for being a thief!"

She opened a new bag of chips and set them in front of me.

"And you're not gonna get any water either, until you finish the bag!"

She watched Peter Falk play *Columbo* on TV while I ate my way through the chips. I pondered the logic of her punishment. Eating a bag of salty potato chips didn't seem so terrible to me. Halfway through the chore, my opinion changed.

Virgil got up to investigate when *Columbo* was over. He peaked into the bag. It was more than half empty.

He brought me a glass of water and removed the bag from the table.

"Why don't you go to bed," he said.

Not long after, Vic came over with a baseball mitt to play catch. To his surprise, I didn't own a baseball glove. Vic said something that someone didn't like, so Dad sent Fluffy on a mission to buy me a glove. A few days later, I got a new baseball glove to wear on my right hand.

"Right-handed baseball players should wear gloves on their left hands," I told Fluffy.

"What difference does it make? After you catch the ball, just take your glove off and then throw the ball back!" she answered.

Fluffy won't let me take my new baseball mitt to school...she says it'll get stolen. It doesn't matter, anyway, 'cause children shouldn't play sports. The Bible says so. First Timothy 4:8 says "Bodily exercise is beneficial for a little, but godly devotion is beneficial for all things." So they say I need to spend more time reading the Watchtower and learning to serve Jehovah, and that's why I don't really need a baseball mitt. And you can't play sports after school anyhow, 'cause that would be associating with people who aren't in The Truth and that's bad association. The Bible says that, too.

I played my first baseball game that year, in fourth grade, at the age of nine. A fellow classmate on the opposing team let me borrow his mitt and we swapped it back and forth when each team changed sides...a warm, soft, well-worn, flexible mitt that made me believe I was just like everyone else.

I reveled in that feeling, stretching my left hand inside the sweaty glove, catching whiffs of the pungent leather, knowing experienced baseball-playing kids had caught thousands of balls in it. I stood patiently out in the south-forty end of the ball field and waited for some kid to slug a never-gonna-happen baseball out to my impossible to reach patch of field.

The inning ended, and I stood alone at home plate, my first and only time at bat. I let loose with my first tentative swing.

Fellow teammates screamed at me.

"Choke up! Choke up on the bat!"

I frantically analyzed the possible meanings of "choke up" while being yelled at by pre-pubescent jock boys who already knew.

My fourth grade teacher interrupted my first baseball game to demonstrate the meaning of choke up, and then banned me from baseball when I took an enormous swing at the next pitch and let loose, only to watch the bat fly over the backstop and nearly brain some other kid who didn't deserve to get hit in the head by some foolish first-timer who didn't know you're supposed to hang on to the bat for a split second. Just to prevent someone from getting killed. That teacher never let me get near a baseball bat again. And I never cared to ask.

—∞—

I have "WC Fields" shoes. That's what everyone says when they see me coming in my shoes. They have three colors, kinda like a Paint horse...but in shoes. They were on sale and were supposed to be my "going to meeting" shoes, but they got turned into school shoes instead. Fluffy says it doesn't matter what people say about them. They were on sale, she said. After they got turned into school shoes, they got unglued in front, so by the time I get to school in the morning, my socks have snuck down around my foot and slipped out the hole and the sock just kinda flops around in front. Like a tongue stickin' out front of my shoe.

Nothin' will make Dad go mental faster than catching us outdoors without shoes, 'cause he says everyone will think we're poor Okies if they see us barefoot. He'll get really pissed if he thinks people are talking about him, even if they have something better to do and probably aren't. Or if they think he can't afford to buy shoes. Or if they think we're Okies, 'cause he says 'Okie' is a bad word. He's scared to death that people will think he's an Okie.

He killed a deer out in Grimes Canyon and brought it home in the back of his truck and hung it from the rafters in the garage. People could see it from out on the sidewalk, and then we cut the horns off with a hacksaw and stacked them in the corner, right on top of the pile of horns from all of his other deer kills, and under his old army surplus backpack that's hanging up on the wall. He says his old arrowhead collection used to be in that backpack, the ones he dug up in Newville, but I've never seen them. He swears that I snuck them to school and lost everything when he wasn't lookin', but he's wrong. I've never seen his arrowheads, and if I'd ever seen them, I'd remember it. And I wouldn't ever lose them, either, but he doesn't believe me. I think Fluffy threw them out when he wasn't looking, but he'd never believe that if anyone told him so.

I rolled the hide out of the way, just so we didn't get hair all over the meat while Dad was dressing it out.

"That was really smart," he said. "How come you can't be smart like that when I leave you home without me? Why are you always causing trouble for your mother?"

I don't know why he asks things like that. People try to tell him about how things are with Fluffy, but he doesn't believe them. When brothers in the Kingdom Hall ask questions, the kind you don't want them to ask, Dad gets mad. He says we spread stories, things that aren't true, but it isn't true. I don't tell anyone anything.

⎯⎯⎯ ⊗⊗⊗ ⎯⎯⎯

Later that year we got chickens. Like about twenty. Dad bought baby chicks from the Fillmore feed store and brought them home in a box. They lived on top of the clothes dryer in the kitchen for a few weeks, a light bulb hanging over top, where they chirped incessantly until we turned them loose at Aunt Jackie's house.

Aunt Jackie was raised in The Truth with Fluffy, and she had graduated from a southern California high school with the Beach Boys. She didn't really know them well on account of them being bad association, but after graduation, she slipped away from the Kingdom Hall and married a worldly guy named John. She gave birth to a child before John left her—a child whom they named Angel Star.

Aunt Jackie followed us to Fillmore and spent her days in and out of the hospital or asleep on pain-killers. She eventually found herself with mental problems and physical ailments and unemployed and dependant on Social Security disability checks. Aunt Jackie smoked, had bad hair, and was hopelessly absorbed in the task of growing her fingernails grotesquely long and stressing out over the potential tragedy of them breaking off—which happened regularly. She had three, four at most, gnarly and twisted nails on each hand, curling every which way, unrestrained. She might have saved the broken nails in a box and hid them in her closet, like treasure. Perhaps she visited them every now and then, wishing they still adorned her fingers, like a graffiti artist who can't see the ugliness of his work.

She had a fondness for gigantic dogs. Her pet at the time was a massive and gangly Great Dane named "Thor" who Virgil insisted was dumb as a fencepost. Aunt Jackie couldn't find an apartment in town that was willing to accommodate Thor, so they ended up in a decrepit and lonely little yellow farmhouse out in the orange groves on Grand Avenue where she didn't have any neighbors, and that's where our chickens went, too. We built a flimsy coop on the back side of her garage, and Thor lived his life chained to the back of her house, laying around the weeds with a twelve foot length of heavy steel chain secured to his neck.

Aunt Jackie's house was littered with candy, all stuck together in little bowls. Sucking on hard candy all day was supposed to help her stop smoking, but didn't. And she had Pepsi, 'cause she was a Pepsi drinker, too. We didn't know how she survived on candy and cigarettes and Pepsi, but there wasn't anything else to eat in her fridge except for horsemeat that she mixed with dry kibble for Thor. The horse flesh cost a fortune, but she said Thor was worth it.

On her frequent visits to the medical facilities, I walked alone to Aunt Jackie's house on weekends to feed Thor and the chickens—one of the few acceptable excuses for an unencumbered escape from Fluffy's. It took an hour at least, through the orange groves and over the Sespe Creek Bridge.

I picked green apples along Sespe Creek and stashed them in the Indian Hawthorne bushes in front of Fluffy's house. Each school day, I carried a few to school for lunch until I found myself so sick of sour green apples that I didn't finish them.

I climbed through the blackberry thickets blanketing both sides of Sespe Creek and threw rocks at the sucker fish in shallow pools of stagnant summer water.

Virgil said, "Only Mexicans would eat sucker fish."

I gently carried a sack of blackberries home as a present for Granny M.

She poured them into a bowl with milk and sugar. "You shouldn't be picking things without adult supervision," she said. "You might pick something that's poisonous and get sick and die."

"I won't get sick," I insisted. "Grandma Terry showed me how to pick blackberries. And I've been reading Indian books for when Armageddon comes and we have to run to the hills. I've been reading about wild plants we can eat when persecution comes."

"I don't care what you've been reading. You shouldn't be picking things without adult supervision," she answered.

Granny M didn't have a nickel to her name and survived on minimal Social Security retirement checks. She slept with Angel in a second bedroom in Aunt Jackie's little yellow rental out in the orange groves, but ultimately spent most of her time at Fluffy's house on account of the fact that Fluffy had four children and Jackie only had one.

Granny M had enormous concerns of whether or not Angel was spending enough time in service to Jehovah, and she got in the habit of driving Angel over to Fluffy's house on meeting nights for a ride to the Kingdom Hall. Angel was the subject of frequent conversation when adults speculated that it would be her demise to be raised under the influence of Aunt Jackie who no longer believed in The Truth.

Aunt Jackie's landlord was an old man without children who owned the vast orange orchards surrounding her rental house. He gave Angel a ten-dollar bill for her tenth birthday, but she kept it a secret. Aunt Jackie would have been fine with the birthday gift, but Granny M would have declared it a sin and made Angel give it back.

Angel ate meals at our house often. There was nothing to eat in her home, most days, except horse meat for Thor. Granny M often drove her over to Fluffy's for breakfast of Post Toasties with made-up milk, and then Angel and I walked to Sespe Elementary School together. With her landlord's ten-dollar birthday gift, we stopped at the donut shop in the Safeway strip mall for a second breakfast of milk and donuts. A regular glazed donut was thirteen cents. A plump, round, and soft donut stuffed with raspberry jelly was fifteen. An apple fritter was an outrageous thirty cents, which meant we never had one.

Angel's father, John, had moved away to Dallas for a new wife and a new life, and she could scarcely mention his name without getting all fluttery. He would come and save her some day, she was sure. She was similar to Sissy in that respect, in that both shared dreams of a distant parent coming to their rescue, but the truth is that Angel rarely saw her father. He called occasionally, never often enough, and Angel loved him to death. Aunt Jackie hated his guts and was always ready to tell you about it, if you let her.

Aunt Jackie used to be a Jehovah's Witness but isn't anymore, and she got a letter from Satan once. I don't know what it said, but she freaked out and cried and called our house, so Dad and Fluffy

*rushed over and tried to burn the letter in her kitchen sink, except
they couldn't get it to burn and that's how they knew it was from
Satan. So they called the elders over and everyone stood around the
sink and prayed to Jehovah and tried to put the letter on fire and
told Aunt Jackie that if she came back to The Truth and devoted her
life to serving Jehovah, she wouldn't get any more mail from Satan.
Everyone in the Kingdom Hall whispers when they talk about it.*

Six months after delivering chickens to the backside of Aunt
Jackie's garage, we had eggs comin' out our ears. Eggs threatened
to bust out of our refrigerator, and the rules in Fluffy's house then
changed. She stayed in bed to sleep in each morning, and Sissy
was instructed to scramble eggs for our breakfast, as many as we
wanted, with one slice of toast each. That lasted for about two
months, until Thor got loose and killed our chickens. He didn't
even eat them. He killed them out of sheer boredom, so our egg
supply disappeared and Sissy and I were banned from touching
anything in the kitchen again. We went back to the old rules for
breakfast—Post Toasties poured by Dad.

Fluffy's house had rules.

*Like clinking spoons. There's a rule about that. You can't
clink your spoon against your cereal bowl when you eat your Post
Toasties. Fluffy will yell at you from her bedroom if she hears your
spoon clink against your bowl. She doesn't want to hear any noise
when she's in bed, so you gotta be quiet when you eat your cereal.
And you can't clink your spoon against your teeth at dinnertime
either, 'cause Fluffy doesn't want to hear your teeth touch your
spoon.*

—∞∞—

I was a thief all through childhood. I couldn't possibly name all
the places that Sissy and I stole from. My oldest memory of stealing

is when I stole a plastic baggie of shelled sunflower seeds from a little girl in kindergarten whose mother always sent her to school with more than one snack. My thievery was discovered when that little girl cried. She bawled while I assured our teacher that the seeds were mine. I had never before come to school with a snack for snack time, so she took the remaining sunflower seeds away from me and gave them to the little girl who then stopped crying.

The next year, at my age of six, Sissy and I frequently pulled what looked edible out of the neighbor's trashcans in Redondo Beach. We once found a mostly-whole chocolate cake, wrapped in a plastic bag, and in the privacy of the narrow walkway between their house and ours, we ate it with our bare hands. The neighbors who had disposed of the cake watched us through their living room window and then complained to Dad. He got embarrassed and spanked us.

After we moved to Fillmore, we stole food from the spare refrigerator in the next door neighbor's garage, until they complained and Dad spanked us.

We stole peaches off the tree from the old retired couple who lived behind us in Fillmore, until they called the police and Dad spanked us.

We stole a can of black olives from the Rodriquez' garage and hacked it open with a hammer.

We stole a box of dietary Aid's hunger-suppressant caramel candy from a Witness lady who temporarily stored her kitchen supplies in our garage when she moved to a new apartment. Unaware that they weren't the simple candy we imagined, we finished off the box in a couple of days. For ten years after, the taste of caramel made me sick.

When I was punished and sent to bed without dinner, Sissy sometimes stole scraps from the dinner table for me. I like to think that I did the same for her, but I don't remember ever doing so.

On our walk to school, we sometimes snuck into the lemon plant across the railroad tracks and stole lemonade from the juice machine in the lobby.

On our walks home from school, we stole oranges from the orange groves until Sissy went through an honorable phase when she felt guilty for picking oranges that didn't belong to us. She convinced herself that eating oranges that had fallen into the dirt might not be stealing—until we overheard a comment that oranges on the ground were raked up and sold for juice. We found that hard to believe. It just didn't seem possible that people would pay good money for juice if they knew the oranges—some of which were split and rotten—had been lying in the dirt. So the specifics of honesty in an orange orchard became too confusing. Sissy conceded to again picking oranges from trees, stolen or not.

We stole from the penny candy store next to the Fillmore pool hall on Main Street...dozens of times. The old man at the register was too old, or too disinterested, to recognize what we were doing, but Sissy eventually felt guilty and put the kibosh on that as well.

We stole from Safeway on a three block diversionary walk to school. Often. Candy bars were easiest to fit in my pocket or down my pants, but I got tired of candy bars, so I once stole a package of hot dogs. They got hot and slimy before I could eat them all, so I never stole hot dogs again.

I once stole alcohol from Fluffy's refrigerator. My first ever self-created cocktail was a nasty mixture of approximately half Southern Comfort and half Tyrolia wine from screw-cap bottles, Fluffy's favorites, poured in a pink Tupperware glass at my age of nine after climbing through the bathroom window to steal something to eat when no one was looking. It wasn't drinkable. Not by me.

In the summer of 1974, at my age of ten, I stole a Hershey bar from Safeway on a day when I shouldn't have been a thief. I was only there to purchase Kool-Aid for Grant, but I broke my own self-imposed limitation for thievery. I had invented a funny little rule that, when stealing, I should only take something that customers wouldn't buy. A damaged candy bar, one that Safeway couldn't sell, one with a broken wrapper perhaps, because it seemed slightly less sinful to steal that way. It eased my guilt and was my backup plan, as it were. I envisioned that if I was ever caught and threatened with prison, I would just point to the torn wrapper and explain that customers wouldn't pay for an imperfect candy bar, and then the authorities would nod their heads in acknowledgement and agree that, certainly, stealing a damaged candy bar wasn't, in reality, stealing. At least not the sort that should receive punishment, and I would then walk home with my defective and certainly not pilfered bar of chocolate because Safeway would have seen the wisdom of my logic and realized that particular candy bar wasn't going to do them a bit of good.

But there were no damaged candy bars on the shelf that day, so I ripped the label on a perfectly good Hershey bar and slid it into my pocket, and when the officers pulled me into a dimly lit storage room in the back of the store, the stark lameness of my invented alibi crumbled. It sounded so ridiculous at the moment I needed it, not to mention a lie, that I never used it. I stood in front of the two loss prevention officers, ready to cry, feeling their interrogation, giving up my name and phone number and knowing Virgil would beat the holy hell out me when I got home. The Safeway people called my house and then escorted me out the back door.

After a stern lecture about the reproach I had brought on Jehovah's name for being a thief, Dad beat me with his belt on Fluffy's king-sized bed. The neighbors heard me scream.

Not long after, Grant and I were playing the rocket game on Fluffy's front lawn. I lay on my back with my feet in the air. Grant sat on top and I pushed him off, like a rocket.

Grant strained his back and ran to the front door, crying. He stumbled over the step and went down.

Fluffy went into hysterics. She said I hurt Grant on purpose.

Virgil threw me on the couch and beat me. The neighbors heard me scream. Virgil picked me up and threw me across the room. I landed against his black recliner. My ribs hurt, and I kinda made a wheezy noise when I breathed.

He came to my room that night and told me he loved me.

Fluffy's never said she loves me, but that's okay. It wouldn't mean anything either, 'cause I know she doesn't.

They love Grant. Grant never has to worry about being hungry, and he's gonna grow up to be really tall and handsome with dark wavy hair. Fluffy says that men named Grant are always tall and good-looking. And she says Grant will be taller than me and he's gonna be better looking. I'm not sure what I'll be when I grow up, but for sure it won't be tall and handsome. And I won't get dark wavy hair, either, 'cause Fluffy says I have hair "like straw." It isn't good to have hair like straw. Grant will never have hair like straw.

Grant's favorite TV show was *Emergency* with two firemen named Johnny and Roy. Fluffy bought him a toy Emergency kit after he got out of the hospital from getting tubes put in his ears. He ran around the house in his underwear for months after, pretending he was Johnny. Or Roy. I talked him into using the toy paramedic briefcase to sneak food from the kitchen to me by promising him a secret party in our bedroom after everyone else went to bed, convincing him to steal the food, until Grant figured out that our secret party was pretty damn boring and lost interest.

Grant was allergic to milk and was plagued by ear infections, so Fluffy gave him Carnation chocolate bars for breakfast instead. I usually ate what he didn't want—the leftover piece, his fingerprints and tooth marks embedded in the chocolate coating.

While washing the dishes and cleaning the kitchen, Sissy set Grant's leftovers aside.

"Grant? Are you gonna finish your food?" she asked.

"Neeevvveeerrrr miiiindd......leeeeaavee it therrre," he answered. He thought it was a game to say "Neeever miiiind. Leave it theeeerreee."

Fifteen minutes later, Sissy again asked for permission to throw it out.

"Grant! Are you gonna finish your food?"

Fluffy got mad when Sissy asked Grant too many times if he was gonna finish his food. Later in the day, Sissy snuck the leftover food out the garage to share with me.

———

Virgil's bird dog, Britty, got quarantined again. He had a tendency to bite people he hadn't been officially introduced to, the PG&E utility worker being the unfortunate target this time around. Britty escaped from our yard often, an event that concerned Fluffy enough to send us on a mission to retrieve him before he sunk his teeth into someone's leg. Sissy and I used Britty's freedom as our own excuse to escape confinement, running all over town, chasing our dog and returning to an inquisition as to why it had taken us so long. We once caught Britty deep in the orange groves and over fits of laughter, we turned him loose again, enjoying our freedom, not yet wanting to go home.

I often walked to Safeway on hot summer afternoons to buy Pepsi for Fluffy and Kool-Aid for her children...any flavor except Orange because Grant didn't like Orange Kool-Aid. I picked Kool-Aid flavors off the shelf, knowing Sissy and I wouldn't taste a drop. Kool-Aid meant nothing and meant everything, and it was incredibly effective at letting us know our place in life. It defined our childhood. As we watched Grant and Amber drink daily Kool-Aid, any flavor except Orange, we knew who we were.

—∞—

In August of 1974, we took our fifth and final trip to Orland. Grams picked us up at the Sacramento airport, and then got sidetracked by a tomato field alongside the freeway that was being mechanically harvested. Unable to make sharp turns, the combine was bypassing the corners, which was exactly the kind of mistake my grandmother would notice. Aunt Letha had come down to the airport that year with Grams, just to keep her company, so they pulled over to park in the freshly plowed dirt and the two of them wandered out to ask permission to pick what the harvester had missed. The guy in charge of the operation gave Grams a couple of cardboard boxes, and we picked free tomatoes for what felt like forever to an impatient ten-year-old who wanted to get to Orland.

The next day, I tucked a *Watchtower* magazine in my grandfather's dresser drawer, right on top of his underwear, hoping its discovery would cause him to miraculously convert to The Truth.

My cousin Jason ruined our talent show that summer. It was Sissy's big dream every year to coordinate an evening performance for all the aunts and uncles and miscellaneous Okie relatives in a summer gathering on my grandparents' back lawn, with a collection of a cappella tunes from all seven cousins and homemade ice cream churned with rock salt on the back steps for all the relatives after dinner. With my grandparents' encouragement, Sissy granted approval of appropriate music to our cousins, and the neighbor girl down the road whose name was Sherry.

Sherry lived a little further down Road FF in another Okie shack, and she had a pink bedroom all to herself with magazine clippings and posters plastered all over her pink walls.

Sissy invited her to participate in our show on our grandparent's back step that year, but Jason ruined the show, at his age of eight, when he stood on the back porch for a spontaneous solo performance that wasn't part of Sissy's approved agenda and confidently adlibbed a thirty-second song with approximately eight words, repeated over and over.

"I got an old buck horse and an old buck cow...an old buck horse and an old buck cow...I got an old buck horse and an old buck cow..."

Sissy was horrified. It made no sense to her, but perfect sense to him.

Sissy can sing like a bird. The really pretty kind. People say she's going to grow up to be famous. Sissy was pissed when Jason sang the made-up song about the old buck horse and old buck cow, but what really ruined the show was when we all joined hands and went out to dance on the lawn, but Dad and Fluffy were there to visit that year and they got mad and stopped our show to make us go put shoes on. They don't like it when we don't wear shoes. My dad feels like an Okie when we don't wear shoes.

—ᆢ—

Sissy and I returned from our trip to Orland in August of 1974, and she left for junior high each school morning while I walked to Sespe Elementary for 5th grade. At lunch time, I then walked the seven blocks to San Cayetano Elementary where I washed dishes and emptied garbage cans and passed out cartons of milk in exchange for a free lunch in the San Cayetano Elementary cafeteria.

The following summer, 1975, Sissy and I did not go to Orland. We went to summer school instead, with the complete freedom to pick any subjects we wanted, feeling incredibly unencumbered and independent to choose classes without asking permission.

I chose macramé and swimming. Macramé was a big deal in the 1970s, the basic concept being the intricate braiding of string into creative objects, the most popular item being a hanging planter. After arriving back at Fluffy's on my very first day of summer school, I requested some cheap balls of twine for macramé.

"I'm not spending money on string," she complained. "If you want to learn macramé, you can do it by watching other people."

I abandoned macramé for tennis.

Tennis was a sneak peek into a fantasy world where rich kids with the financial means to outright own a tennis racket showed up in cute outfits. The instructor let me borrow a cheap aluminum racket on my first day, one he kept for a spare, and I pounded balls across the net and over the fence for an hour, pretending I was a rich kid with no barriers to playing sports. I would conquer tennis. I would smash balls across the net and inside the court, rather than repeatedly knocking them over the fence and having to chase them down the street. I would pretend to be a rich kid. No one would know I wasn't.

The following day, I returned to the courts, expecting to hone my new appreciation for tennis, only to have the tennis pro pull me aside and explain that students were required to bring their own rackets. He suggested that I ask my parents to buy one and sent me on my way. I slunk out of the tennis complex, ashamed, not wanting him to know that my parents wouldn't spend money on me. I wasn't a rich kid.

I wandered into Beginning Typing, a room crammed with tall stools to bring short kids up to the heights of the keyboards where they laboriously pounded away at manual typewriters, struggling to master the dexterity of typing, especially the pinky key, wondering why they couldn't learn to type on the new electric model displayed up front except the teacher wouldn't allow anyone to touch it on account of the fact that it was so expensive. And on account of her prediction that we would never enjoy the luxury of an electric typewriter, due to its cost, so it was important to learn typing skills on a manual machine, she said. And on account of the fact that my vision was so bad that I couldn't see what was written on the chalkboard and therefore didn't know which letters I was supposed to be punching, which meant I couldn't really learn to type, which made the whole idea pointless.

I escaped to a math class a few days later, with a pinched-face teacher who displayed a new hand calculator on her desk. It was a new invention and "very expensive," she claimed. It was important to learn math the old-fashioned way, she said, given that calculators cost a lot of money and she predicted that none of us would ever be able to afford one. I truly believed she was an idiot. She wasn't, of course. She was stressed out, but still not an idiot. Learning math the old-fashioned way is generally the point of math class, but I thought her logic was seriously warped, given the presence of a miraculous new invention called a calculator.

Out of boredom, I leaned against her desk one afternoon, fiddling around with her stapler, and unintentionally stuck a steel staple through my finger. She dislodged it, then taped a Band-Aid over the bloody spot and assured me that I wasn't gonna die. I thought we had a warm little bonding session, until the next day when I gave up on understanding her version of math. So, having bonded with her and everything, I informed her that math class didn't make a lick of sense. I even used the word "stupid," which just seemed like a helpful piece of information to pass along, but she got mad and sent me to the principal's office.

So I bailed from math class, getting increasingly worried that any one of the teachers I had abandoned would report my absence to Fluffy, until I found a craft room where they were dissecting bottles with a glasscutter. I pulled a bunch of dirty brown beer bottles out from under the Sespe Creek Bridge and hauled them to school in a paper sack. After cutting the tops off and grinding down the edges with sandpaper, I delivered a six-pack of drinking glasses to Granny M and Aunt Jackie. Within a month, every single one of those non-tempered glass cups had shattered in their kitchen sink, scattering a million pieces of brown glass at the bottom of a sink of soapy water.

Sissy had enrolled in a summer school cooking class and was asked to bring food items to share. She and Fluffy got into a big argument over that requirement, in raised voices. It was the first time I had ever seen Sissy be so bold. Their argument, for the first time, was heated. Later that night, Dad convinced Fluffy to spend the money for a cheap cake mix in a box.

A cake from a box seemed so contrary to what we had seen Grandma Terry bake. Her cakes were from scratch. Fluffy didn't bake cakes, but Sissy gingerly hauled her box cake home after school, down the street, through the orange grove, wrapped in plastic to protect the pink frosting. She was thirteen. Her two-layer cake sat on the dining room table with a few dents from traveling six blocks from school, waiting for the end of dinner, a little off kilter, covered in cellophane and very slightly lopsided and deliciously pink. It sat next to a flat, square, and easy-to-make single layer cake from Fluffy.

Virgil arrived home and declined to confront the competing cakes, or declare a winner. He lightheartedly added a slice of each to his plate, hoping he had found the only delicate line he could walk between the two cake creators. Sissy watched him eat, her pride deflated, waiting for praise from a father that wasn't about to give any.

Sissy and I had enrolled in the same summer-school swim session, so we walked to school together each day, and then met up outside the pool for our return home. The swimming pool was a tremendous escape from the boredom of home, and only marred by the trauma of sitting on the pavement in our group circle with my legs spread and looking down to discover that without the constraint of underwear, my penis had flopped out for everyone to see. The high school girl who was teaching me to swim saw my penis. The next day, she threatened to climb up to the top of the high dive and push me off if I didn't jump.

Fluffy timed how long it took us to walk the six blocks from school. Uncertain if a mid-day meal would exist when we arrived home, Sissy and I rushed out of the gymnasium each day and buried ourselves in an orange grove, out of sight, for a fast picnic under the obscurity of the orange trees.

A block from home, bellies full, we inspected each other for tell-tale signs of what we had done.

"Check me out," Sissy said. "How do I look?"

I pointed at a sticky spot on her cheek. "You have juice on your face. Right there. Lick your lips."

Erase the evidence. Wipe your hands on the grass. Dig the pith out from under your fingernails.

We snuck off campus with Sissy's school friend Linda to play hooky from summer school. We sprawled out over her living room floor while her parents were at work, watching a re-run episode of The Brady Bunch, basking in freedom, wondering if she would offer us something to eat, thinking her parents would be pissed if she did.

Linda drug a pornographic magazine out of her parent's room, and an 11-year-old boy and two 13-year-old girls scanned through porn at her kitchen table. We flipped pages from one naked woman to another, and another, and then…there it was!!! A picture of a man. With his clothes off!

It was just a "Here's a snapshot of my hairy boyfriend standing next to the palm tree in our backyard with his clothes off" kind of picture, not particularly large, about a quarter page.

I played with myself that night, thinking of him. I thought about his body hair, and the hair that was growing on my own legs. I had something in common with the naked man in the porn magazine. That pleased me.

RUN TO THE HILLS

"But before all these things people will lay their hands upon you and persecute you, delivering you up to the synagogues and prisons, you being haled before kings and governors for the sake of my name." Luke 21:12 - The New World Translation of the Holy Scriptures

"...when you see all these things, know that he is near at the doors. Truly I say to you that this generation will be no means pass away until all these things occur." Matthew 24:33-34 - The New World Translation of the Holy Scriptures

Jehovah's Witnesses were eagerly awaiting the end of the world. Matthew 24:33-34 was interpreted in a manner that guaranteed the arrival of Armageddon within our lifetimes. We understood the term 'generation' in that scripture to refer to the generation of people who were alive in 1914, and old enough at the time to understand its significance. The generation of 1914 would have been born around the year 1900 or earlier, and they were very close to dying out. There wasn't much time left on this wicked earth for them, or us. The end would come before the generation of 1914 had departed from the planet, we were told.

By following a strict Jewish calendar, we also believed that 1975 would precisely mark 6,000 years since Adam and Eve's creation, which made for a very convenient and significant year for God to destroy an earth that we were assured had clearly gone to hell.

Discussions of persecution dominated the conversation and lectures in the Kingdom Hall. There were many instructive conversations to prepare us for the day when Sissy and I would arrive home after school to discover that our parents had been dragged off to jail for worshipping Jehovah and we would flee to the hills to look for other Witnesses who had also run to the hills. I don't know what the fascination was with "the hills," but it was clearly where we would end up, along with other JW's who were also wandering the hills in avoidance of persecution.

Fluffy was convinced that disobedient children would get all the Witnesses killed during persecution. She worried that disobedient kids might not be quiet, and that's how the mobs of people hunting us in the hills would discover where we were hiding…cause the bad kids forgot to be quiet.

I overheard Fluffy discussing plans with her mother to stash a collection of their most crucial prescription medications next to the kitchen door in anticipation of the immediacy of needing to flee. Under the influence of their conversation, I built a bow and arrow out of a five-foot length of willow branch from Sespe Creek and hid it behind a sheet of plywood against the garage wall, ready to embrace my new role as the chief rabbit hunter. Never mind that I'd never successfully shot a rabbit before. And never mind that I was never really clear about exactly *which* hills we would be running to.

A month later when I dared to draw my first flimsy arrow from the string of my handmade bow, it snapped in two.

I spent many investigative hours in the school library, devouring Indian books and learning to identify edible flora and fauna—prickly pear cactus, yucca roots, shepherds purse, acorn meal. I memorized animal trapping instructions, thinking I might run to the hills and never be hungry but other Witnesses would starve to death because they wouldn't listen to a ten-year-old who spent an inordinate amount of time scouring the library in preparation for persecution.

Worries of persecution and Armageddon dominated our life. Our Kingdom Hall meetings were centered on helping us prepare for the impending end, and there were occasional congratulatory reports of brothers and sisters around the globe who had sold their homes and were living off of the proceeds while spending their final days in this "wicked system" by being full-time Pioneers for Jehovah, abandoning their jobs and going door to door to spread His word on a daily basis.

—∞—

The Truth has never been a religion for lukewarm adherents. It's an "all or nothing" faith, and devotional gatherings don't occur just once a week. It's an arduous schedule of meetings, all of which require advance preparation at home by all literate family members who are expected to read that evening's study guide and highlight text to answer the questions printed at the bottom of each page.

Topics for worship and discussion in the Kingdom Hall are controlled by the Governing Body who prints two magazines every other week—*The Watchtower* and *Awake!*.

The *Awake!* was designed to give hope to the hopeless with articles entitled, "How Can I Break Free?" and "Overcoming Life's Challenges." The *Awake!* described itself, on the inside cover of each issue, as, "*Awake! is for the enlightenment of the entire family. It shows how to cope with today's problems. Most important, this magazine builds confidence in the Creator's promise of a peaceful and secure new world before the generation that saw the events of*

1914 pass away." The magazine frequently included illustrations of what we expected the New Order to be—a beautiful cleansed earth where Jehovah's Witnesses would live forever and gather for picnics in serene mountain meadows with lions and tigers lying casually amongst sheep nearby.

Our weekly schedule of worship began with a two-hour Sunday meeting. The first hour was devoted to the Public Talk which was a prepared speech handed down from the governing body in New York and delivered by a chosen elder in each congregation. Why it was referred to as the Public Talk is unclear, because essentially all Witness meetings are public. Anyone who shows an interest in absorbing Witness beliefs is more than welcome to enter, and they will discover a very friendly but insulated congregation if they demonstrate any willingness to convert.

Major sermons and topics are not created by favorite elders in Jehovah's Witness congregations. They are prepared by the Governing Body in New York, so generally speaking, the Public Talk in a Los Angeles Kingdom Hall is identical to the one given that same day in Mobile, Alabama.

The Sunday Public Talk is followed by a one-hour review of an article in the most recent issue of *The Watchtower*. *The Watchtower* is also printed twice each month, and each issue contains two articles for two weekends of Sunday afternoon worship. It is a certainty that on any given Sunday, every single Witness congregation around the globe is studying the exact same topic, as supplied by *The Watchtower*. Study of *The Watchtower* encourages audience participation in a very polite and controlled question and answer format, and it allows those members who had actually studied the text at home to prove that they had done so. And there are, of course, a few songs and prayers sprinkled before, in between, and after each half of the Sunday meeting.

Tuesday night worship was devoted to The Book Study, an intimate one-hour discussion of a recent Witness publication. Those Tuesday meetings were held in the living rooms of various members' homes, scattered all across town, just to encourage Christian fellowship and socialization. Like *The Watchtower* study, this meeting required advanced study, a homework assignment, per se. It also encouraged the same sort of "participation," which is limited to a moderator's vocal reading of a question printed at the bottom of each page from the study material, followed by many members raising their hands. The moderator then chooses from the raised hands a member who has located the proper answer in the written material, and that chosen individual then reads the answer as it is printed. At no time are you encouraged to form your own conclusions or question the accuracy of what you are being taught, but if you have a vocabulary that enables you to re-phrase the supplied answer in your own words, rather than reading verbatim from the text, that is considered highly commendable.

Thursday's meetings were the most interesting. That was another two-hour gathering in the Kingdom Hall, divided into two sections. The second portion was the Ministry School, which primarily centered on experiences and instructions for converting non-believers to The Truth. That hour was broken into pieces and portioned out to various male members of the congregation. Women were allowed to share one small piece where they re-enacted a short skit of a biblical discussion with a potential convert, but generally speaking, this meeting was like all others and dominated by men.

It is in this meeting that young boys are given a five-minute scriptural reading as their first entry into public speaking from the podium. I gave many of them, starting at the age of nine, and if there were moments in my childhood when I thought my father envisioned my potentially having some redeeming qualities, these were it. I could write my own analysis of the assigned scripture without his help—an interpretation I typically wrote on the very same day that I would deliver it.

I mounted the Kingdom Hall stage in my short-sleeved dress shirt and clip-on tie to read my assigned Bible passage and give a self-determined interpretation of what it meant, and then wallowed in praise from congregation members afterwards, hoping Dad and Fluffy were paying attention. I loved the Kingdom Hall.

More than once during those Thursday meetings, women practiced how, what with the anticipated persecution and all, they would dress up in costume to continue our door-to-door work. They sauntered up and down the Kingdom Hall aisle, pretending they were out in service to Jehovah, carrying a change of clothes in a paper bag, demonstrating how they could quickly switch clothes into a new disguise if the threat of jail or police loomed.

We were cautioned to immediately flee if we were at someone's front door and the homeowners said, "Excuse me, we'll be back in a moment," because they were likely calling the authorities to have us thrown in jail. Persecution had to include time in jail. It just did. Some Witnesses were going to spend time in jail. That was the price for having The Truth, we were told.

I had visions of Witnesses slinking out of the hills under the cover of darkness, secretly wandering neighborhoods the next morning with a spare set of clothes and *Watchtower* magazines. Some would die for serving Jehovah. Others would get caught and thrown in the clinker, and others might make it back to the hills where the rest of us were hiding.

I wouldn't have been caught. My imagined Indian skills would have served me well in those trying times, sneaking in and out of the hills to convert people to The Truth. I would have been really good at that. You could have asked me when I was ten. I would have told you so, even though I didn't understand why we would go door to door while being persecuted. Nor did I understand why any right-thinking person would willingly convert to a religion of such torment. It seemed to me we should just hang out in the hills and hide in the sagebrush while hunting rabbits and waiting for Armageddon to arrive.

Sissy and I had a silly childish conversation one afternoon, choosing names for our future offspring, debating popular choices and ranking favorites, forgetting the fact that Armageddon was fast approaching. "Rachel" was Sissy's favorite girl name. I don't remember her choice for boys or remember having an opinion of my own one way or the other, but Fluffy pitched a fit.

"You kids shut up! You don't need to be having such a stupid conversation. You're never gonna have kids! Armageddon will be here soon!"

I was once allowed to spend the night with my friend Scott Smith. I only knew him through the Kingdom Hall where he was a Witness, too. Our faith was unbelievably fragile, balancing on the edge of an overly sharp knife, in danger of being sliced wide open by the slightest touch from a non-believer. Heaven forbid that we might actually allow worldly people into our home as friends or equals, because of course, they weren't. We lived and breathed a life of separation, so it was a really big deal to spend a Saturday night away from home, protected by the companionship of the only other Witness family with a son my age.

The Smiths lived in a doublewide trailer out in the orange groves, halfway out to the neighboring town of Piru. They didn't own the property, but Brother Smith managed a portion of the vast orange and lemon groves between Fillmore and Piru. On the single weekend when I was allowed to visit, Scott S. and I spent our time constructing animal traps in the shelterbelt—a windbreak of trees on the far side of their barn. In my mind, it was a practice run for Armageddon. An initial attempt at killing critters for supper. Scott S. had big dreams of killing bobcats, but Scott T. was hoping for rabbits, not knowing what to do with a bobcat but certain we couldn't eat it for dinner.

Virgil had shown me how to bleed a rabbit for dinner. The optimal method of bleeding a screaming rabbit, as instructed by my dad, is to stand heavy on its head, grab the hind legs, and pull. Rabbits scream when wounded, but the screaming stops once you pull their heads off.

I shared my rabbit trapping adventure with Dad the next day, wanting to impress upon him my recently acquired skill in preventing our starvation, only to be crushed when he reminded me that not only did rabbits likely have tularemia, but the Bible said it was a sin to eat animals that hadn't been bled properly. A rabbit hung in a snare obviously wouldn't have been bled properly, so we couldn't eat any that were foolish enough to wander through my traps. I was really concerned about that and wondered how we would get rabbits for dinner if we couldn't trap them. And terribly bummed out to realize that all of my research into Indian hunting techniques had been a ridiculous waste of time.

The year 1975 came and went. There was never any persecution, no one got thrown in jail, we didn't run to the hills, and the Jehovah's Witness faith lost a massive number of disillusioned members around the globe when the promised "End" never materialized.

JIXTH GRADE

When the last of the orange groves disappeared from Fillmore under the weight of new subdivisions where modern 1970s architecture required that each house look exactly like the one next to it, the schools became overcrowded and parents were asked for volunteers to have their children bussed to a less populated school in the neighboring town of Piru. Six Fillmore families volunteered to send their sixth graders to Piru, and mine was one of them.

Piru was a quiet little town with a small and friendly elementary campus tucked up against the hills. Mr. Taylor was principal, and he knew the name of every kid on campus, including mine.

Scott Smith also went to Piru Elementary, so for the first time, I attended school with another Witness in my class.

George Ferry had been my best friend for years. He wasn't in The Truth and was considered to be an extreme example of bad association on account of the fact that he and I ran away from home twice, which was determined to be mostly his fault but certainly wasn't. He was my best friend, but he never once set foot in my house, nor I in his. We were only friends at school. After another summer of being separated, I boarded the bus for my first day of sixth grade and discovered that ironically and unexpectedly, George's mother had also sent him to Piru.

Every school morning, a small yellow van drove to the little community of Bardsdale to get George, outside of Fillmore, and then stopped around the corner from my house to get me and four other neighborhood kids for the ten mile drive to Piru.

I missed the bus once. I'd been in that predicament before. I wasn't sure what to do, other than pray that Fluffy would give me a ride to Piru when she drove Grant to San Cayetano Elementary for kindergarten.

She emerged from her bedroom, still in her nightgown, red hair askew, and found me sitting on the floor of her living room, watching cartoons with Grant.

"Why aren't you at school?" she screamed.

"I missed the bus!"

"I don't care. Get to school! Get out of here!"

I ran out the backdoor and walked to the edge of town.

East Telegraph Road, a two lane highway leading out of Fillmore, stretched out in front of me. I wondered if I'd reach school in time for lunch.

No more than two miles down the road, Scott Smith's dad drove by in his truck, on his way from one orchard to another. He stopped hard, then drove backwards to get me.

Seconds later, I was sitting in his front seat, uncomfortably aware of his shock, trying to find an off-the-cuff explanation for my odd circumstances.

Incredulous, he asked, "What are you doing?"

"I missed the school bus," I answered. "I'm just walking to Piru. It's not that far."

Walking to Piru wasn't anything to get all worked up over, I told him. I would protect Fluffy. I wouldn't cause trouble.

After school, Granny M met me at the back door. She was there to console Fluffy, who was barricaded in her room.

"Shhhhhh," she said. "Your mother's crying. Brother Smith wasn't very nice to her."

Brother Smith had called and tore her up one side and down the other.

For weeks after, I felt a bit of fear and unease about what Fluffy might do to me for causing trouble.

Sissy did not share my anxiety. She had a growing fiery streak and was beginning to lose her fear of telling friends about what went on at Fluffy's. Unlike Sissy, I wouldn't have shared that information with anyone. I thought secrets should be kept at home. Dad got mad if we didn't keep secrets. I would never have invited Scott Smith or George Ferry to visit. My vision of allowing school acquaintances to enter her home was composed of their horrible discovery that I wasn't allowed to have anything from her kitchen. And anxiety over their inability to understand why I couldn't touch Fluffy's TV. And disastrous observations that I had no toys. And fears of those discoveries reverberating all over school....

The American Bicentennial, 1976, was a huge deal to my school music teacher, Mr. English. He decided that an afternoon parent assembly when older students gathered to sing a collection of popular television jingles...all strung together into one horrendous song...was an appropriate celebration. All fifth and sixth graders were required to practice for hours on end in the auditorium until they got it right.

Except for me and Scott Smith. Bicentennials were a sin, so we sat together in the auditorium and listened to classmates memorize the proper order to sing TV lyrics. Sometimes Scott's mother pulled him out of school early, leaving me to sit by myself.

When Mr. English left the room during practice, the chorus of students sometimes warped the song into an unapproved version of the Burger King part....

Burn the pickles burn the lettuce shut up lady don't upset
  us all you have to do is throw it away.
Have it youuuuuur way, at Burger King.
Have it youuuuuur way, at Burger King
Aren't you glaaaad, you use Dial
Don't you wish, Eeeeeverybody did
Aaaaren't you glaaad,
You uuuuuse
Diiiallllll
Come to the Florida Sunshine tree
For great tasting orange juice, naturaleeeeee
Orange juice, with natural vitamin ceeeeee,
At the Florida sunshine tree
Haaaave aaaaa great great. Day day. To double your
  pleasure and fun fun
Chew chew double double good good double mint double
  mint gum.
Come on and flyyyy with meeeeeee..........

━━━⚬⚬⚬━━━

I realized we were poor in sixth grade.

Our poverty wasn't obvious to outsiders. Fluffy got a new house and a brand new station wagon with wood trim running the full length and tailgate. Virgil already had a horse and two dogs that had to be fed, and he unexpectedly showed up on our Fillmore driveway with a third dog in the back of his truck— a second Australian Kelpie named Andy. Andy was a mate for Virgil's first Kelpie, Flo. Virgil had a plan.

He walked in the back door of our Fillmore house that day...a bouquet of flowers in hand...a contrite smile on his face...hoping the combination would offset the fact that he'd bought another dog. He laid out a money-making scheme of puppy breeding and swore they would make a fortune by selling dogs for hundreds of dollars, but Fluffy threw his flowers in the trash. She hated him that day. We couldn't afford to feed another dog, she said.

The proof of our poverty, to me, was when Granny M started baking bread at home which every once in a while turned out just fine, and when we qualified for free food from the US Department of Agriculture.

Free USDA food consisted mostly of enormous bricks of processed cheese. Virgil took one look at the first orange and square block and said, "That's not good for anything except fish bait," so the cheese blocks got turned into weekend lunch sandwiches for me and Sissy on Granny M's occasionally edible bread. Free food also included bottles of white corn syrup that I volunteered to use in place of more expensive Log Cabin syrup on Dad's pancakes, and packages of freeze dried powdered eggs that stunk up the house when we cooked them. We only gave those a try once.

Sissy and I were then accepted into the free school lunch program. The application for free lunch required the disclosure of income and assets.

Fluffy couldn't have been more pissed.

"It's none of their business how much money we make!"

But after an enormous argument in the kitchen, Dad convinced her that free lunches were worth the sharing of private financial information and he submitted the paperwork.

Sissy was incredibly self-conscious about being poor, not wanting any of her friends to know...but I loved it. Every afternoon, my class lined up outside the Piru cafeteria while Mrs. Frost handed out lunch tickets to all the students who could afford to pay for them, and then they watched her dispense free tickets to the poor kids like me. The free tickets were a different color, a really obvious way to embarrass children with low self-esteem who didn't want to be poor, but I wasn't one of those kids. In Piru, you could ask for second helpings, even thirds, so long as you had eaten everything else on your tray, and I thought being poor was fabulous. Food was plentiful in Piru.

About that time, Fluffy experimented with a Roquefort cheese casserole for Dad's evening meal. It was a present from the *Better Homes and Garden* magazine, she said, but none of us could choke it down. My father had a serious taste for moldy cheese, but I like to have puked. He was late as usual that night and I don't remember what he ate for dinner, but it wasn't Roquefort casserole, because the bulk of it was buried at the bottom of the kitchen garbage can by the time he showed up.

Sometimes Fluffy cooked a special halibut dinner to entice Virgil to come home early for dinner, rather than abandoning us for playtime with his horse. He ate halibut for dinner those nights while the rest of us ate fish sticks with tater tots. It was a rule…you gotta have tater tots with fish sticks.

Virgil generally cooked on weekends. He wasn't very good at it. He pan-fried deer meat with garlic salt for dinner, and made French toast for breakfast some days and thick pancakes on other days. He couldn't make pancakes like everyone else, the normal way, flat, but it didn't matter because he always gave us enough to eat.

When breakfast is ready he yells, "Come and get it before I slop it to the hogs!!"
We don't have any hogs.

I learned what it meant to be a homo from a fellow sixth grader. Michael was the most "grown up" kid I knew. He had blond hair that was so blond it was white and I always wanted to ask why he had white hair but that wouldn't have been nice, so I never asked. I wanted to spend private time with him, making him my friend, which wasn't going to happen. I admired his independence, and his confidence. His mom was a psychologist which I assumed was the obvious reason for his being so grown up. He stole a centerfold from his father's *Playboy* magazine and unfolded the page in front of friends at school.

Three boys huddled around the image, totally absorbed by the female nudity. Bobby Prescott giggled uncontrollably. I watched them, starkly aware of the disparity between my boredom and the spell my classmates seemed to be under.

Michael's older brother, Matt, showed up at Piru Elementary every now and then. He was in high school, and he thought his own muscles were impressive enough to show off. Matt pulled up his pant legs, displaying his muscular calves to sixth graders. When he flexed them into a knot, I felt an instant attraction.

Michael had a crush on Monica, another sixth grader. They chased each other around the playground and called each other 'retard' while throwing out accusations of being infected with cooties, and when she called him a 'homo' he laughed hysterically and explained to her what a homo was…and that if he liked *her*, he certainly wasn't a homo.

That cleared up my confusion regarding the literal definition of homo, something that had been the butt of my dad's jokes for years and a phrase I had never understood. I got the concept that homo, fruit, and queer were synonymous, but I had never understood the defining characteristics of those afflictions. My eyes were finally opened in sixth grade, thanks to Michael, and I was quite shocked to realize that my fascination for his older brother was considered queer.

That realization sent me on a long and arduous journey of prayer. If I was a queer, as I was beginning to suspect, Jehovah would fix it. So I prayed about it. I prayed at least four times a day, asking Him to stop the persecution that Witnesses in other parts of the world were experiencing. I prayed to thank Him for the food I had been given. In sixth grade, I added a request to not be a homo to my private prayers.

I thought those prayers were answered in 1976 when the Witnesses produced a new study book for kids. It was a little red book to help young congregation members understand sinful things, and I got my copy at our massive three-day assembly in Dodger Stadium. Witnesses worldwide had two assemblies to attend each year—a smaller and remotely local Circuit Assembly, and a larger District Assembly where attendees traveled for hundreds of miles and numbered into the hundreds of thousands. Dodger Stadium was the nearest location for our District assembly, and that's where the Witnesses introduced the new book that I thought would answer my prayers. It had a long and complicated title, so we called it *"The Youth Book"* for short. When the assembly concluded, Fluffy drove us back to Fillmore in her station wagon while I curled up in back of the car and scanned *The Youth Book's* table of contents of to see what great questions would be resolved.

Chapter Five, "Masturbation and Homosexuality," caught my eye.

I had just recently learned about homosexuality from Michael, but I wasn't familiar with the term masturbation.

In a loud voice, without even leaning over the seat, I asked, "What's Masturbation?"

I could have stunk up the car with a fart at that moment and no one would have said a word. Granny M made breathing noises... followed by a glance at Fluffy and a stunned silence...concluded by, "Why don't you ask your father when you get home?"

Silence can sometimes tell you everything you need to know. It was a simple question. I was only asking for a definition, not a demonstration, before deciding which subject to tackle first...so I opened to the chapter about homos and masturbation and began to read...

Should you experiment with your sex organs? Is there anything wrong with rubbing them in some way until the excitement is climaxed?

This practice is called masturbation. It is very common. Lying and stealing are also common today. Yet you wouldn't say this makes them natural and proper, would you? The "common" cold is quite universal, but this certainly doesn't mean that you want it, does it?

Weakly giving in to sexual desires by masturbation will certainly not give you strength when faced with a situation tempting you to commit fornication—or even homosexuality. Just the opposite, it cultivates wrong thinking and wrong desire. In fact, masturbation can lead into homosexuality. In such instances the person, not satisfied with his lonely sexual activity, seeks a partner for mutual sex play.

This happens much more frequently than you may realize. Contrary to what many persons think, homosexuals are not born that way, but their homosexual behavior is learned. And often a person gets started when very young by playing with another's sexual parts, and then engaging in homosexual acts. (Your Youth—Getting the Best out of It, 1976, p. 35, 36, 39)

So I prayed a lot. I prayed before breakfast. I was supposed to pray before lunch too, except sometimes I forgot 'cause none of the other kids at school prayed before lunch. So I lied about it when Fluffy asked if I said my prayers at school, and then I had to pray about lying. And we prayed before dinner, too. And we always said a prayer before going to bed at night, 'cause that was the most important one. I prayed every time I thought about masturbation too, and that seemed to be happening an awful lot.

Dear Jehovah God,
We thank you for this day, and we thank you for the food you provided. We thank you for the good association in our congregation, and we pray that you look after the brothers all over the world. And we pray that you help Aunt Jackie get better and we thank you for Granny M. And we pray that your Will be done and that we spend each day in service to you, and we pray that you bring this wicked system to an end soon. And please help me stop the masturbation. And please make my dad and stepmom like me. We ask these things in Jesus' name,
Amen.

To my way of thinking, *The Youth Book* was a wonderful and enlightening study guide from Jehovah, and it dropped in my lap on the cusp of puberty, an adolescent problem I didn't understand. There was an entire chapter devoted to that concept: Chapter Three—Growing Into Manhood. Chapter Three explained my physical changes and the appearance of body hair in private areas.

About thirteen or fourteen years after your birth, you begin another rapid spurt of growth. At this particular time you start changing from a boy into a man. The entire transitional period, which is known as adolescence, lasts for a number of years. It ends when you reach physical maturity, generally between the ages of twenty and twenty-three. Puberty covers the earlier period of adolescence. (Your Youth—Getting the Best out of It, 1976, p. 19-20)

Finally! An answer that made sense! I was not a homo! I just had to wait for puberty. It was all about puberty. Age twenty. That's when I would find a desire to get naked with girls. That seemed like plenty of time for puberty to work its magic.

The Youth Book also gave a woefully inadequate tutorial about heterosexual relations. It painted a sterile picture of a tranquil and gentle procedure that resulted in women becoming pregnant.

The husband lies close to his wife so that his male organ fits naturally into her birth canal. (Your Youth—Getting the Best out of It, 1976, p. 22)

Birth canal? What the hell is a birth canal? I was twelve. The tutorial from *The Youth Book* didn't really work for me. I was confused with the lack of specifics and no explanation as to which side of the woman would be receiving the man's organ. Is it the front or back? Women had two entrance holes, in my mind. One in front, one in back, either one of which could have led to a birth canal. I feared that I would grow up and, on my wedding day, be forced to ask my dad which side of the woman would lead to the birth canal.

—∞—

"Suck my dick!"

The most emasculating insult possible from a sixth grade boy was a command to suck dick. Worldly boys in Piru who were about to enter junior high had outgrown the taunt of being infected with cooties and replaced it with "Suck my dick!"

Dick was for sure a cuss word. I would never have said it. Jehovah wouldn't like it. It was the crudest insult imaginable. No one would ever suck dick. Would they? Of course not. Dicks were not for sucking.

On the walk to Aunt Jackie's house, I found several tattered and discarded pages of a porn magazine alongside the road—pictures of a woman sucking dick. A penis in her mouth, like a cherry lollipop. I didn't think it was real. It was staged, in my mind, like a Hollywood movie where people do things that aren't believable. People wouldn't put dicks in their mouth. Would they? Of course not.

I snuck one page home and hid it in the garage. We had visits every now and then.

Not long after, Virgil spanked me with my *Tom Sawyer* book for masturbating, but I wasn't masturbating. I was home sick.

I was laying in bed, home from school with a cold, reading about Huck Finn and Nigger Jim floatin' down the river catching catfish. I'd read that book a thousand times, and once made the mistake of saying "Nigger Jim" when telling Granny M how much I liked Mark Twain's writing.

Virgil threatened to beat the hell out of me if I ever said "nigger" again. I didn't understand why that was a problem because the slave's name, according to the book, was in fact, "Nigger Jim."

But by mid-morning, I was tired of reading *Tom Sawyer* for the millionth time, so when faced with an entire day of isolation in my room, I stole a needle and thread out of Fluffy's sewing kit in the old red cookie tin in the kitchen cabinet to hand sew a bean bag. I had no beans to put inside, but never mind about that. I had nothing else to do that day except dream up ways to make use of the clown costume that had been hanging in my closet for two years. Two years prior, on my last visit to Orland, Aunt Donnis had given me a red and white polka dot clown costume that Grams had made for my cousin Lisa to wear for Halloween.

We don't believe in Halloween, so it's not like it's going to do anyone any good, so I cut it into squares. Grandma Terry showed me how to sew, so I cut it up and tried to make some bean bags while I was in bed sick. I had to shove everything under my pillow real fast when Fluffy came to see if I was doing something she doesn't like.

She didn't know what I was doing and I wouldn't tell her, so she told Dad she caught me masturbating except that's not what she called it because we would never say that word. She told him she caught me "playing with myself" and he asked if I was and I told him I wasn't but he spanked me with the Tom Sawyer book anyway, 'cause Fluffy said I was. It wasn't true.

He didn't spank me very hard. He just grabbed Tom Sawyer and swatted me a couple of times. It makes a lot of noise when you get hit with a book. A big "whump" noise which makes everyone think you're really getting whaled on and that makes everyone happy because masturbation's a sin.

It would have been worse if Fluffy knew I stole a needle and thread out of her sewing kit. She doesn't like it if you touch her things.

Jehovah doesn't like it if I touch my things. The Youth Book says touching my things will lead to homosexuality. The Youth Book says it will be easier to not masturbate if I sleep on my side, instead of face down.

I tried sleeping on my side.

It doesn't help. The Youth Book is wrong.

—✺—

Towards the end of sixth grade, the entire country was gearing up to fan the flames of nationalist pride in the upcoming 1976 summer Olympics, so Mr. Taylor decided to hold a mini-Olympics of our own. On the last day of school, June 9, 1976, we celebrated the Piru Olympic Games.

Some kids fulfilled the minimum requirement of competing in two events, others chose four, and I entered all six. It seemed to me that when the opportunity arises to participate in the Olympics, you should enter every event, and besides, I had a secret weapon.

Sugar lumps—discovered from the *Hardy Boys*, where I learned that sugar and chocolate were life saving tonics of energy, especially when evading capture from bad guys who might be chasing your skinny and tired body down the road after you've been locked up for uncountable hours and barely have the strength to untie yourself. I stored away that valuable piece of Hardy Boy information as my secret weapon for the Olympics.

For an entire week beforehand, I splashed water droplets into the kitchen sugar bowl while washing dishes, then fished out the hardened lumps when Fluffy wasn't watching and hoarded the stolen pile in the garage. Over the course of our amateur Olympics, I sucked on crystallized lumps of raw sugar from a sticky and disintegrating mess in my pocket, convinced they would empower me with an extra special energy. The Hardy Boys said so.

With the assistance of sugar lumps, I got first place in the Long Jump, second in Sit Ups and Sidestep, third in 50 Yard Dash, and sixth in Pull Ups. I missed the first place award in Sit Ups by one.

We held an awards ceremony at the end of the day, in a hot auditorium packed with sweaty kids and proud parents who had spent the afternoon watching their children compete. I sat in back with Scott Smith and his parents, on top of a table. There were no seats left in the crowded assembly hall. The Smiths were so proud every time I walked up on stage to receive an award…even though I wasn't their son. I carried my ribbons back to Fillmore and walked in the back door of Fluffy's house to discover that they had called and yelled at her for not showing up to watch.

It wasn't her fault. She didn't know about the Olympics. I never told anyone. Granny M wanted to know why I didn't invite them to attend, and I stammered something along the lines of, "uuuuummmm…well, you wouldn't be interested in that kind of thing."

Her answer, which I remember perfectly, was, "That doesn't matter. We should have been told about it, anyway."

The police came over to visit. Sissy's gym teacher saw her bruises and asked where Sissy got them from, but Sissy said she didn't know. The teacher didn't believe her because most times people know where they get their bruises from, so a police officer got sent over to our house. He didn't come in, he just talked to Dad and Fluffy on the driveway. I got sent out to the backyard with Sissy, and we peeked out at them through a hole in the fence.

Sissy's best friends are Lori and Kelly. They're worldly girls. Not in The Truth. It's not a sin to be around worldly people, but almost, so Sissy's friends are a secret. They would never be allowed in our house, but it doesn't matter, 'cause Sissy would never ask them. They're only her friends at school.

Lori wrote a letter to Sissy and said she wished Sissy could come live with Lori's family so Sissy wouldn't get bruises. Sissy hid the letter under her dresser, but Fluffy found it. She cried, although

*I don't know that for sure 'cause I wasn't there, but Sissy told me
Fluffy cried and promised she was trying really hard to love us,
except everyone knows she doesn't.*
    I've never seen Fluffy cry, but Sissy says she did.
Sissy doesn't think it means anything.
I don't either.

Me and Grandpa Terry
in Squaw Camp, 1970.
I was six.

Me and Aunt Letha, with
a string of catfish on Road
FF in Orland. I was nine.

Me, 1977, at age thirteen. The coat
was a hand-me-down from another
Jehovah's Witness family.

My grandparents at their 50th wedding anniversary.

Me on Coors Light at the Oroville Junior Rodeo, 1980. I was sixteen.

Me and Aunt Donnis, college graduation in 1989. I was twenty-five.

Me at the San Diego gay rodeo, 1996, age thirty-two.

Me on the cover of *Roundup Magazine*, at age thirty-four.

Scott Terry today

ONE DOWN, ONE TO GO

Sissy escaped from Fluffy's house on my twelfth birthday, April 4, 1976. She was 13, almost 14, and her departure was sadly uncomplicated.

We didn't try to keep her. There was no debate, to my knowledge, about whether or not anyone wanted her to stay.

Like me, Sissy had shoes that were well beyond being on their last legs, so two days before my birthday, on a Friday, she borrowed a replacement pair from a school friend. We didn't wear shoes in Fluffy's house, so Sissy left them outside, pushed under the geranium bush where she imagined they wouldn't be seen.

Aunt Jackie came over to visit and inquired about the unfamiliar shoes sitting outside the door.

Fluffy lost it.

"Where did you get those shoes?" she demanded to know.

"I got them from a friend," Sissy said.

"No you didn't! You stole them."

"I did not! My friend Lori gave them to me!"

"Really? Okay, what's her phone number? I'll just call her. You stole them. Give me her number!" Fluffy insisted. "And get that look off your face!"

Their fight escalated...starting in the kitchen.

Sissy ran to her bedroom...Fluffy chased her, mere steps behind...I wanted to follow, but couldn't free myself from the kitchen table. I leaned against it, feeling helpless and watching their fight progress to a level I had never before seen, stifling my own anger and knowing my day would be hell too, even though it wasn't my argument.

Sissy reached her bedroom. She turned to face Fluffy.

"I want to go live with my real mother!"

Fluffy backed off, pondering Sissy's announcement.

Two hours later, Virgil came home.

Two days after, on a Sunday, we got rid of Sissy.

We should have gone to the Kingdom Hall for the Watchtower study that day, but didn't. We stayed home and Dad gave away his first child while I wondered how she found the strength to get out.

People might wonder why I didn't do likewise, which is silly. That thought would never have occurred to me. I hadn't seen my mother since I was three and my singular memory of her dabbing smudges off my face with spit didn't count. Two years had gone by since we'd last seen our relatives in Orland. Six years had passed since we'd been cut off from Mom's parents. Sissy often dreamed of our mother coming to save us, but Mom wasn't real to me. No photos of her existed in Fluffy's home.

Through a series of phone calls, Virgil tracked her down.

"It's your turn to take care of Sissy," he informed her.

"What about Scott?" my mother asked.

"Oh no, Scott's fine," he answered. "Sissy is the problem."

Mom showed up that Sunday to take Sissy away. Craving a glimpse, I peeked my head out the kitchen door to watch the cold, stark, and amazingly simple interaction between my mother and father. The trade-off lasted about two minutes. Mom drove up the driveway. Dad went out to meet her. Fluffy and her mother sat frozen to the couch. Sissy got in Mom's car. They drove away. I cried. Dad followed me back to the bedroom and hugged me.

Sissy's name was instantly taboo in Fluffy's house. We never talked about her again. Ever.

Unless you count the day a few months later when Sissy came back to Fillmore for a summer slumber party with the worldly girls, unannounced. She spent the night with her girlfriend Kelly who lived just three doors up the street.

I about keeled over and died when she unexpectedly showed up on our driveway to see me.

The change in her demeanor was palpable. I felt it, envied it, and wanted to indulge in it, too. We stood on the sidewalk and laughed and bonded for all of about fifteen minutes, during which time Fluffy peeked out the window and then ran to the phone to call my father who was away discussing Witness business on a Saturday afternoon with other elders.

He drove back home to confront Sissy at the end of his driveway.

Her staying mere steps down the block with no advanced notice burned him with embarrassment.

"Go back to your worldly friends," he told her. "Scott…Get in the house."

He herded the family out to Fluffy's station wagon and drove us outside of town to where he kept his horse. We stayed there for several hours, watching him feed his horse, while he made it clear that under no circumstances would I be allowed to have any contact with Sissy while she was in town.

In a sense, it didn't matter. Her brief visit reignited our connection, and I carried memories of it for years, knowing she hadn't forgotten me.

PEOPLE IN HELL WANT ICE WATER

"Virgil's as useless as tits on a boar," Fluffy complained. She laughed.

"Too bad you didn't marry someone like Vic Percival," her mother answered. "Vic Percival is incredibly talented. He can fix anything."

I was bored by their conversation. I'd heard it before. I sat in the dirt under the kitchen window, next to the propane barbecue, unintentionally eavesdropping on a private conversation between Fluffy and her mother, listening to their discussion about my dad, thinking that Fluffy had just sinned. Tits were for sure a cuss word. Cuss words were anything Jesus wouldn't say.

But Virgil could say it. Tits, poop, and Sam Hell were regular parts of his vocabulary, and I had a hard time wrapping my head around the double standard.

He drove his truck into the Safeway parking lot. An absentminded woman pulled out in front of him and froze. Unaware that she was in my father's way, she sat behind the wheel of her car, the engine running.

He leaned out the window, "Come on lady! Either poop or get off the pot!"

I was horrified.

"What does that mean?" I asked.

"It means she needs to make up her mind! Is she gonna move, or is she just gonna sit there? That's what it means."

My world was dominated by good words and bad words. Double standards. Impossible definitions:

Hallelujah: *Hallelujah means "praise Jah" in Hebrew. Hallelujah takes Jehovah's name in vain, so it's a bad word and Jehovah's Witnesses can't say it.*

Jeez: *Duh. Everyone knows 'Jeez' is a bad word.*

Nuh-uh: *For sure a bad word, 'cause only Ignoramuses would say "Nuh-uh"...as in, "Did you eat Grant's sandwich?" to which an appropriate answer would never be "Nuh-uh." Dad says if he catches me saying "Nuh-uh" one more time, he's gonna whip me with his belt because only an Ignoramus would say "Nuh-uh."*

Ignoramus: *I don't know any Ignoramuses, but they're bad. See above.*

Okie: *Just as bad as Ignoramus. You hope no one ever finds out you're an Okie. Or an Ignoramus.*

Masturbation: *We don't talk about that word.*

Homo: *Or that one, either.*

Pissed Off: *I got spanked for saying pissed off. Jesus never got pissed off. Can you picture Jesus getting pissed off? That's why it's a bad word.*

Satan: *Satan is bad, but it can be good if used to explain all the things that we don't understand. Like Sissy's mood ring that was given to her by one of her worldly friends at school. The stone changes color when she wears it. Fluffy doesn't know how mood rings work, so she thinks they're from Satan. She got really pissed and threw Sissy's ring in the trash.*

Or when I was nine years old and brought the book Escape to Witch Mountain *home. Fluffy got mad and took it out to the garage and threw it in the trash because she doesn't want books about witches in her house.*

Food-For-Thought: *Everyone at the Kingdom Hall likes to say this, especially when my dad is teaching them about The Truth. He likes it most when he discusses Bible scriptures that don't make sense, and then he says "Now there's some food-for-thought." I hate that word. You shouldn't mix food with thoughts. It's gross, but people who read the Bible like to say it a lot.*

I was convinced that my father probably apologized to Jehovah when he said his private evening prayers. I listened to him spout words like "poop" and "Sam Hell" and "tits on a boar," knowing that Jesus never talked about poop or tits or hell. For sure, Jesus would never say "hell." Or "tits," either.

But I figured my dad said he was sorry when he said his private prayers.

I would have.

—∞—

Two months after Sissy escaped, we took a long drive into the mountain states in Fluffy's station wagon, looking for a new place to live. Nevada, Utah, Wyoming, Idaho, Montana. Three months after that, we packed up for a new life in Evanston, Wyoming. That's three states and 1,362 miles from Fillmore, if you drive the most direct route and don't mess around on the way, which we didn't.

We crossed the state lines of Utah and Wyoming in the middle of October—patches of windblown snow along the Wyoming interstate. At the truck scales, Grant and I wandered off to touch snow for the first time. I was disappointed with my first snow. The desiccated snowflakes were dried out by the wind, ice crystals really, a handful of white dust that wouldn't stick together, and we stood out on the windswept edge of Highway 80 where Dad reminded me that it wasn't my first snow.

"Your first snow was that time when we took a drive up to Big Bear when you were four," he said. "I stuffed snow down your pants and you cried like a bawl baby. We took pictures of you crying."

Within days of arrival in Evanston, we were introduced to an obnoxious and permanent resident of the western high desert. The wind was persistent, monotonous, and dry, even in a snow storm. It blew hot and dusty in summer. The brittle Wyoming cold bit through clothes in winter.

We rented a little three-bedroom singlewide partially-furnished trailer on a barren gravel lot at the northern end of Evanston. A barbed wire fence surrounded the vacant field behind us, the Bear River running behind it.

Virgil went to work for an oil company who gave him a new truck. When he changed jobs for a new oil company, he had to give the truck back. Fluffy's furniture sat in storage with the Global Van Lines moving company while she and Dad perused countless flyers of new homes to purchase in Evanston. Fluffy bought an inexpensive little black and white TV with rabbit ears for the tin can trailer while Dad fantasized about custom built log homes and ordered sales literature and house plans from developers and mail order companies.

Evanston was an ugly and desolate little community on the cusp of an oil boom with an interstate that took travelers around town instead of through it. People drove across the interstate and ran over ground squirrels that were called "squeakies" by the thousands. Hordes of magpies turned squeaky pancakes into dinner.

It was ridiculously cold in Evanston, so people who knew what they were doing hung a spare key on their turn signal levers during winter months, just to lock their doors and leave their vehicles running as they ran through the snow with an extra key to replenish their supply of Hamburger Helper and Folgers instant coffee from Safeway.

Downtown Evanston was a depressing little railroad business district with a Greyhound bus station that had been intentionally split in two—a mostly vacant diner that didn't promise to deliver quality food from tired waitresses off to one side, and a souvenir shop on the other side with miscellaneous items to be purchased by people who were travelling through Evanston on their way to places more interesting.

Like porno mags. The bus depot displayed an enormous selection of pornography on the top shelf of a gigantic magazine rack, and I discovered the whole mess at the age of 12 when I stopped in on my walk home from school. I learned that *Playboys* didn't have pictures of boys in them. Not a one, even though it advertised boys, right there on the title.

I pulled a *Oui* magazine off the rack and imagined it was probably pronounced Oy. Or Ooey. I flipped through its pages and saw that, like *Playboy*, it only had pictures of girls inside.

The grouchy old man hired for the unpleasant task of protecting valuable bus stop porn quickly put an end to my searching porno mags.

"Hey! You're not old enough to be looking at that stuff."

I placed the *Oui* back on the shelf. It had nothing I wanted to see.

—∞—

My light California clothes didn't wear well in frigid Wyoming. I was in junior high, the most volatile time in school for most kids, often the cruelest days of adolescence when you discover you aren't handsome or popular. Folks in Wyoming generally don't take well to Californians who come to town and kill Wyoming deer. And I was a Jehovah's Witness. No one seemed to like them.

My Wyoming classmates didn't know what to make of my refusal to salute the flag or participate in Mormon prayers that preceded our school assemblies. I was an alien who dropped into their campus—their first exposure to The Truth.

The previous month of junior high I had attended in Fillmore was a pleasant experience. The boy's locker room in Fillmore was immaculate, well lit, and monitored by Coach Fauver. The only trace of unpleasantness was when Coach Fauver wouldn't allow anyone to leave the gym without showering first. He was an old Marine, and he made everyone stand in line and memorize the proper way to right-face and left-face and ten-hut when calling roll before class. He docked points from kids who didn't ten-hut properly, and he was consumed by fears that boys wouldn't shower after class.

A week after school started, Fluffy made me deliver a note to him.

"Scott's not allowed to play football," it read.

Coach took the restriction in stride, and in place of the physical exercise provided by football, he allowed me to be his assistant—measuring out the football field and hauling equipment back and forth from the gym. I thought he was unbelievably kind. He didn't dock points for not participating like everyone else. My equipment hauling task wasn't complicated, so I stood on the sidelines each day and watched my classmates play flag football while they stared back at me, wondering what affliction was preventing me from participating.

After class, Coach Fauver stood in front of the showers and folded his thick tattooed arms to oversee the handing out of perfectly folded clean white towels while taking roll call a second time, just to prevent anyone from avoiding the mandatory strip and shower. It didn't matter that I hadn't an ounce of sweat on my body. I was required to get naked too.

No one wanted to be naked while soaping up in a massive shower with no privacy...unless you saw Matt Spiterri, 'cause you had to look at him. Matt Spiterri wasn't a little boy. Matt had matured faster than the rest of us. His penis wasn't small. Dark hair crawled up from the crack of his ass, and I couldn't get thoughts of his naked body out of my head. His penis invaded my fantasies often, and I wanted to do something with that information. I thought about writing it on the bathroom wall... "Matt Spiterri has a hairy butt!" And then we moved to Evanston.

The locker room in Evanston had nothing in common with the locker room in Fillmore. They didn't give out clean white gym towels in Evanston. You had to bring your own, but I didn't know that on my first day. I undressed for my first gym class, shocked at the disparity between Fillmore and Evanston schools. The Evanston locker room was a virtual hell hole in the basement, only accessible via two narrow sets of stairs leading down from the gymnasium. The air was damp and odorous. It stunk. Like a dungeon. A worn, cold, concrete floor. Broken doors hung from lockers. Meager streaks of sunlight struggled through a narrow row of windows, high up on a single wall.

I dressed in shorts for my first class and wondered where the towels were located. I wondered where the teachers were hiding. I wished I was back in Fillmore.

I removed my gym clothes in the locker room after class, including my jock strap. Jock straps were required in gym class.

I pulled my underwear up to my waist. Seth Agnitsch shoved me into the showers.

"You gotta shower, you loser!"

I picked myself up off the wet floor. "I can't shower. I didn't know I was supposed to bring a towel."

He cornered me up against the lockers, and I wilted in fear.

"Too fuckin' bad! You're gonna shower like the rest of us, you fuckin' Jehovie!"

A girl who, moments earlier, had been standing just outside the locker room entrance, saved me. She was rumored to be a slut. Boys were attempting to drag her into the locker room. Seth went to help.

He shoved her through the door. She screamed as naked boys ran for cover.

"No! No!" she cried. "I don't want to see anything!!" In my mind, her screams were proof that she was not, in fact, a slut.

While Seth was distracted by the slut girl, I dressed and ran to my next class. Home Ec was an elective class that I had chosen on the hopes that they would give us something to eat but turned out to be a disappointing hour of lectures about food groups and setting a table properly. There was very little food to eat in Home Ec.

Seth Agnitsch shared a table in Home Ec with me. We made fruit frappes once. The Home Ec teacher had an honest to God recipe for depositing a scoop of vanilla ice cream in a deep glass and spooning canned fruit cocktail over top, then pouring 7-Up over the whole mess. She passed out written recipes for fruit frappes, just in case we wanted to impress our parents by making fruit frappes at home. When her back was turned, Seth dumped salt in my frappe. The whole table laughed.

"Blessed are they who are meek, for they will inherit the earth."

Matthew 5:5

Defending oneself was contrary to everything my religion stood for. Persecution was proof that we were His favorite people. Persecution was a badge of honor. Persecution meant The End was near. Fighting didn't exist in my vocabulary, or in my demeanor.

Roger Malone was the star of junior high, a fact that he was aware of. He basked in the attention, and all the boys in school wished they were his best friend. All the girls hoped he would breathe in their direction. He dominated the lunch room while playing foosball. Roger generally ate FunYuns and Orange Fanta during the lunch break. People in Evanston drank massive amounts of Orange Fanta. And Root Beer Fanta and Grape Fanta. And they ate FunYuns and chewed Bubble Yum. Unlike California, people in Wyoming seemed to love Fanta.

Roger often asked me to run to the snack store across the street to retrieve FunYuns and Fanta for his lunch. If I agreed to be his delivery boy, he would let me buy a couple penny suckers for myself, too.

I once set his Fanta and FunYuns on the table next to the foosball machine, waiting for him to finish playing before handing over his change.

In a loud voice, he asked, "Hey Scott. Do you want to FFF?"

"No." I answered, not knowing what it meant but assuming it was bad.

The whole room erupted in laughter.

"That means you're a homo! Scott's a homo!!"

All the foosball boys wanted to FFF. All the foosball boys wanted to Fuck Farrah Fawcett. Everyone heard me say I don't want to fuck Farrah Fawcett. Everyone said I must be a homo.

Jehovah's Witnesses don't talk about fucking, or Farrah Fawcett. The foosball crowd's gonna be really sorry when Armageddon comes. They're gonna wish they hadn't called me "Jehovie" or given me crap for not wanting to fuck Farrah Fawcett. They're gonna be really sorry someday.

Fluffy was miserable in Wyoming, packed into our narrow trailer. To escape her awful existence in Evanston, she periodically drove to Salt Lake City, craving civilization and shopping excursions.

Amber was three. Grant was in second grade, and Fluffy often pulled him out of school early for an eighty mile drive to Salt Lake. The oil fields kept Dad at work until late and he still needed to take care of his horse, so I often came home in the middle of a Wyoming winter…locked out of the house with no place to go.

I sat on the front stairs, hoping the neighbors we didn't know would invite me to their trailer to stay warm. Winter darkness arrived early in Wyoming. I sat alone on our welded steel stairs, three steps up to the front door, wondering how long I would wait for someone to come home. Sometimes I waited for fifteen minutes. Sometimes hours. My stomach growled from after-school hunger. I often thought of Sissy, remembering the day she stood up to Fluffy, and wished I could be more like her.

Sometimes Fluffy comes home before dark. Sometimes she doesn't. Sometimes I crawl into the tack compartment of the horse trailer to get out of the snow. I curl up with the saddle blankets and wonder why Jehovah doesn't answer my prayers.

And sometimes I cry angry tears in the horse trailer and get mad...

"Jeeezuz, what the fuck am I cryin' for! It doesn't mean anything...grow up for cryin' out loud, you're not gonna die for having to crawl into the fuckin' trailer!"

Unless they find out I say "fuck." Dad would beat the hell out of me with the Brown Stick if he knew how much I cuss when I cry. The Brown Stick moved to Wyoming too, all the way from Fillmore, packed in a box, and they would use it if they heard me say "fuck."

Sometimes I pretend this isn't my life, but it is my life, so sometimes I cry and sometimes I just tell myself to, "Quit bein' a fuckin' bawl baby"...then Fluffy comes home and I crawl out of the horse trailer. It's just how it is.

I once slammed my shoulder against the front door of the trailer in frustration...and it opened!! I literally fell inside the entry and couldn't believe my luck.

The front door didn't latch properly if it wasn't slammed hard, but Fluffy was apparently unaware of that fact.

I shoved my shoulder against the door often, and if it opened, I investigated each room in the trailer, ensuring they were, in fact, empty, before daring to steal food from the kitchen.

I parked myself at the kitchen table, eating bits of food I was confident no one would miss. A single slice of bread with peanut butter. A piece of leftover venison from the fridge.

I peered through the curtains at the gravel parking lot.

When Fluffy's car rolled up to the front door, I slipped out the back.

Fluffy started asking questions.

"What are you doing behind the trailer?"

There was no reason for me to be in back of the trailer.

Virgil began asking questions.

"What are you doing back there?"

I ignored the inner voices warning me that they were getting suspicious.

Weeks later, I warmed up some leftover biscuits in the oven. I guessed that the oven should be turned on high, then burned the biscuits black. Fluffy and Virgil came home while I was frantically trying to get the burnt smell out of the house...the front door was open...the back door ajar...fanning fresh air through the interior... oh shit...

"How'd you get in the house?"

"How dare you steal some biscuits!!!?"

"How'd you get in the house?"

"You could have burnt the trailer down!!!"

"How'd you get in the house?"

Not long after, while sitting at the kitchen table and peering through the kitchen curtains, I watched my father's truck pull onto the lot. I ran to the back door, only to discover that instead of stopping in front of the trailer, he had driven another 15 feet until parallel to the backside. The whole family saw me sneaking out. From then on, the front door was always latched properly.

———————

Granny M visited us often in Wyoming. Her limited Social Security income didn't allow her the luxury of living on her own, so she shuttled back and forth between Los Angeles and Wyoming, dividing time between her two daughters' homes. When she stayed with us, she took over Amber's bed and Amber either shared it with her or went to sleep with Dad and Fluffy. Granny M also had a tendency to take over the cooking chores and prepare my sack lunch for school. I spent less time thinking about food and hunger when Granny M was around.

Granny M says her father used to beat her until the blood ran down her legs. Her father was really abusive, she says. She says that a lot. Her other favorite thing to say is, "If wishes were horses, then all would ride." That's kind of like saying, "People in hell want ice water," except you can't say that because there's no such thing as hell.

BLOW JOBS AND CAR SEX

Sissy wrote a short letter to me, then mailed it to her worldly friend Kelly who had slipped it to me at school in Fillmore.

I smuggled it up to Wyoming under the seat of Fluffy's car, stuffed up between the cushions and the seat spring. It was my most precious possession.

Shortly after arriving in Evanston, I cornered an unusually independent and loner kid in gym class I had spent a few weeks getting to know.

"I have a sister who doesn't live with me," I eventually told him. "Can she send letters to you? And then you'll give them to me?"

"Why?" he asked.

"I don't want my mom and dad to know I'm talking to her, so I need to find someone that she can write to."

"Okay. That's weird, but okay. She can send letters to me."

I wrote my first letter to Sissy that night in the bedroom I shared with Grant.

He wanted to play. I ignored him.

"Shhhhhh! Leave me alone! I'm writing a letter to Sissy," I whispered.

Grant tore the unfinished page from my hand and took it to Fluffy. She passed it to Dad that evening.

He confronted me in the hallway. "Why are you sneaking around behind my back, trying to talk to Sissy?" he asked.

"Because I thought you would want to read it first," I answered.

"Of course we want to read it first," he said. "You don't need to be talking to Sissy about anything we don't know about."

Sissy's letter soon disappeared from underneath my bedroom dresser. I no longer had her address. I pulled a California map out of the school library and searched the metropolitan area around San Francisco, wondering where my sister might be. She lived in a town that started with a 'P', I thought. It might be Pleasanton. Pittsburg? Palo Alto? No. I decided it was probably Pittsburg. I couldn't remember.

—∞—

My seventh grade English teacher was a short and energetic lady with blond hair in a pixie cut. I adored Mrs. Ronci. She took an interest in me that I hadn't known before, and when I wrote a very long short story about two teenage boys who ran away from home, she divvied it up over a week's worth of classes and read it out loud.

When I wrote a second short story entitled *Dusty the Lonesome Dog*, she submitted to the Young Wyoming Writes competition. It was four pages of misery, detailing the short life of a starving dog…searching for love and a home, and it was published in 1977 in a thick, spiral-bound volume of miscellaneous poetry and short stories by other Wyoming students.

Mrs. Ronci then gave me the study manual for the National Spelling Bee.

Grant offered to help me practice, but he was only seven and couldn't yet read. One of the really smart girls in school asked to study with me after school, but that would have been bad association. She offered to meet up at lunchtime, but I had taken a cafeteria job in return for free lunch and wasn't about to trade free lunch in place of spelling bee study.

The city Bee was held in the junior high library. I won First Place and my picture was displayed in the Evanston *Herald* newspaper.

The county Bee arrived a few weeks later. It was too big for the library, so we held it in the auditorium instead. All the kids who had won spelling bees from other towns in our county sat on stage, gazing down at all the parents who came to watch.

Near the end of the competition, I misspelled the word "raisin." Seriously. I spelled it raisAn. With an A. That mistake threw me out of the County Spelling Bee in Fourth Place, which meant I was the alternate to go to the State Bee in Cheyenne. I got my picture in the paper for that, too.

That night, during dinner, I told Dad I might qualify to go to the State Spelling Bee. I was in fourth place. I was the alternate. I might have to go to Cheyenne for the competition.

"You don't need to be going to things like that," he said.

—⁚⁚⁚—

In 1977, Elvis died. Fluffy cried. I discovered car sex and blowjobs.

Just the concept, not the actual thing. The junior high library sponsored a read-a-thon, just to encourage students to pick up a book now and then, and to crown the most prolific reader at the end of a two-week contest. I was a shoo-in, the undeclared but understood winner before the contest ever started. Books were my only outlet to hide inside fantasies and worlds that were impossible to conjure up on my own, and the whole school was aware that my days were always buried inside the pages of those dreams. I wallowed in books, scoured shelves, squandered days, consumed

by worlds unbelievably different from mine. I fell in love with
libraries and buried my brain so deeply in books that I carried home
more than one report card with a teacher's handwritten notation,
"Scott reads too much."

I eventually exhausted the library's supply of children's books,
and found myself in the adult section, eagerly searching for new
and undiscovered material. My first encounter into this new world
of entertainment was *The Thorn Birds* which included colorful
descriptions of good looking Irish men having sex in cars. There
were vague descriptions of events in the back seats that sounded to
me like blowjobs. I still wasn't sure if dick sucking existed in real
life, but dick sucking was real in adult books and porn magazines,
apparently. I next read the book *One on One*, shortly after the movie
came out with Robby Benson. It appeared to me, according to
written descriptions in the book, that Robby Benson got a blowjob
in his car while his girlfriend's fingers "danced in his crotch."

I won the school reading contest. The reward was a free meal,
donated by the lunch counter at City Drug, and I found my name
and photo in the local paper again. The *Herald* posted a photo of
me in plaid polyester JC Penny Toughskin pants at the City Drug
counter, next to a freckle-faced and red-headed girl who was the
second place winner. No one could tell that she had red hair from
that black and white cutout, but I remember the long and curly
brightness of her hair and the inaccurate photo caption that assured
readers we "enjoyed our lunch very much."

It wasn't true. I never enjoyed my lunch because I never
found the nerve to ask for it. For several weeks after the contest, I
took occasional walks down the hill at noon to linger outside the
drugstore and struggle to pull the courage I couldn't find to occupy
a vacant stool and endure the scrutiny of old people who ate lunch
at drugstore counters.

———∞∞∞———

Later that year, we moved out of the trailer and into a brand new two-bedroom, one-bath house with an electric dishwasher and a totally vacant and unfinished concrete basement in a barren subdivision on top of rocks. That was our first experience with a dishwasher, and it removed me from kitchen cleanup duty. A week after moving in, Fluffy again assigned a daily chore of dusting baseboards to me, a task that she didn't find necessary when we lived in the trailer.

Our new home site had less than an inch of dirt, masking an impenetrable layer of rocks. Lots of rocks. Rocks from an ancient riverbed, cemented together over the centuries and a terrible place to think you could grow anything other than sagebrush. Most of our neighbors hauled in real dirt and planted front lawns, but we only had a yard full of rocks. And dog dirt, 'cause Virgil had four dogs in the backyard—Britty, Flo, Andy, and Turk.

The dogs were my friends. The dog breeding business had worked out well. Andy was the stud and Flo, the bitch, was pregnant on our drive to Wyoming. Their first puppies were born in the horse trailer in the middle of a Wyoming winter and we raised several litters after that, selling pups to ranchers around the country for $100 each, via an ad in *Western Horseman*.

First there were three, then eight. Then four, then ten. Then three, and back down to two. 'Cause there was always a leftover, at least one. Sometimes two. Usually just one that didn't get sold quickly and turned into a temporary pet, like Turk.

Our four dogs turned into three when we took a weekend roadtrip to Jackson Hole and Dad's bird dog Britty went along. Britty was nine years old and arthritic. He had a tendency to bite people he didn't know, so we had no choice but to take him to Jackson Hole. Someone from the Kingdom Hall agreed to feed the three other dogs we left at home—dogs that had never shown an inclination to bite people.

Britty rode to Jackson Hole in the back of our truck, and I tied him up behind our rented cabin for the night. When we awoke the next morning, he was gone. Nowhere to be found. My simple knot had not restrained him from breaking loose.

We drove around town for hours, yelling "BRITTYYYYYY" at the top of our lungs, which was pointlessly stupid because he'd spent most of his miserable life chained to the backyard and was desperate enough to be impossible to catch on the rare occasions when he broke free. After a long afternoon of searching and screaming his name in Jackson Hole, we abandoned our search.

Halfway back to Evanston, Fluffy informed me, "Britty was worth $50. You owe me $50. And you still owe me for the scratch you put on my car and the broken screen door, too."

—∞—

Grandma and Grandpa Terry came to visit us in 1977. I hadn't seen them since I was ten, but the DDT that was sprayed around the ranches in Newville had caused blood clots in Gramps' lungs, so he had a lung removed and then they were going to retire back to Anderson, Missouri where poverty was the norm. Midway through their cross-country drive in a U-Haul van, they stopped to spend the night with us in Evanston.

Grandma took a picture of me early the next morning.

I was convinced it was our last contact. Armageddon was coming. They weren't in The Truth. They were bad association, not to mention that Fluffy didn't like them. And they didn't like her. And she didn't like me.

—∞—

Fluffy craved an escape from Wyoming, so she announced plans to fly back to Los Angeles with Grant and Amber. She needed to revisit civilization, she said. For weeks leading up to her departure, I wondered what they would do with me. Where would I go?

When they walked out the door, Virgil driving Fluffy to the airport in Salt Lake, she handed me a temporary key to the back door of the house. I was free to come and go at will, with a house key strung around my neck from an extra shoelace.

On my first day alone, after Virgil left for work, I made two cups of International Foods mocha flavored instant coffee for breakfast. The can had been sitting in the kitchen cabinet for several years, and no one would miss it. I mixed up a box of raspberry Jell-O and ate the whole bowl while jerking off to images of a shirtless Marlon Brando crawling through underground tunnels in the movie *The Great Escape*.

I dug old bottles from the long-abandoned town dump, a short one minute walk from the house, and then sold them at the Trash and Treasures Antique shop on the far side of town.

I discovered Professional Wrestling on Channel 13 WTBS Super Station from Atlanta. Hours of my day were spent in front of the TV, my heart pounding with arousal at the spectacle of beefy naked guys pounding on each other inside a wrestling ring—until Virgil came home and discovered how I was spending my day. He said it was "fake" and wasn't "real" wrestling, and I remember thinking of course it was fake; I could see that for myself. I sat on the living room floor that evening, five feet from the TV, watching Dad open mail in the kitchen with more attention than you really need to give mail, wondering why he got so worked up over the discovery of how I spent my afternoons. I changed the channel, and we never talked about that again.

When he was off to work, I parked myself in front of the TV for daily doses of wrestling fantasies, pants around my knees, fondling my dick and imagining wrestlers doing the same. Rick Rude, in particular. Rick Rude was a monster of a man. Thoughts of him engaging in solitary exploration of his own body got me off. Sexual activity was a solitary proposition, in my mind. I fantasized of Rick Rude with clothes on, clothes off, fondling himself, just as I did in Fluffy's living room. I stretched out in front of the TV and shot sperm across Fluffy's carpet until my testicles were wrung dry. Grant's baby picture was displayed on top of the TV, in a fancy metal frame with his first baby shoes preserved in bronze. A large photo of Amber decorated Fluffy's stereo, equally visible… and it suddenly occurred to me that there were no pictures of me anywhere. And none of Sissy.

I zipped my pants and ransacked the house, starting with the two nightstands in Fluffy's bedroom. In the bottom of Dad's short cabinet was a folder with all the personal items he had cleaned out of Sissy's school locker two years earlier. Inside was a stack of gossipy notes that Sissy had traded back and forth with the worldly girls, and cute greeting cards from young boys with equally young crushes on my sister—things she kept at school because they would have been cause for instant trouble at home.

What compelled Dad to keep those insignificant items was a complete mystery to me. I couldn't make any sense of that folder in my head. He had retained the personal effects of a lost child—a child he had given up so easily. I sat on his bedroom floor for a long afternoon, troubled by that realization.

I tucked everything back into Dad's nightstand and continued my exhaustive search, finding few intentional photos of me, or Sissy. Mostly accidental snapshots when we happened to be in a group photo. Two school pictures from second and third grade. Nothing since.

In the hall linen closet, behind the bathroom towels, I found an old transistor radio—a radio I had never before seen and had never before found its way out of the closet. I took it down to the basement.

Each night, after the sun went down, I laid in bed, alone in my basement, the volume turned low, listening to an unexpected world of entertainment from across the country. My stolen radio picked up signals from Texas, talk shows from Nevada. Music from California. Radio stations unfolded their tales in the high desert of Wyoming.

After a two week vacation in Los Angeles, Fluffy flew home and Virgil retrieved her from the Salt Lake airport. The next evening, she heard the faint music from my stolen radio wafting its way upstairs.

I heard Virgil coming in his cowboy boots, walking across the upper floor with enough advance notice to hide the radio. That's the beauty of living in a basement. No one can sneak up on you.

Virgil stood at the top step and peered down below.

"Scott! Is that a radio I hear down there?"

"No, uh-uh."

He said, "Hmmmm, your mother said she heard a radio down there."

"No, I don't have a radio."

Fluffy searched the basement the next day when I was at school. She found her radio hidden between two stacks of old paint cans.

She was furious.

"You're a thief! The next time I go to California," she warned, "you're not gonna be allowed in my house."

—⊶—

Her next trip to California arrived at Christmas time. Virgil drove her down to the airport, but just before leaving, they held a loud discussion in my presence, debating whether or not I could be trusted in her house. He insisted they couldn't lock me out all day for weeks on end during winter.

I again got a key to the house.

Fluffy got her vacation to Los Angeles.

Virgil got to play with his horse each night after working in the oil fields during the day.

I got unrestricted time to jerk off to professional wrestling.

I killed a rabbit while she was gone. On purpose. It snowed like crazy over Christmas, and the wind howled across Evanston and piled snow into gigantic white snow dunes. I've never seen so much snow in all my life, coming from California like we did, but it was amazing...huge drifts of snow banked up next to the fence in back. They're so high that you can stand on top and see into our backyard. Not that there's any point to that because everybody knows there's nothin' in our backyard except rocks and dog dirt. And rabbits, 'cause the snow's so deep that the whole town is swarmin' with starving rabbits searching for somethin' to eat.

I cornered a rabbit up against the foundation and whacked it in the head with the curved rocker that came off of Grant's broken baby rocking chair.

I skinned it and taped the hide to my wall in the basement, just for decoration.

The basement was unfinished, except for Grant's bunk bed that we had separated into two individual beds—one for me and one for Grant, except he hardly ever slept down there. At the age of eight, he often still slept with Dad and Fluffy.

Fluffy's washer and dryer were down in the basement too, and the upright freezer to store Dad's deer meat. And my rabbit hide, taped to the concrete wall.

Fluffy came home after her Christmas trip to LA and flipped out at the sight of it.

"Virgil!!" she screamed. "Get down here! Do you see that? Where did that come from? So help me, if anyone gets sick...What knife did he use? I want that knife out of my house! You better have a talk with him!"

"Honey. Calm down," Virgil said. "No one's gonna get sick, now that the knife has been run through the dishwasher and all. It'll be okay."

He turned to me, "Scott, as punishment for upsetting your mother, I want you to do some research at school and write a report about rabbits and tularemia disease."

~~~

Halfway through eighth grade, Dad allowed me to take on a paper route. It had taken three years to convince him, starting in Fillmore, because another Witness kid named Frankie Rodriquez had one there and he worked his butt off and didn't make much. You wouldn't want to ever take a job that requires you to work hard and earn so little. It would be better to stay broke. But Virgil finally agreed to let me deliver the *Casper Star*, which promised to pay all of $40 a month—a teenage fortune in 1977.

"I don't want to hear you complaining about it, or asking for help," he said. "If you take that job, it's all on your own. Don't come to me for help."

Fluffy added, "And save your money. You can start buying your own clothes."

Wyoming paperboys must get out of bed at the crack of dawn and meet the delivery truck at the post office at 6 am, a fact that was carefully explained to me prior to signing on. Virgil loaned me a few dollars to purchase a cheap wind-up clock, and I slept next to the constant tick-tock until the alarm blasted me out of bed in the basement, only to find myself sitting on the post office loading dock thirty minutes later, struggling to stay warm and awake while waiting for the truck that was often stuck in the snow between Evanston and Casper. On some dark winter mornings, I gave up on walking the ice covered streets and simply dumped the undelivered papers in my gym locker, then delivered them after school, not understanding why anyone wanted a newspaper at the crack-of-dumb-ass-dawn, anyway.

I was a terrible paperboy. Before my customers discovered that fact, some thought it nice to offer Christmas presents. The first present was a hand-crocheted green and yellow beanie with a fuzzy ball on top, and it came from a little old lady who lived in what appeared to be the oldest two-story white Victorian house in town, on a corner. I imagined she had lived there her entire life.

That sweet lady delivered her homemade beanie to me on her front porch in exchange for the paper I usually folded and tucked inside her screen door, along with a Christmas card and an explanation that she had watched me deliver papers for weeks with nothing on my head. Her enormous beanie was wonderful. Too big, but wonderful, nonetheless.

I wore it home, feeling pleasantly warm at the unexpected comfort of a gift. I walked in the back door of Fluffy's with a green beanie on my head.

"You shouldn't be taking Christmas presents from people," Virgil said. "You should have given it back. You could have witnessed to her about The Truth instead."

I removed the hat from my head.

"Do you want me to give it back to her tomorrow?" I asked.

"No, you can't give it back after you've worn it, but you should have given it back and told her that Christmas is a pagan celebration. Jesus wasn't born in December. Remember that next time."

I struggled with that. I couldn't imagine handing a present back to someone with the words, "No thanks. Christmas is a sin."

I was so struck by the unfamiliar power of unexpected presents that, after listening to Virgil's lecture, I convinced myself that Jehovah didn't really care. He really wouldn't. It would be our secret. No one would know about the gifts from my customers, except Him.

Like the two dollars folded inside a friendly holiday card that I received a few days later.

And a silver Ben Franklin 50-cent piece from a lady who advised me to "Put it somewhere safe, 'cause it'll be worth a lot of money someday." I didn't. I added that silver coin to the two dollar present on a hungry day, and I used the combination to buy a full-size meatball sandwich and root beer Fanta in the basement of The Dugout, a block from school.

And a box of chocolate covered cherries from the little old lady who had a quart of milk delivered to the dairy coldbox on her front porch twice a week, every Monday and Thursday, except for the single Thursday when I stole it. She gave the chocolates to me a few weeks later, and when I bit the tops off to suck out the cherry liquor, I felt shame for stealing milk from a little old lady who didn't know anything about me but cared enough about Christmas to give me a box of chocolates. I never stole her milk again.

Shortly after Christmas, I met another customer for the first time—a handsome mid-twenties guy with a beautiful white smile and big thick hands that looked like they swung a hammer all day. He lived in a little brown dump of a house, a rental probably, the front seat of an old car leaned against his porch. I collected the first month's subscription money on his doorstep, propping his screen door open with my leg, watching his muscular fingers unfold bills from his wallet, my mouth going dry, wanting to blabber something in the way of conversation, totally out of words, wondering when I might see him again. Wondering what I might do to make him my friend.

He had beautiful teeth. I thought of him often—his beautiful white smile, his massive hands.

A few days after meeting, I jumped up on his porch to deposit a paper and eavesdropped on the obvious sound of water running down the drain, his shower on full blast. He was naked. Hot water cascaded over his beautiful naked body, in the privacy of his shower. He was probably tan. His muscular hands were browned by the sun. His body would be covered in muscle. Big, solid, tanned muscles, like a professional wrestler.

I stood on his porch, listening to the water pour off his body, wanting to lure him to the door, craving a glimpse of what would step out of the shower, maybe wrapped in a towel, maybe wrapped in nothing, inventing every excuse imaginable for why I should stay, thinking he would become my friend. He would sit on his porch every day and wait for me to deliver his paper after school. And we would talk. We would talk every day. And maybe he would take another shower. And maybe he would invite me in to talk. Just once. He would be my friend. But I would say no. I would for sure say no. A naked friend would be a sin.

After a two minute battle between desire and fear, I couldn't invent a reason to stay on his porch. Flush and frustrated, I left his home to deliver the rest of my papers. Thoughts of him helped me jerk off that night, as it had several nights before. I prayed about it afterwards, asking Jehovah to forgive me.

A week later, I handed over a partially-itemized mess of cash and checks to my boss, Dick McCloster.

It had never occurred to me to keep detailed records or issue receipts. I assumed the responsibility of being honest and paying what they owed was up to subscribers. They were adults. Dick spilled it out over his kitchen counter, trying to make sense of the jumble, which wasn't possible, and then he refused to compensate me for delivering papers.

I went back to customers, attempting to collect the amount I was short, but some weren't willing to pay again. Some refused to pay because I was a lousy paperboy. I didn't understand the importance of delivering a newspaper early in the morning. We didn't read worldly papers in my house. The only reading material delivered to our address was *Western Horseman*.

In my mind, the irregular delivery of the *Casper Star* didn't seem to be anything worth crying over, but some of my customers were sure upset about it. None of them saw a Sunday paper until mid-afternoon because an early morning delivery would have interfered with my obligation to worship Jehovah in the Kingdom Hall. People who savor a Sunday newspaper over a hot pot of morning coffee don't like seeing it show up at the end of the day…but I didn't know that. I just became hopelessly lost in the nightmare I had created.

I agonized over fears of Dad finding out.

The problems grew exponentially larger and I never received a paycheck. Some of my customers refused to pay their subscription fees, and a few others paid in cash. The temptation was too great. I used some of the cash to buy candy bars and over-ripe pineapples from Safeway. I occasionally bought lunch in the school cafeteria. Two months into my paper route, on a night when Virgil took us out to dinner at the local steakhouse, I reimbursed him for the cost of my dinner with funds he assumed came from my paycheck, but didn't. I stole subscription money to pay for that dinner, just to prevent him from discovering that I wasn't being paid.

After three months of thievery and accounting disasters, the whole paper route business blew up. My boss called Virgil and demanded a little over $600 for the funds I had either stolen or was unable to collect. Virgil was unbelievably pissed. I had brought reproach on Jehovah's name, he said. He feared the news of my thievery splashed across the Evanston *Herald*..."Jehovah's Witness Boy is a Thief!"

Fluffy was more than furious. Not only had I cost them an enormous sum of money, but I was clearly a worthless kid. They needed to get rid of me. She felt vindicated by my thievery.

A month later when school closed for the summer, I walked the business streets of Evanston, inquiring into work that would repay my $600 debt. On my first day of job interviews, the Whirl Inn Motel hired me as a laundry boy. For five and six days a week, I carried clean linen to each room, taking the wear and tear of climbing the stairs off of the maids.

The Whirl Inn introduced me to coffee with cream and sugar on lunch breaks, and a stack of porn magazines in the basement office for the perusal of the motel owner. They gave me a pass key to open newly vacated rooms and strip the dirty sheets off the beds and haul new ones in. There's really no way to know if a room is empty unless you stick your head in, so after knocking repeatedly and feeling certain that there was no living soul inside, I cautiously unlocked each door and unloaded a pile of clean replacement linens on the dirty beds. Halfway through the middle of one room with an armload of clean sheets, a 40-something guy stepped out from the privacy of the sink divider, stark naked, with an erection. His penis waved at me. It swung to the side and waved back the other direction.

My heart stopped beating. I stammered, "Sorry," and ran back out, leaving my stack of sheets behind.

I have a suspicion that his exposure was intentional. I think he was hoping for a hotel maid of the opposite gender to wave his penis at, but that's not what he got. He got a skinny fourteen year-old boy with acne, and I got a great mental picture to jerk off to in my basement.

Each week, when I collected my paycheck from the Whirl Inn, I turned it over to Fluffy. By the end of summer, my newspaper debt was paid off. When I delivered the final check to her, she insisted that I pay the long overdue bills for Britty and the broken screen door and scratch on her car too.

Virgil disagreed. I still needed to buy clothes for school, he reminded her.

All of the old items on Fluffy's list were forgiven, and I spent my last two Whirl Inn paychecks at the Salt Lake City Mall on clothes.

THE EPIPHANIES

My father never discussed the specifics of his divorce from my mother—not with me except for one solitary occasion in Wyoming when we left the Evanston house under the pretense of "going hunting," but what instead became a dishonest afternoon retreat while Virgil sprawled out over the truck bed, dozing off for a nap.

I was fourteen and wasn't in need of a nap. We parked under the shade of pine trees on a lonesome dirt road outside of Evanston while I considered the possibility, for the first time ever, that perhaps this is what my father did on his frequent disappearances—took naps in back of his truck while the rest of us believed he was off with a gun procuring dinner for our table.

Having nothing to do, I poked around under the trees and scuffed dirt across the road. I hiked up the hill, out from under the shade, enjoying the sun, and then went back to the truck, unintentionally waking Virgil.

Irritated, he gave up his snooze. He wasn't yet ready to go home.

Virgil talked a bit of his childhood. He explained how he became a single father of two babies at the age of twenty-one with no education beyond high school.

He touched on stories of his sinful days, things he had done before finding The Truth, his poor judgment in previous years, vague generalities, no specifics except for a mention of how he gave up smoking after becoming a Jehovah's Witness by simply throwing the pack of cigarettes out the car window and never looking back. He said his previous mistakes in life were resolved when the Witnesses showed up. They explained why life was difficult and promised him a better one when Armageddon arrived...a message that resonated with him and arrived when he needed it most, the lowest point in his life. And that, he said, was how he knew they had "the truth."

It was the only heart-to-heart moment we ever had, an exclusive but brief glimpse of his adult world. I listened to his one-way discussion, nodded my head, and agreed that it was indeed fortunate for him to have found The Truth.

It wasn't the first time I felt gratitude for being a Witness. I wrapped my arms around my religion often. Unlike what I had known in California, the Evanston congregation was a small and intimate group where everyone was closely acquainted.

Shortly after arriving in Wyoming, the Witnesses scheduled 1978 as the year in which all missionaries around the globe would be sent home for special assemblies on their home turf. It was a "regrouping" attempt to assuage the unanticipated effects of Armageddon's failure to arrive in 1975. To fund the cost of bringing everyone home, each congregation created a special contribution can to solicit donations.

Our can came out at the end of a weeknight Bible study. We gathered to greet the empty soup can, a handmade white paper label taped to the side, soliciting donations.

Fluffy looked at it and declared, "Surely, the brothers don't believe this old system will still be around in 1978."

She was probably correct, our small congregation agreed. The End will be here soon, they said.

I was shaken by that discussion.

I had been a JW ever since my father married Fluffy, but before that moment, I had never questioned whether or not there was such a thing as the "true" religion, or wondered how we knew that our religion was it. Never for a moment did I doubt the validity of my church. I didn't ask questions when Armageddon failed to arrive in 1975, or that evening when my congregation discussed our expectation that it would surely show up by 1978. I just believed what I was told. Would a Catholic child walk out of Mass and request a visit to the local Baptist church? Would a Mormon boy request literature on opposing religious beliefs, or ask for exposure to an alternative point of view? Would an Indian child who has known nothing but Hinduism in his short life be receptive to Jewish teachings, or be mature enough to understand the difference? I didn't ask questions as a child. I didn't doubt. I didn't debate. I just accepted and believed what my parents told me.

But I wasn't a little kid on that evening. I was a teenager. On that evening in 1977, my religious epiphany arrived. On that evening, I understood how lucky I was to be a Witness. I realized, for the first time, that a belief in Armageddon and the New Order wasn't just my belief. It wasn't only a belief of Witnesses in California. It was shared by the Witnesses in Wyoming. It was shared by Witnesses all over the globe. Jehovah's Witnesses were the lucky few who understood that Armageddon would arrive soon. We were in the last days, Armageddon was on its way, and we were the only ones who knew it. On that evening, I completely accepted my faith as the truth.

Energized over the newfound embrace of my religion, I went searching for conversion opportunities at school. That's what you do when you have The Truth. You share it with everyone else, because you want them to have it, too. When you believe you have the one and only path to God, you want everyone else to know about it too. Feeling powerful, I chased weaker students around campus, intending to share it.

My first Bible study came courtesy of a geeky Catholic kid with thick black hair that wouldn't lay down. David was a school outcast like me, but unlike me, he wasn't very well versed in the Bible. I chose him as my target for the simple reason that we were both unpopular, not to mention that he was Catholic in a school dominated by Mormonism. The more we talked, the more I realized that his Catholic upbringing had failed to include any meaningful reading of scripture. The more apparent it became that his faith did not require him to find his way around Bible pages, the easier he appeared as a convert. Like me, David spent his lunch hour holed up in a vacant room with his nose buried in homework, and after several weeks of engaging him in biblical conversations, he gave up on combating my interpretation of scripture and suggested we pay a lunchtime visit to his priest. Shortly after, I followed him to the Catholic Church a few blocks down the street.

I walked into that church with the boy who I believed would be my first conquest, my first convert to The Truth, and was completely fascinated by the discovery that Catholics didn't worship in the same manner as Witnesses. My Kingdom Halls were spare, plain, and full of poor people on cheap folding chairs. My religion was not a place to put on airs, after all. We were just there to read the Bible and thank God that we were His favorite people and weren't a sinner on the same scale as everyone else. Kingdom Halls did not allocate space for parties or basketball, which was rumored to take place inside the Evanston Mormon Church. That's why the Mormon churches were so big, I was told. You gotta build them huge if you're gonna stick a basketball court in the middle of it.

I'd never seen the interior of another church in my life, other than a partial glimpse when Grandma Terry dragged me into the Orland Baptist Church at my age of nine. We didn't enter her church proper. We just stopped in to visit some little old ladies who were off in a side room working on handmade quilts. I felt terribly guilty with Grams that day, knowing I would be in so much trouble if my parents discovered that I had set foot in her Orland church, even if we did nothing other than chat with old ladies about quilts.

My heart pounded with excitement as I entered that Evanston Catholic church with David, completely overwhelmed with an unexpected desire to soak up the unfamiliar details of my potential convert's religion, and grateful for an opportunity to introduce Jehovah to some non-believers.

David splashed his fingers in water from a bowl mounted near the front door, then dipped his knee and crossed his heart and mumbled something that wasn't really intelligible. David said he had to do that stuff before he could walk down the rows of benches, since he was a Catholic and all. He wasn't sure why, but he said everybody did it and God would like me better if I did it, too, but it was okay if I skipped that requirement on my first visit to Catholicism.

I gazed at the rows of beautiful and polished wooden pews before us, then followed him down the aisle and into a tiny windowless room behind the pulpit—an office lined with books. David introduced me to his priest—a man who turned out to be very patient and welcoming.

I was disappointed by his demeanor. I wanted an argument. I wanted to point out the wickedness of his ways. I was prepared to prove him wrong and bring him to Jehovah, but the priest wouldn't argue back. He just smiled a lot, a soft and defenseless grin, and after a pointless discussion and gentle sharing of scripture, we parted ways with the understanding that he wouldn't change my beliefs, nor would I alter his. I walked home that afternoon, disappointed in the priest's passivity but expecting to be congratulated for having the bravery to preach to him.

I proudly unraveled my conversion attempt to Granny M—a story that concerned her, immensely.

"You shouldn't have done that," she said. "You shouldn't be going inside a Catholic Church."

"I was just witnessing to them."

"Do you think Jehovah will protect you inside a Catholic church? He's not going to protect you from Satan in places like that."

She relayed my indiscretion to Virgil when he arrived home.

"Why would you do that?" he asked. "Didn't it occur to you that Satan might occupy worldly churches?"

"No," I answered. It had never occurred to me that Jehovah would cast me aside for entering the church of someone who didn't share my faith. At no time during my Catholic Church visit did I feel the presence of Satan. I carried my religion and my God into that church and was certain I carried them back out.

My next Bible study was found in Tracee Colgate. Tracee was a chunky girl. We had few friends, but I found her to be a very willing audience for a discussion of my religion. We studied the Bible together during lunch while I quoted scriptures to prove that every holiday she had ever enjoyed were, in fact, the sins of a worldly society. I explained how wonderful it was to be in The Truth and invited her to a meeting at the Kingdom Hall, and that's when I discovered she wasn't really interested in my religion, after all. Tracee was only interested in me, because I was the first boy who paid attention to her.

The Evanston Kingdom Hall was a little brown box, an inexpensive building of cheap construction for a very poor Wyoming congregation. There were perhaps five other Witness families in town, none of whom had children my age. I was the only teenage JW, unless you count Brother MacDonald's daughter. He was a divorced guy with three children, and they had HBO which seemed unbelievably extravagant. His oldest daughter was two years older than me, but she was disobedient and had been quietly disassociated from the congregation, effectively cutting her off from our fellowship.

I only saw her once, but she was rumored to be rebellious, refusing to listen to her father's instruction in The Truth. I thought of her as evil, an apostate from my religion, but she had freedoms I dreamed about, not to mention HBO.

Out of boredom, I often explored the shelves of literature in the Kingdom Hall storage room, occasionally borrowing old volumes of *The Watchtower* and *Awake!* magazines just to read historical discussions about my faith and to enjoy the recognition and praise it generated for showing an interest in wanting to learn more about Jehovah.

There were many printed discussions about whether or not Witnesses should attend college—an issue that was becoming pertinent to me.

> *"Many schools now have student counselors who encourage one to pursue higher education after high school, to pursue a career with a future in this system of things. Do not be influenced by them. Do not let them brainwash you with the Devil's propaganda to get ahead, to make something of yourself in this world. The world has very little time left! Any 'future' this world offers is no future. Make pioneer service, the full-time ministry, with possibility of Bethel or missionary service your goal. This is a life that offers an everlasting future!"* (*The Watchtower*, 1969 March 15, p. 17)

> *"If you are a young person, you also need to face the fact that you will never grow old in this present system of*

things...you will never fulfill any career that this system offers. If you are in high school and thinking about a college career, it means at least four, perhaps even six or eight more years to graduate into a specialized career. But where will this system of things be by that time? It will be well on its way towards its finish, if not actually gone! This is why parents who base their lives on God's prophetic Word find it much more practical to direct their young ones into trades that do not require such long periods of additional schooling. And trades such as carpentry, plumbing, and others will be useful...in the reconstruction work that will take place in God's new order." (Awake! 1969 May 22, p. 15)

I set my sights on missionary school. That's what I would do. I would finish high school and devote my life to trading Watchtowers for cans of beans and live chickens overseas...sharing God's word in countries overrun by poor people. It would be a beautiful life. One better than I was worthy of. Traveling through jungles, trading *Watchtowers* for chickens. Converting dark-skinned people to my faith. Serving Jehovah until Armageddon arrived.

Missionary dreams pumped Virgil's ego. Shortly after announcing my missionary intent, we attended the Circuit Assembly in Salt Lake City where he sought out the Circuit Overseer for a chat. The CO is the grand poobah for The Truth on a region by region basis, so Virgil went looking for him to introduce us, blatantly vain for producing a son who would become a "future missionary for Jehovah."

After a brief chat with the Circuit Overseer about my plans to serve Jehovah, we drove back to our motel for a pizza dinner. Fluffy phoned in the order, then drove to the pizza parlor to get it.

I went with her and absentmindedly sat on a lobby bench, watching customers go in and out while Fluffy paid at the register. We walked out, Fluffy carrying our pizza. She was livid.

"Did you see those homosexuals? They sat down right next to you!! Why weren't you paying attention? If they had so much as laid one hand on you, I would have been all over them!!"

I didn't know what she was talking about. I had noticed two men enter the pizza parlor together, one was white and the other black, but other than that stark disparity, it was Utah after all, I didn't pay them any attention. But Fluffy overheard one ask the other, "What do you want, dear?" and was just burned that a homosexual had dared to sit next to me.

By then, I knew what a homosexual was. My classmate Michael had described them to me. The Youth Book had condemned them. Jehovah hated homosexuals, as did my father. But I had never before knowingly associated with a homosexual, and my close encounter with them in Salt Lake left me conflicted and titillated.

There were a million thoughts and confusions running through my head that night. I wondered why Fluffy feared that the homosexuals might touch me. What would they have done in the middle of the pizza parlor? And I was floored by her threat to be "all over them" if they had. And I was pissed that I had blown my first opportunity to meet a real homosexual. I wanted to go back and look for them.

But that wasn't possible, so I settled into the motel room... Dad and Fluffy in one bed, Grant and Amber in the other, me on the floor in a sleeping bag with my pants rolled up for a pillow, and I spent the night dreaming of regrets for missing my one and only opportunity to meet some genuine homosexuals. And I tried to make sense of Fluffy's declaration that she would protect me. And I thought about my future as a missionary.

Sissy needed me. I fantasized of saving her from Satan—an achievement so great that everyone would talk about me afterwards. I assumed that Sissy was no longer in The Truth and that bothered me terribly because I was in The Truth and it was the truth after all. I dreamed of turning 18, when I would escape from Fluffy's house to go find my sister and return her to The Truth. Everyone would talk about me after that. I would have my sister back. And Jehovah would like me, for sure. Then Armageddon would arrive and everyone would know I was responsible for saving Sissy from Satan in the nick of time, and life would be good. What a great fantasy that was.

Sometimes you shouldn't believe what people tell you. Sometimes you just have to think it through for yourself. It's better that way sometimes, but not always because you can get yourself in trouble by trying to think. Like when I had the Bible study with the Mormon kids at school, like about ten, which was awesome, 'cause odds are, with that many, at least one would join The Truth.

So they brought over some Mormon elders to talk to me at school, which is allowed because practically everyone in town is a Mormon and that's why we always say a Mormon prayer at every school assembly to ask God for help to win the football game. And they needed elders to help explain things, so we had lots of discussions for several weeks, right in the middle of the library.

The elders wanted to know why Jehovah's Witnesses celebrate baby showers before you're born, but aren't allowed to celebrate your birthday after. I didn't know the answer, so I asked Dad when I got home.

That was a mistake. You're not supposed to ask questions like that. It isn't important to understand the logic behind your religion; you're just supposed to believe it. He explained why it's okay to

celebrate baby showers but not birthdays, but it still didn't make
sense and Dad said he's gonna knock the snot out of me if I ask
him one more time, 'cause I should already understand the answer.
Except I don't. It doesn't make sense. It's just as stupid as the
Mormons who ask God for help to win a football game when they
know the Mormon kids at the other school are praying for the same
damn thing. And it's stupid that Grandma Terry changed churches
to become a Baptist but Aunt Letha is a Seventh Day something or
other which means she can't go see a doctor when she gets sick
because she thinks it's a sin. Or wait, that's not right. I think Aunt
Letha still goes to the Assembly of God. That's where Grams used
to go a long time ago, until she started dressing her kids weird
and Grandpa said he had enough of that "foolishness" and made
Grams go find a new church. But the last I heard, Aunt Letha still
goes there. It's an Okie church, so she won't cut her hair. She wears
it long in braids with old dresses that cover her arms and go all the
way down to her ankles. Even in summer. 'Cause she thinks it's a
sin to wear pants because women in the Bible didn't wear pants. It
makes no sense, and it makes my head hurt trying to figure it out,
and maybe that's why you're not supposed to understand things.
'Cause they don't make sense, no matter how many times you turn
them around in your head.

──⊶⊷──

In 1978, two Hollywood homosexuals got married.

The *Awake!* reported on their wedding on a back page titled
"Eye On the World"—a section that was generally occupied by
little snippets of information demonstrating clear indications of
Satan's control over this system and Armageddon's near arrival.
In that particular issue, a brief section described two men from
Hollywood who had recently been married. Not officially, but they

belonged to a church that performed a ceremony to unite them, they called it a wedding, and it didn't matter if their marriage was legal or not. Just the thought of such a travesty was enough to inspire horror in good Christian folk.

I leaned up against the counter at the conclusion of a Kingdom Hall meeting and casually selected bits of the *Awake!* to read... killing time...unexpectedly discovering a short discussion of two homos who had been married...trying to imagine what a homosexual-marrying-church would look like...envisioning a wedding procession with a man wearing a dress...closing the *Awake!* out of fear that other congregation members had seen me reading about homosexuals...intrigued to learn about others who might be like me but might as well have been in another solar system, a million miles from Wyoming...feeling horrible pangs of guilt for being titillated by a few trivial words describing them.

It had never occurred to me that the people my father referred to as "homos" would marry each other. I thought that being a homo was all about sex and effeminate behavior. It was a terrible and dirty thing and I had never figured out what two men might do for sexual gratification together. My fantasies were frequent, and all were composed of single men engaged in self-fulfillment. Later, they began to revolve around Tom Selleck on *Magnum PI* having sex with women, the key ingredient being Magnum PI. Women had just recently begun to enter my sexual fantasies, but not as participants. They served no useful purpose in getting me off. Women were in the fantasies simply because that's what I saw on TV. I had a basic understanding of the mechanics of heterosexual sex, but no details. Television did not include details at that time.

People did not chase members of their own gender on TV. Everything I had ever seen was of the heterosexual variety. I was the only one of my kind, in my mind.

I did not really view myself as a homosexual, at least not the sort that I understood to exist in Hollywood. At best, I thought of myself as potentially being a homosexual hybrid. I wasn't a real homosexual and the men in my fantasies weren't either because my recognition of homosexuals was made up of confusing pantomimes from my father of limp-wristed, word-slurring, speech-impaired men who wore women's clothes and referred to each other as "Sweets." God hated homosexuals, and that fact came up in conversation frequently.

None of those discussions included mention of women. Homos were exclusively male with the exception of Laverne and Shirley on TV who Granny M once accused of being lesbians. I'd never heard of lesbians before then and didn't understand any of it. My previous missed exposure to the homosexuals in Salt Lake didn't leave me with any lasting impressions, other than regret for not noticing them. I didn't understand how effeminate mannerisms connected to homosexuals either, or how they related to me, or how I could possibly be a homo if I wasn't that way. My prayers frequently included the heartfelt request for help to not be a homo, but the discovery that one homosexual wanted to marry another caused me to question my perception of what it really meant to be one, and to question all the things my father said about them.

I was 14 and imagined myself growing up to find an incredibly understanding wife who lacked the urge to have sex, and somehow we would have children because that's what you're supposed to do when you grow up...you get married and produce kids. I couldn't envision any other possible future, other than getting hitched to some luckless lady and having babies after the arrival of Armageddon, and by that time, I'd figured out how women became pregnant and was relieved I wouldn't have to ask my dad how that worked...but the knowledge that two homos wanted to marry each other completely challenged my perspective on what it meant to be one.

But I was a little unclear on how a homosexual wedding might unfold. Which one has to wear the dress? That's what happens in a wedding. One person dons a suit and tie, the other wears a dress, so I wondered how those two guys in Hollywood decided who had to take on the woman's role. I did not ever want to wear a dress, nor was I interested in getting naked with anyone else who wore a dress. I was only able to fantasize about men in pants, thank you. I just preferred things that way. So I was really stumped with wondering how they solved that problem and spent many subsequent months trying to visualize the two homos in Hollywood, pondering the dilemma they faced when choosing which one had to dress up like a woman. Eventually, I decided that they probably just flipped a coin.

BENDING MORALITY

J ehovah's Witness missionaries around the globe went back home for special assemblies in the summer of 1978, and we drove to a Canadian assembly that year for our very first family vacation together. We tacked a week of vacation at the beginning and end of the convention, but other than gathering to worship for three days and meet the missionaries, our sole purpose during that time was to drive. Miles and miles...hours and hours...endless days of driving to see the country, with "country" not meaning Canada. Or the United States. Or urban locations with tall buildings and hordes of people. "Country" referred to isolated regions with mountains and trees. Places that made Virgil's heart go thump-thump while fantasizing of horseback rides through the newly discovered country, chasing potential dinner quarry with a gun.

We drove through the beautiful Canadian countryside on our first vacation, rarely stopping to actually do something because that would cost money and we had little of that. We just drove around to see as much country as possible, through the windows of the truck, collecting memories of places we drove past so Virgil could have future conversations of, "Yup, that's some beautiful country up there" and hear the reply, "Yup, it surely is."

Actually, Fluffy had numerous vacations, if you count her trips back to Los Angeles with Grant and Amber. They always went to summer Dodger games and the Magic Mountain theme park to ride roller coasters. Virgil took vacations too, if you count his solitary weeks of elk hunting. But as a family, the trip to Canada was our first...unless you count our two-week drive in 1976, three months after Sissy left home. We drove from Fillmore across the western states of Nevada, Utah, Wyoming, and Idaho, but that wasn't an intentional vacation. It was a scouting trip, looking for a new state to abandon California for.

So in 1978, we rented a travel trailer to pull behind the truck for our first official vacation, with Calgary as our ultimate destination.

Grant and I sprawled out under the camper shell while the rest of the family crowded into the cab. There was an order to it, a proper way to fill the front seat.

Virgil drove.

Fluffy got the middle.

Granny M took the window seat.

Five year old Amber shuffled back and forth between their laps, occasionally sticking her head through the slider to see what Grant and I were up to in back. When we stopped each evening at a roadside campground, the family crowded into the trailer to sleep while I stretched out in the bed of the truck.

We pulled over alongside a beautiful Canadian river one afternoon with nothing to do but marvel at the incredible scenery and take a break from driving. It was a welcome stop for the afternoon, alongside a spectacular river fronting the highway... massive granite boulders strewn across a wide riverbed originating from a glacier, with glacier melt that turned the water into a replica of made-up milk—white and cloudy and unusual.

After a short hike through the boulders, I went back to the camper for lunch, watching Fluffy make sandwiches. Grant and Amber snacked on Doritos from the open bag on the table. I watched them eat...so close to the chips I could smell them.

I reminded myself of the rules in Fluffy's house. My breakfast cereal was still portioned out each morning by her. Made-up milk had long since disappeared, but the real milk that replaced it was not poured by me. There could have been a bowl of green beans sitting six inches in front of me on the dinner table, but if I wanted more, I was required to ask permission. If approval was given, I would have waited for Dad or Fluffy to dish it out.

I wondered if the rules would be different while on our first vacation, but I hesitated.

Maybe if I only take one? But I still hesitated.

I sat there for the longest time, playing out the pros and cons of helping myself, knowing full well the rules of my life, debating whether or not it was worth getting yelled at for attempting anyway, and wondering if things would be different in Canada. We were on vacation, after all.

After a tremendous amount of thought and hesitation, I decided to commit what had always been an unforgivable sin. I waited until I was clearly in Fluffy's line of vision, and then I lifted a chip from the pile.

"Stay out of things!" she snapped. "You'll get something when I'm ready to give it to you!"

I cried. I was 14 and I cried about a stupid Dorito chip. I ran outside and slammed the trailer door, the first time I ever had the nerve to do something so bold. I crashed into Dad who was standing outside, and he threatened to spank me right out there in the middle of the parking lot if I didn't apologize for being disrespectful to Fluffy.

We arrived in Banff, Canada, a few days later. Virgil pulled into an empty ski resort and decided we should ride the gondola up the mountain to gawk at the summer view. It was a rare opportunity for the family to crawl out of the truck and actually do something, and I watched them walk away to the gondola, wishing someone might offer to pay for my ticket. My money had dwindled, so I walked back across a hot and desolate parking lot to stretch out across the bed of the truck and take a nap while the rest of the family burned an hour riding to the top of the mountain and back. Two minutes later, Granny M came back to keep me company.

"I don't really care about riding the gondola, anyway," she said.

——∞——

I started my first year of high school after we returned from Canada. The Evanston Red Devils—a mascot that was announced in my house as an obvious sin.

I was still likely to be called "Jehovie" on a daily basis.

"Hey Jehovie!"

My tormentors would pay for it when Armageddon arrived, I thought. The more I saw my world as complicated and pointless, the harder I grabbed for my faith. I took absolute joy in my frequent speeches in the Kingdom Hall. I adored going door to door, and I took every possible opportunity in school to be known as a Jehovah's Witness. I had The Truth.

The beginning of school brought an end to my job at the Whirl Inn Motel. All my summer savings had been spent on school clothes and the trip to Canada. The high school cafeteria didn't hire students, so I was back to irregular visits with hunger, determined by whether or not Granny M was visiting at the time. On the backside of Safeway, while on my walk to school, I scrounged through the produce thrown out back. During winter, on lunch breaks, I often walked the two block perimeter of school, knocking on doors and searching for snow shoveling jobs from elderly ladies who paid me fifty cents to clear their walks.

And I quickly discovered the tranquility and solitude of the boys' locker room. The locker room was vacant during lunch. People didn't hang out there—they were on their way in or out.

Three rows of lockers. A group shower. A wall mirror that steamed up in winter. Not a soul in sight at lunchtime.

Off to the left side of the locker room entrance was a rarely used gorilla of machinery, pulleys and weights hanging off the ends, a leg press with a seat upholstered in red vinyl. I escaped there often during lunch to read a book and eat the remaining pieces of my sack lunch that I hadn't eaten for breakfast, undisturbed. It was a respite from the social world of high school. Peaceful. Antisocial.

The far wall was lined with private offices, changing rooms, really, for coaches who never seemed to be around…except one. I'd seen him walking the halls many times. I didn't know his name—sports weren't part of my world. He was a beautiful specimen who strode manly through school…an enormous Italian mountain of muscle with barn door shoulders swinging side to side, curly black hair, filling the school with as much attitude as size. I viewed him as a real and up close version of a professional wrestler. He was a Greek God. Or an Italian God…fuck, I didn't care. My breath stalled every time he came within twenty feet of my presence…and that is precisely what he did one day while I was minding my own business in the weight room, my nose buried between the pages of a book.

I watched him fumble with his keys as he walked in. He didn't notice me. He unlocked one of the offices…I thought I should probably leave. I should definitely leave. It was a private room for coaches. I didn't belong there. I should get up and leave.

But I didn't.

He took his shirt off, and through the tangled wall of machinery, I stared at his thick but hairless chest…not what I expected, given the amount of hair on his head.

I was afraid of him. Afraid of what I saw. Afraid he would catch me looking.

My eyes shifted down to my book. I would keep my eyes downcast into my book. Yes, that's what I would do. I would focus on my book. I should definitely leave.

He slipped his shoes off, and my eyes momentarily shifted upwards...he unzipped his pants. I reminded myself that I should leave.

He turned away and dropped his pants, then folded them neatly and laid them on the desk.

I stared at his back and shoulders, wide as a house. His butt filled out his white briefs. I watched him fumble with a towel, wondering what he would do next. I didn't need to see more. He had already fulfilled every fantasy I ever had of him.

He still seemed oblivious to my presence. It was time for me to get up and leave.

But I didn't leave. He dropped his underwear, exposing his pale bare ass, and I quit breathing when he turned around to face me, stark naked. I watched him walk out to the showers, flipping a towel over his gigantic shoulders. A stubby little penis peeked out from his pubic hair.

Visions of that beautiful coach fueled my masturbation that night when I jerked off in my basement...but I gave him a bigger penis. That's the beauty of a fantasy. You can turn it into anything you want.

I never saw him naked again. The weight room returned to being my peaceful and secluded escape, and I finished many novels and peanut butter sandwiches in the comfort of the leg press over the next few weeks—until I felt tempted by clothes and wallets in unsecured lockers.

It's easy to bend morality when you're hungry. I gave in to temptation and stole money from those lockers to buy lunch in the school cafeteria. I believed I was an ethical thief. I only stole pocket change, enough for lunch, on that day only. Nickels, dimes, and quarters. Nothing else. I once opened a wallet that contained a twenty-dollar bill. It annoyed the hell out of me to find that twenty. It was too big, too significant to steal and not feel guilty…so I put it back and spent the day hungry and irritated that some other kid was walking around with a twenty that was of no value to me.

Small-scale stealing somehow seemed less egregious. I stole enough for lunch and then held off until the cafeteria was almost cleared out and the line was reduced to nothing before daring to inhale a tray of food in the final few minutes before the resumption of class while unaccompanied in an almost vacant lunch room without anyone inquiring as to where someone like me might have acquired the minimal amount needed to afford it. *Someone like me*, a skinny kid who had no money and imagined the entire student body was aware of it. They talked about it amongst themselves, in my fears…I could hear them, imagine them, and cowered at nonexistent conversations that echoed in my ears…

"Hey! What's he doing here? Jehovie doesn't have any money! Ask where he got it from! He doesn't belong here! Someone tell him to leave!"

After stealing several times, I terminated my locker raids. But if I am truthful today, stealing didn't end on account of honorable ethics. I ended my swiping for the simple fact that I was scared to death of getting caught.

That fear began to taint my peace and quiet in the weight room. I had shit in my own backyard. Knowing I had stolen from lockers mere steps away layered the room with discomfort. Occupying the scene of the crime seemed an obvious clue to brand me as the most likely suspect.

Those fears permeated the weight room, and before I could resolve the quandary of finding a new location for lunch, a second fear slammed the locker room door shut. I was standing alone at the urinal, taking a piss at a long line of porcelain receptacles, not a sound in the world, watching my yellow urine travel down the drain. Coach Karst came in to take a leak. He was a part-time coach. Overweight. Balding. A bad complexion. Approaching fifty, I thought. An old man, in my eyes. Nothing like a professional wrestler.

I heard him open the door. I felt him pass behind me. He stood two urinals away and unzipped his pants.

Mr. Karst pulled out a stiff dick and stroked it once, then put his hands on his hips, his erection on display.

I peeked at him. I didn't have any desire to see him naked. He wasn't beautiful. I peeked at it again.

His cock was the thickest, ugliest, and most beautiful thing I'd ever seen.

It scared the shit out of me. I wanted to look at it. I wanted to touch it. No, I couldn't touch it. That would be a sin. I was a sinner. I wanted to see it up close. I was confused by his presence, his erection, and why he chose to show it to me. Torn over feelings of titillation and fear, I zipped my pants and fled. I didn't ever want to see him again. I didn't know what he wanted. Maybe he wanted nothing. Maybe he was just there to piss.

I abandoned the locker room as my lunch-break sanctuary, and soon joined a group of boys who were pitching pennies in the hallway between Mr. Smith and Mr. Orton's classrooms. Gambling felt natural to me. You don't have to be rich to become a penny pitcher. A nickel will do if you're good enough.

We got caught more than once by teachers who weren't particularly happy to find students honing their gambling skills, but we continued anyway, mostly under my encouragement. The teachers never administered a lick of punishment, and I sometimes won enough for lunch in the cafeteria. Sometimes enough for a Snickers bar from the vending machine.

A Snickers wrapper announced a rebate… "Buy twenty candy bars and receive $2."

I pulled twenty candy wrappers out of the school garbage cans and mailed them off with a used stamp I had carefully peeled off a discarded envelope. Those two dollars would change my life for a week. With two dollars, I could buy three days of sixty-cent lunches in the school cafeteria. The small sack lunch packed by Fluffy would become my breakfast.

After months of waiting, I casually slipped a comment to Dad in the privacy of his truck.

"I was just wondering if anything has shown up for me in the mail. I sent in for a candy bar rebate, and they're supposed to send me two bucks."

"That's what that was? Oh, yeah, we got that. Weeks ago," he said. "The check was payable to Mr. Terry, so I cashed it. I thought it was for me."

"Can I have it?"

He laughed. "No. I figure you owe me for what it costs to feed and put a roof over your head, anyway."

———

Virgil talked to my grandparents by telephone every once in a while. They usually did the calling. Their conversations were odd and simplistic. Once or twice a year he would sit at the kitchen table, the phone in his ear, and by its sound alone, I knew he was talking to them. The odd cadence of their Okie slang made it impossible to disguise a conversation between my father and his parents. Their discussions were generally dominated by horses, or a quick brag of the big Wyoming buck that Dad had shot that year, bigger than anything you'd kill in California. His parental interactions were shallow. Any mention of the religion that dominated our lives was off limits. It always sounded to me like he was in trouble.

I wasn't part of those conversations. The phone was off limits to me.

Grandpa Terry shipped an unexpected present to me that fall—a shiny new Winchester lever action 30-30 rifle. I was never clear on why.

When the rifle showed up in the mail, unbeknownst to me, Virgil picked up the package from the post office. He drove out to the hills north of town and shot a few rounds of shells through it, just to make sure it worked fine.

He pulled me aside a few days later with the news. "You got a present from Grandpa Terry," he said. "Gramps sent you a deer rifle."

"Really?" I answered, stunned.

"Yeah. It's out in the truck. I already shot a few shells through it. I'll let you look at it later."

The simple recognition of a gift was bizarre. Presents were not part of my life. Hunting wasn't part of my life either, not as a participant. Virgil had never once allowed me to fire one of his guns.

We squeezed a short hunt into the two hours of daylight between school and winter sunset. Virgil had already filled his tag for the year. This hunting trip was for me to kill my first buck.

I followed him through the sagebrush. No more than fifteen minutes into our walk, we stopped on the side of a hill to gaze at a couple of bucks across the ravine, emerging from an aspen thicket.

Virgil pointed them out.

"Shoot one," he said.

"Where are they? Which group of trees are they next to?" I asked.

"That clump off to the right. "Can't you see them?"

204 ⸺ Scott Terry

"Oh yeah, I see them."

I held up my new Winchester, aimed in the general location...
and fired.

The deer didn't run. I asked for a more specific description
of the appropriate trees, assured Dad I had located my intended
target...and fired a second time. Again, not even close.

I didn't get a buck for my first year of deer hunting. I couldn't
even see a buck, let alone shoot one.

A week later, Fluffy drove me to the town optometrist who
prescribed thick, Coke-bottle glasses. Mountains in Wyoming were
no longer big fuzzy globs of green to me. They had trees on them.

⸺⸺⸺

In the summer of 1979, I took a job as a box boy at the Evanston
IGA grocery store. It was my third vocation in a line of commonality:
Paper boy-Laundry boy-Box boy. I bought all my clothes that year
by scouring JC Penney catalogs for cheap socks and eight-dollar
Toughskin pants. Bulges on male underwear models distracted me.
I earned enough at IGA for an occasional lunch at the store deli, and
I bought a new 10-speed bike for $90 from the downtown corner
hardware store. It was such an incomprehensibly massive amount
of money, almost all I had, that I asked the clerk if he would finance
the purchase with monthly payments. He declined.

The IGA produce manager, Richard Ridley, was a great guy.
When he talked, I wished he was mine. He had a son about my
age, and I wondered how it would be to have Richard Ridley for a
father.

I helped him stock the frozen vegetable bins one afternoon
while he poked his nose into my plans for college.

"Given any thoughts to where you're going to college?" he
asked.

"No. I'm a Jehovah's Witness. The Bible says we're in the last days, so I'm not really thinking about college."

Mr. Ridley let me have the loose grapes that were rolling around in the bottom of the shipping crate that day—grapes that people weren't willing to pay good money for.

IT'ſ OVER...OR JUſT BEGUN...DEPENDſ ON HOW YOU LOOK AT IT

I n August of 1979, we left Wyoming and moved to Cedar City, Utah, in between which we drove to Los Angeles for our annual three-day Jehovah's Witness assembly at Dodger Stadium and to celebrate Aunt Jackie successfully passing what was described as "the really difficult bar exam." She got a new job as a bartender, and we crashed her apartment for a week of vacation. Virgil and Fluffy stayed in a hotel and all the kids sprawled out over Aunt Jackie's floor and couch each night to sleep.

On her first day of work, Aunt Jackie came out of her bedroom in her new bartending outfit. She twirled around and asked me, "Aren't I pretty?"

Being a Christian and all, I replied, "You kinda look like a prostitute."

After she left for work, I snuck into her bedroom and stole a *Playgirl* magazine from under her bed. The one with Superman Christopher Reeve on the front.

My cousin Angel told me that her mom bought that Playgirl because she was hoping Christopher Reeve would be inside naked, except he wasn't and that pissed her off since she's really hot for

*him. So I snuck into her room and looked under her bed, and there
it was. A Playgirl magazine with Superman on the front. I stuffed
it inside my cowboy boot and climbed up a tree in her backyard to
read it, and then I snuck back into her room and slid it back under
her bed.*

Our new Utah house was the best ever—a doublewide trailer
with three bedrooms and two bathrooms on five acres of irrigated
alfalfa fields about a mile outside of town. We had our own barns
and corrals on the property, so Virgil kept his three horses at home
for the first time. We still had two dogs, Flo and Andy, with a fifth
litter of puppies on the way, and our new house came with a dozen
chickens.

Our property butted up next to a tract of land that was owned by
a Mormon family with seven kids. Or maybe eight. We never got
an official head count, but they lived in town and had permission to
use our road to get to their livestock because at one time everything
had been a single property. Their barns sat about five feet from
ours. There was no access to their land except through ours, so they
pulled up twice a day in a dirty gray station wagon, and all the kids
piled out to milk their cow, feed the chickens, slop the hogs, and
dig potatoes.

Occasionally the father came to help, but their mother didn't,
which I assumed was on account of the fact that there was no room
for her in the station wagon, what with all the kids. They were never
friendly to us, and we weren't to them. It was a small town. Word
had spread that we were Jehovah's Witnesses and we knew they
had a ton of kids because Mormon heaven has several stages of
righteousness. Apparently, the more desirable parts of heaven are
reserved for Mormons with the most kids, or so it was explained
to us by other Mormons. We thought they were seriously misled
every time they drove up our road, and we would never have been
friends with them.

The previous residents of our Cedar City property left an enormous garden on the backside of our trailer, and I spent the first weekend in a vain attempt to keep the inherited vegetables alive. Fluffy was gone for most of those days, chasing down all the necessary stuff when you move to a new house, like renting a post office box for incoming mail and collecting cleaning supplies to thoroughly sanitize the new trailer because Fluffy's house was always spotless.

Our Allied Van Lines truck had yet to arrive. Our trailer was still empty.

Virgil took a quick trip to the grocery store to buy lunch. I was hot and sweaty from working in the garden and asked if he would buy me a quart of milk—if I gave him a dollar to pay for it.

Fluffy returned that evening and learned of it. She stood in the entry next to the wood stove, angry, while my father tried to turn the debate into a lighthearted joke. The more he tried to laughingly explain that it was okay for me to enjoy milk, the angrier Fluffy became. I backed out of the room while they argued, no longer believing I was the subject.

——⊷——

I loved our new Utah house, but was beginning to get really angry with life. I escaped to the barns often and seethed with frustration and cussed and cried and screamed things I shouldn't say, like "Fuck Off!" except, God Almighty, that was a terrible mistake and I couldn't even think that way yet on account of knowing I was a bad kid, so I just went up to the barns and cussed and choked on all the messages I couldn't throw away because I didn't yet know that was possible. All those messages mixed around in my head and got puked out when cussing where no one could hear me…except for the time when Amber heard me scream "Fuck!" while crying in front of the chickens and since Amber was only six she asked Fluffy, "What does it mean when Scott says 'fuck'?"

A month after settling in Utah, Dad planned a trip back to Wyoming for a final deer hunt. He wanted me to get a deer as well.

He and Fluffy argued about it for weeks.

"We need the meat," he told her, eventually winning the battle.

To me, he explained, "If you want to go back up to Wyoming, you'll have to buy a sleeping bag."

At the local sporting goods store, I bought the cheapest bag I could find, a brown flannel zippered bag for $40, about all the money I had leftover from my IGA paycheck after buying my school clothes.

A week later, we packed up the guns, the ice chest, and Dad's horse Socks, then drove back to Wyoming for a weeklong hunting trip. Into the ice chest went a two pound box of bacon scraps, two dozen eggs that weren't going to survive the journey intact, a five pound bag of potatoes, and several cans of Dinty Moore Beef Stew.

In the high desert of southern Wyoming, we parked off a dirt road in the rolling hills, far from civilization. There was little to break the sagebrush monotony except for occasional groves of quaking aspen, referred to as quakies, and every now and then patches of pine forest. We pulled into the hills just before sunset and rolled our sleeping bags out in the dirt, then walked the perimeter of our first makeshift camp, gathering burnable sagebrush. Sagebrush makes a functional but quick fire, high in sap, burning like pine, blazing hot and fast, exhausting itself quickly and requiring the constant stoking of fresh fuel.

It was my first camping trip, alone with my dad. Our nights were weird and beautiful, under the Wyoming stars, the sun disappeared by 5 pm, a smoky fire for comfort, absolutely nothing to fill the empty hours except talk, which we didn't do. The evening cold settled hard and fast, arriving with the early autumn sunset, wrapping our camp with chilled darkness that promised to get colder as the night progressed. To ward off the frigid air on our first night, I loaded several rocks into the fire, then fished them out of the coals with sagebrush sticks and rolled them into my bed, only to watch the hot stones melt enormous holes in the bottom of my new forty-dollar bag before I could shake them back out.

We awoke the next morning around the cold remnants of our campfire.

I shook the frost from my sleeping bag, then Dad saddled Socks to go one direction while I headed the opposite on foot. At the end of the day, we met up back at the truck and then drove off for a new location and a new camp and a dinner of fried potatoes. The Dinty Moore was reserved as a treat for later, Virgil said. My father was on a diet. His hunting trips were always about diets.

Several days later, I found myself a fair distance from camp, well into the afternoon and again not having eaten breakfast. I fell into the dirt on the side of a hill and cried. I laid there under the cold Wyoming sun, bawling, frustrated, feeling deprivation, wondering how I would make it through the week on Dad's diet.

I wiped my tears and didn't give a fuck anymore. There were plenty of potatoes back in camp.

After hiking back up the hill, I built a sagebrush fire in front of the truck and fried potatoes in hot bacon grease. I luxuriated in a plate of hot and greasy spuds. My back leaned against the wheel well, and I wondered how much trouble it would cause when Dad found out.

We met up around the campfire that evening—the skillet and fire still warm from my lunch. I confessed, and waited for Virgil to mete out punishment.

It never came. He wasn't the least bit angry, although I detected a bit of surprise at my nerve. But there wasn't a hint of punishment. We continued our hunting adventure under that agenda. He stayed on a diet, and I periodically cooked potatoes while wondering why the rules were so drastically different when not in Fluffy's house.

And then it rained. A slow and cold drizzle rolled through the hills on our final night in Wyoming. Neither of us had killed a deer. We had no tent. Our Dinty Moore stew was gone, and the light rain threatened to add a miserably wet and cold end to our unsuccessful trip. Virgil was frustrated.

"We're gonna have to sleep in the truck, I guess. We'll just sit in the cab all night to stay dry."

"I can sleep in the tack compartment of the horse trailer?" I volunteered. "That way you can have the truck?"

He looked at me sideways. "You won't fit in the tack compartment."

"Yes I will. That's where I go to stay warm when I'm locked out of the house."

School in Utah was a kinder and gentler place—compared to Evanston. I took a typing class because several years earlier Dad had said it was really important that Sissy learn to type when she declared that she wanted to sing. Jehovah didn't approve of people who sang for a living, he said. They were all drug addicts, and it was best that she take secretary classes.

So I enrolled in beginning typing, thinking it would make him happy, and when Fluffy complained about the cost of paper, I stole what I needed from the school supply room.

From our inherited garden, I dug up the two rows of carrots on an "as needed" basis, then added them each morning to the small sack lunch prepared by Fluffy. That lasted until Dad chained his dog Andy in the garden…right over top my carrots, and that was the end of that.

Our trailer was the only dwelling about midway down a very long and perfectly straight dirt road through alfalfa fields. On my morning walk to the bus stop, if Grant wasn't walking with me, I often divided my lunch into portions. The fruit became my breakfast and the peanut butter sandwich was saved to eat later under the trees along the football field. When finished, I folded the brown paper sack and tucked it into my jacket pocket, knowing Fluffy would threaten to give me nothing if I didn't get at least two weeks of re-use out of each. On the rare occasions when I failed to protect my well-used sack and delivered it torn and useless, lunch might not exist for me the following day. She sent me to school once with a sandwich inside a discarded graham cracker box, just to teach me a lesson.

My bus route took us by a couple of green apple trees growing wild along the dirt road into town. On mornings when Fluffy drove Grant to school, rather than making him take the bus with me, I left home early to walk the distance to the apples and still make it back to my bus stop in time to catch my ride to school. Then the serious side of winter arrived and there were no more apples.

When the cold showed up, I ate lunch in an empty classroom. Not once did I set foot in the high school cafeteria. I couldn't deal with the social intimacy of a cafeteria. My entire life had been built around warnings that people outside of my religion were "bad association." It was a new school, and there was no point in trying to be friends with anyone who didn't share my belief that Armageddon was coming soon.

My only friend in Cedar City is Alvaro. I only see him at the Kingdom Hall. He's still in Junior High, but his mom just joined The Truth. Her new husband doesn't believe we have the truth. Alvaro says his stepdad beats on him.

I told him I have a real sister who doesn't live with me anymore, and I will go find her when I turn 18 and bring her back to The Truth, but it's a secret, 'cause no one knows about her.

But Alvaro didn't keep it a secret. He told Glenna French who's been hanging out at his house to help his mother learn about The Truth. She's Fluffy's only friend in town and she told Fluffy that I told Alvaro about Sissy.

So Dad met me at the bus stop, all pissed off and everything. Fluffy told him that I've been spreading stories, and she say's I'm going to sneak into the house when they're not home and call Sissy collect and he's really sick and tired of my causing trouble and he doesn't understand why I can't be a good kid instead of spreading rumors, which is just stupid, because I don't know Sissy's number. I don't know where she lives. I used to have her address, but I don't anymore. And if I wanted to call her collect, I wouldn't have to break into the house to do it, but he can't figure that out.

So Glenna told Fluffy that she heard I have a sister who doesn't live with us anymore, and then Glenna had an affair with Alvaro's stepdad and skipped out of town to run away and have sex with him. She got disfellowshipped from our congregation which means she got kicked out and that served her right.

———

We went to the movies that winter to see *The Great Train Robbery*, an unusual opportunity given that, up to that point, the only non-G rated movie I had ever seen was *The Cowboys* with John Wayne. Virgil was still traumatized by guilt for exposing us to all the cussing in that western, so I don't know why he took a chance on the new train robbery flick.

Grant and I sat directly in front of our parents and enjoyed what turned out to be a really good movie. Rolling across the screen was a tremendous, fantasy-spawning sex scene with a hairy-chested guy I'd never heard of named Sean Connery. He stretched out naked in bed while a woman slowly stripped down to a frilly piece of lingerie that served no useful purpose I could identify. Scantily clad, she bent over with her ass in the air and crawled under the sheets from the foot of the bed to do things to him.

His eyes rolled in pleasure.

I wanted to be under those sheets with him. I wanted to suck his dick. I was a horny fifteen-year old boy who wanted to embrace my sin. I wanted to replace the half-naked woman who didn't have a role in my fantasy. I slumped into my seat, swallowing shame, trying to ignore the existence of my parents behind me, certain they were drowning in regret for exposing us to such a disgraceful display of sexuality. Jehovah wouldn't approve.

I walked out of the theatre that evening, consciously aware that neither puberty nor religion would cure my homosexual problem. In the middle of the theatre parking lot, I accepted, for the first time ever, the word "gay" to describe my existence. I was gay. Thank you, Sean Connery.

⸺⸙⸺

Grandma and Grandpa Terry came to visit that winter. They flew into Las Vegas with plans to spend three days with us, and would then head to California to visit old friends and family who were still clustered around Orland.

Fluffy picked them up in her second new station wagon and brought them to Cedar City.

Grandpa spent the afternoon exploring our property in the snow and bitter cold. He wasn't happy with everything he found—the state of Dad's animals being a particular issue. Gramps was furious at the discovery of Andy's steel-barrel doghouse—bereft of any bedding to keep him warm. I found some pleasure in watching Grandpa berate my father, who promptly blamed the neglect on me. The next day, my grandparents asked to be driven back to the airport, cutting their trip short.

Fluffy asked Grandma for the gas money to get them there.

———ಎಂ———

Virgil and I took a long drive out to Pioche, Nevada that spring, across the state border, to help a ranching family that he had recently befriended to herd cattle for the day. Driving to Pioche meant passing by the Mormon polygamist colony, "the pigs" they were called by most other people in town. The polygamists lived together in a stark community of trailers stacked up next to each other…adhering to a hardcore religion and interpreting the Bible literally. When the pig women showed up in town, covered head to toe in long cotton dresses and antique bonnets, appearing to have stepped out of 1885, Cedar City residents subjected them to oinking noises.

"Oink. Oink."

The present-day Mormons in town denied the polygamist's inclusion in their faith. They insisted that the pigs belonged to the "old" Mormon religion when Joseph Smith encouraged the taking of multiple brides.

Apparently, the pigs preferred a life under those original Mormon rules. Their makeshift community was a desolate hellhole. Everything looked temporary. No lawns. No flowers. Just trailers, surrounded by dirt and kids and wives. Their sin seemed obvious as we drove by their compound on our way out to Pioche.

We didn't know the Pioche ranching people well. Most of their family didn't believe in The Truth, but one parent and one teenager were barely hanging on to our religion. Rarely did they show up at the Kingdom Hall. They lived way the hell out in the god forsaken high desert of Nevada and it was a long drive to the nearest Kingdom Hall in Utah. Virgil, being an elder, had the requirement to occasionally venture across the state line to feed their spiritual needs and encourage them to remain steadfast in The Truth, not to mention reconnect with his cattle driving past. So we drove out to help them rope and brand calves on what was purported to be the largest land holding ranch in the State of Nevada. It only took one long glimpse of their barren land to understand why it was necessary to have so much of it.

An old and passive horse named Roanie was assigned to me. I hadn't a clue what to do with him.

The Nevada cowboys watched my father saddle Roanie. He offered basic instructions on how to mount, and the cowboys stared at us, wondering how he could know so much and I could know so little. Virgil was clearly a cowboy, like them, but I was not. Roanie was my first horseback ride, and they found that peculiar.

We stopped for a long lunch break that afternoon. My butt was saddle sore, and the old rancher passed around some jerky that had been rendered inedible by an overabundance of salt. Apparently, he had a colt that was "just a fuckin' bastard and I cain't git the sonabitch broke"…so the rancher went out in a pissed off fit and shot the horse in the head, then carved off its backstrap and turned it into salty jerky.

Dad let me drink a short glass of red wine at dinner because everyone in the cowboy family drank wine with dinner, even the kids. And I took my first solo ride on a motorcycle, screaming through the sage brush at full speed in first gear because everyone assumed I would have a clue or some prior experience with shifting into alternative gears. They were wrong. And Dad let me take a drive into town to see a movie that night with a non-Witness kid I had just met. That boy had his own car with a radar detector on the dashboard. He thought it was impressive. He said it reduced his problem with collecting speeding tickets, and I wondered why he didn't just drive slower.

The roundup came to an end, and we drove back to the house of Fluffy. I wondered why my life was allowed to be so different in Pioche, Nevada.

— ◆ —

Fluffy caught me stealing a cookie out of the Tupperware container on top of the fridge.

She retrieved the Brown Stick from her room, then cornered me in the kitchen.

"Unbutton your pants," she said.

I unzipped my Toughskins and turned around to let her spank me.

"No. Your underwear too. Take your underwear down."

I braced myself against the refrigerator with my pants around my ankles, lowered my underwear just below my ass cheeks, and Fluffy slammed the wooden paddle against my bare skin three times.

I was fifteen.

— ◆ —

My bedtime was 8 o'clock. Most nights, Grant and Amber stayed up after I was sent to my room. From my bed, I listened to the rest of the family watch TV and struggled to fall asleep under the shadow of their conversations. Sometimes they had ice cream. Sometimes Grant practiced blowing on his shiny new trumpet, but he couldn't do anything more than blow spit through it. Fluffy wanted him to learn the clarinet, but she bought him a trumpet and signed him up for school trumpet classes when he insisted he didn't like the clarinet.

Grant was ten. He was a good kid.

Amber was in first grade, and she was Fluffy's "Princess." Princess was a conduit to her mother. If she caught me stealing food from the kitchen, she reported it to Fluffy. At the age of six, Amber knew my rank in her family and wasn't reluctant to capitalize on it.

Grant and Amber provided a comparison from which to evaluate my worth. I lay in bed most nights barraged with sounds of parental affections lavished on them. Sometimes I prayed for Armageddon to show up. Sometimes I prayed and asked Him to make me dream about girlfriends that I didn't have. Sometimes I questioned why Jehovah couldn't hear my prayers.

─ ⚮ ─

Our five acres of irrigated alfalfa fields supplied free hay, so owning horses was no longer restricted by the cost of feeding them. Virgil bought two more registered AQHA horses—one a sorrel gelding and the other a palomino stud that he intended to mate with other mares in the area for a fee. The two new horses were added to our menagerie of three pigs, twelve chickens, Grant's hamster Herbie, Amber's pet duck, varying numbers of dogs, and his existing horse Socks. He underestimated the amount of feed needed for three horses, and by late winter, our home-grown supply of horse hay was depleted. Virgil portioned out the last bale, enough to get us by for two days—four more feedings. When it was gone, he would make nice and go borrow from neighbors we had never once been friendly with.

When he returned from work the next night, Fluffy accused me of not feeding the horses. I should be sent to bed without dinner, she said. Virgil listened to her claims, warned me not to have a smart mouth by arguing about it, and then he walked out to the hay shed and counted the remaining stacks. No punishment was administered. The evening slid into obscurity, Fluffy's claims unmentioned.

A few weeks later, I returned from school to find my room ransacked. Inspections from Fluffy were frequent. It wouldn't have been an exhaustive search. I owned virtually nothing. A few books, some antique bottles saved from the Evanston dump, a Monopoly game given to me by Granny M, and a package of felt pens I had purchased at the beginning of the school year after Dad drove me into town to buy them.

Fluffy found the pens and determined they were hers.

Virgil arrived home from work.

"He's a thief!" she told him. "These are my pens! I found them in his dresser. He stole them from me!"

Virgil listened to her claims, then walked me outside.

Feeling emboldened by the previous hay count, I said, "You know I didn't steal those pens."

"Yeah. Don't worry about it," he replied. "I'll buy you some more."

A week later, on a warm summer morning, I was up at the barns, feeding the animals. School had closed for the summer.

Fluffy called me back to the trailer.

"Scott...I'm running to the store. I want you to peel potatoes for potato salad. Peel them, and then clean up the kitchen. I won't be gone long."

"Okay," I agreed, wanting to please her. "What do I do after I peel them?"

"Just leave them in sink. I'll take care of them when I get back," Fluffy answered. "I won't be gone long."

I hadn't yet finished when Fluffy returned.

She pulled into our gravel carport. Dad's horse, Socks, was standing next to his empty water trough nearby, waiting for a drink. His water barrel needed to be filled twice daily, being an old trash can with holes rusted through the bottom. Our approach to keeping Socks in water was to set the can in the mud, fill it with a foot of sand, then pour water over top. Sand in the bottom of a leaky barrel will prevent water from draining out quickly, an Okie patch job, so that was our method for watering Socks every day.

But I hadn't yet filled his barrel. I had been peeling potatoes.

Fluffy burst into the trailer, irritated as fuck. "You forgot to water Socks!"

I yelled back. She had interrupted me in the middle of my chores, I told her, in a raised voice.

She reached out to smack me, and I grabbed both of her arms, a shock to me. A shock to her.

She tried to jam her knee in my crotch. She missed. Her knee slammed lightly into my thigh, no strength behind it.

I yelled, "Goddamn it! Goddamn it!"

"Get out!" she screamed. "Get out of my house!!!"

I let loose of her, then grabbed a jacket from my bedroom.

I pulled my 10-speed bike out from the carport and walked it down the road into town. I was so angry I could spit.

THE ROAD TO VEGAS

My bike had a flat tire. I hocked it for ten bucks at the second pawnshop in town because the first wasn't interested in a bike with a flat tire. With ten dollars in my pocket, I hitchhiked out of Cedar City. My anger subsided into relief. I had escaped.

I hoofed it down the highway for an hour, assuming someone would stop and offer a ride. People would see me sweating in the summer sun and offer to help because it isn't normal for a kid to be walking along the highway, miles away from anything with nothing but a jacket that ordinary people don't wear or carry on scorching summer days.

People would slow down and veer off the asphalt into the gravel and say hello.

They would ask, "Do you need a ride?"

I would answer in a nonchalant manner, "Sure, I'll take a ride. I'm just heading down to St. George to see my cousins." Yeah, that's what I would say. And they would believe every lie I gave them and everything would appear normal. I would be normal.

But no one stopped. An entire hour went by and no one stopped.

I put my thumb out into the road, low to the ground where it wouldn't be too obvious.

An unattractive but not ugly 50-something bald guy pulled up in an older sedan…he leaned across the seat to roll down his passenger window.

"Where you headed?"

"I'm just heading down to St. George."

"Okay. Get in. I can help you out."

I climbed into the front seat of his sedan and closed the door, leaving the window down. I was sitting in the car of a stranger. People get killed by accepting rides from strangers.

He asked, "St. George, huh?"

"Yeah, I go down there sometimes to see my cousins. Thanks for the ride."

"Hmmm. Okay. Well, I'm not going as far as St. George, but I'll take you part way."

"Great. Thanks."

Twenty minutes later, as promised, he dropped me off on the side of the road. As I exited his vehicle he offered some parting advice.

"You know, if you can make it as far as Las Vegas, you can get just about anywhere from there."

The prospect of Las Vegas scared the holy hell out of me. I had been there before for Jehovah's Witness conventions. Las Vegas was full of drug dealers and hookers and thieves, but I picked up on the bald man's comment as a veiled recommendation and decided it would be my destination. And started walking.

A few miles down the highway, a young couple in a brown Ford pickup pulled over.

"Do you need a ride?" the woman asked.

"Sure, that would be great," I answered. The woman scooted over next to what I assumed to be her husband. He was a Native American, she wasn't. He was red, she was white, and their truck was brown. Light brown. Like coffee with a bit of cream. Tan.

I climbed into their truck.

"What are you doing out in the middle of nowhere?" they asked.

"Oh, I'm just heading down to St. George. I have cousins down there. We're gonna go see a movie. I do it all the time."

We drove to St. George in silence. My dishonesty filled the air. Heavy. Unbelieved.

At the first off ramp on the outskirts of town, I asked to be let out, eager to end the discomfort.

"This is great. I can get out here."

"Here?" they asked.

"Yeah, my cousins live right around the corner."

I jumped out of their truck, and discovered the St. George KOA camp straight ahead.

The KOA camp had bathrooms and water fountains, and people who hadn't a clue that I wasn't an official guest. Cherry trees dotted the grounds—icons of a previous farming lifestyle—surrounded by tents and RVs. It was the first of June and the end of cherry season. Stragglers hung from branches, waiting to be picked. I would have stolen handfuls, but didn't for fear of disclosing the fact that I didn't belong there.

I holed up out of sight for most of the day. I hid in the irrigation ditch out back for a few hours, then sat in the laundry room until I thought it appeared weird to people who were washing their clothes. I barricaded myself inside a bathroom toilet until that seemed even weirder. I lunched on candy bars and Coke from the vending machines and wracked my brain for solutions to where I might go. I thought a bit about Sissy, but I hadn't talked to her in four years. I didn't know Mom's last name. I didn't know where they lived. Somewhere in California. Maybe a town that started with a P.

After the sun went down, I abandoned the KOA camp and walked into town, searching for a dark place to hide and sleep. On the main drag, I stumbled through the blackness of a dumpy hotel property where two residential mini-cabins were tucked in back—no lights to guide me. A big 4x4 pickup was parked nearby. Through the weeds and brush, I poked around for a makeshift bed.

A cabin door abruptly swung open.

An angry man practically blew through it and stood illuminated in the doorway, peering into the blackness. He had a gun. I crouched down into the weeds and shadows, balancing on the balls of my feet, sweating bullets and knowing the fear of a quail who was about to be flushed from hiding.

I froze, and the gun-toting cabin dweller went back indoors, unable to see much of anything in the dark. I snuck out a different way than I came in, and an hour later, I curled up in the bushes behind an apartment building with a blanket from their laundry room to wrap in.

I slept until dawn, restless. A warm night in St. George. A stolen blanket in the dirt. Spiders in the bushes. Never mind. My life had changed.

The next morning, I folded the blanket in a perfect rectangle and left it on a washing machine in the laundry room.

For lunch, I inhaled a McDonald's Chocolate Shake and Quarter Pounder on the Mormon Temple lawn, under the summer sun, pounding my brain for solutions to my predicament. No fries, not wanting to spend precious cash on fries.

I needed money to get to Las Vegas. Stealing would have been embarrassingly easy at the KOA camp.

From behind the door of the KOA bathroom toilet, I watched men drop their pants on the floor, unguarded. I assumed their wallets still occupied their back pockets. I pondered my opportunities to steal while barricaded in the toilet stall. I wondered how things would end.

What are you gonna do now? You're a runaway. You can't go back.

I don't want to go back.

Well then you better think of something else.

Choice A. *Look for a job in St. George. But that's fucked. What're you gonna tell them when they ask where you live? And what if they don't pay you for two weeks? That's normal, you know. They're not going to just hand a pile of cash to you at the end of each day. And what will they think when you show up for work every day in the same stinky clothes? Forget about getting a job. You've got less than $6. You should steal some more.*

Choice B. *Go to Las Vegas. How're you gonna get there?*

I could hitch a ride at the truck stop. Maybe stowaway on back under their cargo.
Oh that's brilliant. What if you're on a truck going somewhere else? Then you'll really be up shit creek. And what're you gonna do when you get to Vegas, anyway? You don't have enough money. You'll have to steal it. And what about when school starts? You have no clothes. You'll have to steal those, too.

I did not pray to Jehovah for help. He had never before answered my prayers.

Instead, I called the police from the payphone in the KOA laundry room.

An idiot answered the phone.

"St. George Police Department."

I stammered and choked out, "Uuuummm...I was just wondering. Is it illegal to run away?"

His curt response was, "No."

.........Long pause......deep breath.........

"Well.........I ran away and I'm just trying to figure out what to do..."

His short and sarcastic reply was, "And NOW you wanna go back home…right?"

"No!" I blurted, horrified. "I don't want to go back. I just don't know what to do!"

I came very close to hanging up on him, until he transferred me to the juvenile officer, Lieutenant Dobson.

Lt. Dobson was the sort of guy you respect before you know him. Even on the phone. He offered to send a squad car to get me, but I refused to tell him where I was. I asked for the location of the police station and promised to show up on my own.

I walked across town to the police headquarters and was greeted by a surly fat guy with unkempt greasy hair haphazardly combed over top. He was in charge of deciding who could enter the front door and he wasn't the least bit interested in letting me in. I disliked him instantly and remember him perfectly.

He was sweaty and out of breath, and I pegged him as the sort of guy who looks forward to getting off work so he can go home and drink a few beers. He hates his job but doesn't have the sense to do something else. I almost walked out because of his sour attitude, and wondered if he was the same idiot who answered the phone. Maybe I made a mistake calling the police? They didn't seem very experienced with helping a kid who had nowhere to go, but eventually, the surly idiot called Lt. Dobson, who came out to greet me.

Lt. Dobson was trim and handsome, originally from England, and carried a strong accent. I wondered how he had the misfortune to end up in a desolate corner of Utah, but never got around to asking. He was kind and reassuring and genuinely interested in my predicament. Lt. Dobson listened and believed; in spite of the fact that I didn't tell him anything of significance. It's not like you can show up at the police station and explain to the juvenile officer that you ran away because you don't get Kool-Aid. Or because you can't touch the TV, since it isn't yours. Or because you've never heard the words "I love you," except for the time after your father threw you across the room. Or because you're hungry. Or because you feel like you're drowning in a life that you wish belonged to someone else.

In his private office, Lt. Dobson listened to my very short story. I told him I had gotten into a fight with my stepmother.

"I don't want to live with my father anymore," I said. "I can't live there."

I sat across from his desk in my filthy worn out tennis shoes—my pig feeding attire. I was dressed in baby blue polyester pants and a brown jacket of genuine imitation leather Naugahyde, both of which were hand-me-down gifts from another Witness in our congregation. I stunk.

I told him my sister had left home earlier too.

"I don't know where she lives, though."

"Okay. I'll see what I can do," he answered. "But I have to tell you, your father reported you missing yesterday, and now that you're here, I am required to send you back. That's the legal requirement. I have to send you back to him. I'm sorry."

I countered with the threat of running away again.

"I'm sorry," he said. "I don't have a choice. Let me go call him, and see what I can do."

Lt. Dobson left the room to make that call. For a moment, I wondered why. His office had a phone.

He returned less than ten minutes later.

"I talked to your dad. He's on his way to get you," Lt. Dobson said. "He'll be here in a couple of hours. But I told him you don't want to live with him anymore, and he promised to send you to live with your mother. Is that okay?"

"Yeah, that's okay."

"Until your father gets here, I'm going to have some friends of mine come get you. They'll take you over to their house. Is that okay?"

"Sure," I answered, wondering why he asked my permission.

Lt. Dobson did some paperwork and kept me company in the police station for the next thirty minutes. We talked briefly about life. He assumed I was a Mormon. He asked about my local church. I told him I was not a Mormon. I was a Jehovah's Witness.

An old gentleman who no longer has a name in my memory showed up to get me. Lt. Dobson introduced him as an old family friend.

The old man escorted me out of the police station to his car.

I sat in the front seat of his sedan.

The stench of my sweaty feet overpowered the interior.

He rolled his window down.

We stopped at the grocery store and roamed the aisles while the old man cheerfully chatted and asked what kind of things I might like to eat and solicited opinions regarding what I thought of various brands of something or other that we might have for dinner. I didn't have any opinions.

We pulled into the driveway of his neat and tidy little house, and after introducing me to his wife, he said, "You're probably wanting to take a shower, huh? There's some towels hanging right there on the wall. Dinner will be ready as soon as you're done."

I luxuriated in the pleasure of a short shower, afraid the old folks would think I was taking advantage of their hospitality by using too much water. I was limited to baths only in Fluffy's house, a few shallow inches of water in the tub.

I dressed in my smelly clothes, negating the shower's benefit, then I joined the elderly couple at their dinner table.

Dinner was fried pork chops, with boiled potatoes, turnips, and butter all mashed together as a side dish. I'd never tasted turnips, but I imagined them to be the sort of food that Grandma Terry would serve.

The doorbell rang. The old man rose from the table, interrupting dinner.

Virgil was at the front door. He laughed and joked like it was just a little accident that I had run away from home. I quietly thanked the old folks for dinner, then walked outside with Virgil.

We drove back to Cedar City, mostly in silence.

Virgil interrupted the silence.

"So I called your mother, but she can't take you right now. She's heading out of town for work, so I don't know what I'm going to do with you. Fluffy doesn't want you in her house. She said I can bring you back for a few days, but she's not going to do any cooking or cleaning for you while you're there. Do you understand me?"

"Yes," I answered. Our conversation required nothing more.

"I'm going to give you a choice," he said. "You can either sit in your room for two weeks until your mother can take you, or you can go to work with me in the oil fields until then. If you stay home, Fluffy won't do any cooking or cleaning for you. You can't set foot out of your room unless you need to use the bathroom. And if I so much as hear one word from Fluffy that you're causing trouble, I'm gonna haul you off to juvenile hall. Do you understand me?"

"Yes," I muttered.

"So the juvenile officer said you told him things. What did you tell him?"

"I didn't tell him much of anything," I answered.

"What did you two talk about?"

"Not much. He's a Mormon. I told him we are Witnesses."

"Are you kidding me? Why would you do that? Why would you bring reproach on Jehovah's name that way?"

The next morning, Virgil brought a bowl of cereal into my room while everyone else ate in the dining room.

The story of my predicament was being passed through the family in California. Virgil's older sister, my Aunt Dot, called. She asked Dad to turn the phone over to me, which he did.

"Hi Scott. This is your Aunt Dot. Do you remember me?"

"Yeah, I remember you."

"Are you okay?"

"Yeah. I'm fine."

"Well, I asked your dad if you could come live with me. How would you feel about that? We'd love to have you. Would that be all right?"

"Yeah. That would be great."

"Okay, I'll get your dad to put you on a plane to Sacramento tomorrow. We'll see you soon honey."

I packed my stuff that evening. Grant helped. He wanted to be my brother.

Grant said Fluffy was going to tell everyone in the congregation that the police had arrested me and I would have a criminal record.

He said, "She won't ever allow you to set foot in her house again, once you're gone."

The next morning, I carried my belongings out to the truck for a drive to the Las Vegas airport. Dad stopped me at the door.

"I want you to go apologize," he said.

I looked back at him with a blank stare. I didn't understand.

"Go apologize," he repeated, motioning to Fluffy's room.

I walked into Fluffy's bedroom to choke out what felt like a requirement of my departure ticket.

I stopped just inside her doorway. Fluffy was sitting on her bed. She wouldn't look at me.

"…Dad told me to come in and apologize." That's what I said.

"I don't want to talk to you." That's what she said.

"Okay," was my answer.

Those were my last words with Fluffy.

On June 7, 1980, Virgil drove me to Las Vegas. Our drive was quiet and difficult. Breaking the silence, he became consumed by silly, brief, and superficial conversation. He suggested I might go fishing in California…the Feather River, perhaps.

In the terminal, a few steps from departure, Virgil gave me a hug. I found an unexpected lump in my throat. The word goodbye got stuck. I walked down the ramp and buried myself in the pleasure and knowledge that my future would be defined by that day. I stared out the window at the barren landscape of Las Vegas, knowing my world was about to change. The lump in my throat faded. I swore to never forget it.

AUNT DOT

The day I ran away from Fluffy's house was the most significant day of my life. The luckiest day was when I found myself at Aunt Dot's house, two days later.

I didn't know that while on the plane bound for Sacramento. I hadn't seen my aunts or cousins since I was ten, and wasn't certain that I could remember everyone. Other than the two brief visits from Grandma and Grandpa Terry, I hadn't talked to any of my relatives in six years.

I only had two memories of Aunt Dot. I remembered visiting her in Angels Camp at my age of seven and feeding bits of pancake to the blue jays on her backyard picnic table. I remembered when, at my age of eight, Grams and I went to visit her brand new ranch-style home in Redding with tomato plants in back while she unabashedly nursed her new baby on the fireplace hearth and I wondered why someone didn't tell her to put her top back on.

I remembered even less of my Aunt Susan. She lived in Auburn, east of Sacramento, and she volunteered to pick me up at the Sacramento airport and deliver me to Redding for my welcoming party. I exited the plane, wondering if I would recognize her. The only memory I had of Aunt Susan was from my age of nine when she collected clothes from her church rummage sale for me and Sissy. She gave me an orange pullover sweater that summer. I remembered it, and I remembered sleeping in my grandparents' living room with her—Aunt Susan on the couch and me on the floor. I waited until she was asleep before daring to sneak over in the darkness to the bowl of butter suckers on my grandmother's coffee table. Under the cover of my blanket, I pulled the wrapper off, believing I had stifled the crackling of the cellophane, and fell asleep with the candy in my mouth. The next morning, around the breakfast table, Aunt Susan asked why I waited until dark to get a butter sucker. That's all I knew of her.

My concern that I wouldn't recognize her was needless. Aunt Susan looked familiar when I spotted her at the bottom of the escalator, her two young children in tow. She was of average height for a woman. Brown hair in a not-fancy cut. Genuinely friendly. She was happy to see me.

Aunt Susan was an elementary school teacher, recently divorced, and we packed the four of us, along with my cargo—a tiny trunk the size of an oversized briefcase holding my precious Bible and Youth Book, and two small boxes containing everything else I owned—into her Volkswagen Beetle for our drive to Redding. We stopped for dinner at a little burger stand along Highway 99, catching up on the names and particulars of the family members who had been lost for so many years. She gave me ten bucks— money she couldn't really afford to give. My entire family was poor, with one exception.

Aunt Dot was not poor. She was a real estate broker in a rural cowboy town, and she looked the part. Her jewelry had some bling. Serious diamond bling. Her clothes did not come from Kmart, or a church rummage sale. Aunt Dot had found success in the real estate industry—a success that did not come from men. She had earned it herself.

We drove up the long, private, gravel road to her house amidst a brief summer thunderstorm— too dark to see beyond what was illuminated by occasional lightning flashes. I smelled rain in the oak trees. Aunt Dot met us at the front door, exuding warmth. I entered her enormous ranch house, believing I had just walked into a castle. I gazed at the antique furniture inside. The pitter-patter of rain out back announced the presence of a swimming pool.

Being late, everyone went to bed.

I awoke the next morning with an overwhelming urge to explore. Aunt Dot's castle was a 1970's custom built ranch house, on top of a thirty foot cliff with a swimming pool out back, surrounded by thousands of acres of open space. A beautiful creek meandered at the base of the cliff—schools of fat and lazy bluegills swam in deep pools under the shade of wild grape vines. A two story barn stood a short walk away—stuffed with horses and rope cattle, a private roping arena a shorter distance down the road. My cousins Todd and Brenda, ages eight and twelve, had their own horses and motorcycles. They had private bathrooms in their bedrooms. They lived in heaven. A castle in heaven.

My cousin Todd was eager to show me around. He was a cute, mischievous, confident, and blond-haired, blue-eyed, eight-year-old with a life totally disparate from mine. Todd walked me down to the barn and introduced me to his pony Half Moon—Moonie, for short. They were preparing for their first junior rodeo competition of the summer that would take place the following weekend in Montague, Todd said. We walked out to the main road to gawk at the longhorn bull who served no purpose other than impregnating rope cows.

Todd suggested we cross the dirt road and explore the oak-studded hills on the other side.

"We should go back and ask your mom," I suggested.

Todd thought I was an idiot.

"Why would we do that?" he wanted to know.

"I just think we should ask your mom if it's okay, before we get too far from the house…"

"Nah, she's not gonna care," he insisted.

Todd wasn't about to go all the way back. He brushed off my recommendation, unable to imagine why we needed permission for a freedom he took for granted.

In our absence, Aunt Susan baked a big flat chocolate cake in the shape of a Teddy Bear with "Welcome Scott" scrawled in yellow frosting over top for my welcoming party that evening.

The welcoming party was a bit of a blur. I remember very little of it, other than sitting in the kitchen with my back to the antique woodstove and eating cake as my aunts attempted to build the self-esteem I clearly didn't have. I remember my aunts wrapping me in affection. I remember not wanting the evening to turn into a confessional about Fluffy's house. I remember wondering how I could possibly live with people who didn't believe in The Truth. From my perspective, the best way to fit into my new life was to pretend that I had been there before. Don't tell them who I am or where I came from. Just act normal. That's what I would do. I would act normal.

My aunts asked questions. They told me that Grandma and Grandpa Terry had been terribly bothered a few months earlier when they abruptly cut short their visit with Fluffy in Cedar City. Something "wasn't right," my grandparents had said, and it had bothered them enough to make them leave.

That surprised the hell out of me. I don't know what my grandparents could have possibly seen.

In retrospect, I don't think they saw anything. I think they *felt* it.

In the privacy of a conversation with her sisters, Aunt Dot referred to me as "one whipped pup." I weighed myself on her bathroom scale. 112 pounds. I was sixteen, underweight, and my life was about to change.

Todd and I were home alone the next day. Around noon, I asked him if we could make peanut butter sandwiches for lunch. The reply I expected to hear, but didn't, was, "Oh no. We can't do that. We have to wait for my mom to come home."

We ate our self-prepared sandwiches in the kitchen while I wondered if Aunt Dot would be angry at what we had done.

A few days later, Aunt Susan drove back to Auburn. Aunt Dot drove into town with Todd and Brenda to run some errands at her office. I found myself on her front porch, alone in her home for the first time, watching her gold Cadillac wind its way down the dirt road, weaving through the oak trees, falling out of sight beyond the roping arena. Before the dust could settle back to earth, I ran to the kitchen to get something to eat.

I became self-aware at that moment. For the first time, I consciously thought about the power that Fluffy had held over me. I went back to the living room and settled into the red recliner, next to the woodstove, and contemplated my unexpected urge to steal. I tried to shake off those thoughts. I didn't need to be a thief in Aunt Dot's house, I hoped. I wasn't hungry, my life had changed, and the heavy varnish that Fluffy and religion had coated over my life was beginning to crack.

While doing laundry, Aunt Dot pulled my dirty underwear out from the clothes hamper. I had purchased them three years earlier when I was 13. She checked the label inside. They were the same size as her son Todd's underwear. She threw every stitch of my clothing in the garbage, then took me shopping for an entire new wardrobe. We wandered the aisles of more than one western wear store where I tried on long sleeved cowboy shirts and Wrangler jeans. Aunt Dot didn't turn over price tags to see how much things cost.

My cousin Brenda suggested that I buy Angel Flight pants, a style that was popular in 1980 and had no back pockets. I was offended at the thought of wearing pants I referred to as "Fairy Flights."

"Only fags would wear Fairy Flights," I told her.

———∞———

Aunt Dot's house had been custom built for her by a bowlegged contractor. Fred was an old rodeo cowboy. Within days of my arrival in Redding, he began teaching me to rope steers and ride bulls. Fred was my rodeo coach, as well as Todd and Brenda's, and he swabbed my bruises in horse liniment when I was injured. He taught me that when you're sick, a large glass of gin and tonic but mostly gin will render the problem insignificant.

Fred celebrated his 55th birthday that summer. For an entire week leading up to the celebration, I agonized over the decision to join the brief celebration and offend Jehovah, or decline and offend my rescuers. I was enjoying the freedom of not being required to attend three religious meetings a week. Not once did I ask to visit the local Kingdom Hall in Redding. I was enjoying life as a cowboy, and one that was free of religion, but Fred's birthday caused some religious angst for me.

On the morning of the event, I let my religion win the battle.

"I'm a Jehovah's Witness," I reminded everyone. "Jehovah doesn't approve of birthday celebrations. I can't participate."

I quoted a few Bible scriptures, and then left the house. An hour later, I returned and asked for a piece of Fred's chocolate cake, now that the party was over, the key difference being "over."

In mid-July, we drove Aunt Dot's motor home up to the rural town of Cedarville for a weekend junior rodeo competition. I wasn't ready to compete and hadn't yet been on a bull, but I was practicing on smaller rope cows in Aunt Dot's arena.

The day after arriving home from Cedarville, Aunt Dot abruptly suggested that having the skill to lead a woman around the dance floor was something I needed to know.

"You can't dance proper on carpet," she said, so on the tile of her front entry, we held an impromptu dance lesson where Aunt Dot showed me how to hold a lady and do a rock step on every third beat to country western music.

Late in July, Aunt Dot drove me down to Sacramento for a quick rendezvous with my mother at the California State Fair. I did not ask for the visit because I did not know my mother. My only interest was in seeing Sissy after four years of separation.

Aunt Dot walked me back behind the grandstand where Mom was camped out on a picnic table, in the middle of a poker game. My mother likes to play poker.

After divorcing my dad, Mom had become a thoroughbred race horse trainer. She had spent the previous fifteen years owning and training race horses that never seemed to hit it big, and Sissy had dropped out of high school to travel the state fair racing circuit with her, working the test barn and collecting horse piss in a jar. Horses are drug tested after running, and Sissy's occupation was to take each one into a private stall, hold a mason jar in front of its penis, and wait for a sample.

I watched my mother play poker. Her Wrangler jeans and work boots were splattered with manure—an obvious hazard of working in horse barns. She had the rough language of a blue collar woman.

I tried to wrap my head around the idea that she was my mother. We didn't look alike. Robin resembled her, I thought. There was not an immediate connection between us. We did not know each other. Unbeknownst to me, she had recently celebrated her 36th birthday.

She introduced me to her poker buddies, and then her short break was over. She went back to the barns for work, and Aunt Dot drove me back to Redding.

Two months later, Aunt Dot put me on a Greyhound bus to have a second and more intimate connection with my mother over Labor Day weekend. Mom lived in Pleasanton, about 40 miles outside of San Francisco.

I rode the bus from Redding to Oakland with an itinerary to transfer to a Pleasanton bus in Oakland.

In the Oakland bus terminal, I walked upstairs to the men's room on the second floor, needing to take a piss. The Oakland Greyhound bus depot is a hellhole. Halfway up the stairs, a worn and haggard black man blocked my path. His eyes weren't right.

"Hey son...look at this."

He opened his fist, revealing a grimy and colorful assortment of pills.

I waived him off, disturbed by the pinkness of his palms, a collection of white and blue pills clutched inside. I had already waived off a similar offer in my brief one-hour stop in Oakland.

The Pleasanton bus pulled in. First in line, I stepped up to board, relieved. I handed my ticket to the driver. He stopped me.

"Hey, this says you're headed to Pleasanton?" he asked, staring at my ticket.

"Yeah."

"Well, I'm not going to Pleasanton."

I pointed out that my ticket indicated that's where he was headed.

"Sorry. I can't help you. That's not where I'm going. Someone wrote the wrong bus number on your ticket."

I had my mother's home phone number and called her frequently. There was no answer. She was still working at the track.

I found myself back at the ticket counter shortly before closing, asking for a solution to their error, wondering how I would get out of Oakland, a veritable den of sin, with nightfall coming and my having no clue that Pleasanton was a mere twenty-five miles away.

There were two customer-service-type people at the counter, and they suggested that I ride the last bus out of Oakland and go home.

When the last bus came in, the only one heading back to Redding, I boarded. We arrived in Redding the following morning, and Aunt Dot promptly put me on another back to Pleasanton.

The bus let me off on the bridge next to the old Pleasanton Hotel that evening...that's where the bus stops when it pulls into town. Five minutes later, Mom picked me up.

I stretched out across the yellow shag carpet in her two-bedroom apartment on Vineyard Avenue and realized that relationships aren't instantaneous. You can't make up for years of non-existent contact. You really can't.

Sissy and I wallowed in the emotions we couldn't embrace when Dad let her go, and all the things we wanted to say but couldn't in the ensuing years. It was an emotional but painless re-discovery as we laughed our asses off, cussed out Fluffy, and re-established a bond that hadn't withered. We sprawled out over Mom's living room, laughing and sampling selections of music from a stack of eight track tapes that Sissy had collected.

She cranked up Lover Boy, The Cars and Van Halen, and quizzed me on her favorite bands.

"Who's your favorite?" she asked. "I love Stevie Nicks... Do you?"

"Yeah, I like him too."

"Him? You mean her...right? Stevie Nicks is a woman."

"Oh...yeah, that's what I meant...I was thinkin' about someone else..."

Sissy probably thinks I'm a dork...I don't know anything about music.

It's just like when Aunt Dot took Brenda to San Francisco to buy a dress. They bumped into some famous guy named Dudley Moore and Brenda got her picture standing next to him. I've never heard of Dudley Moore, but Brenda didn't believe me.

She didn't believe it when we went to the party after the Cedarville junior rodeo either, when I confessed I don't know how to dance. That's why Aunt Dot tried to teach me when we got home, because I was scared to death to go to that party. I've never danced before, or listened to music much, or watched popular movies or had friends, but Brenda thinks I'm just making it up.

It isn't her fault. She doesn't understand where I come from, and I don't know how to tell her.

———

By August, Aunt Dot's bathroom scale recorded my weight as 135. At her insistence, I had been listening to hours of Dale Carnegie motivational tapes to build some self-confidence. By late summer, I was ready for my first bull riding competition in the nearby town of Yuba City.

Aunt Dot called Virgil, asking for his signature on the entry form that would grant approval for me to ride. He refused to sign it, so she signed it herself.

In Yuba City, I drew a big black Brahma bull named Superstar. He trashed me hard within two seconds of the gate opening. All two seconds of my first bull ride were a blur of blackness.

A few weeks later I entered the Red Bluff Junior rodeo, and found the same results. That bull dumped me hard and fast.

On September 14, 1980, I won my first bull-riding prize at the Oroville Junior Rodeo. It was my third competition, and I took third place and winnings of $65. My bull's name was Coors Light.

Aunt Dot taught me to pull calves in the mud in the middle of a midnight winter rain when a confused calf insisted on entering the world backwards. A black angus-cross heifer had served as our practice rope cow for months, and when she got tired of being roped, we converted her to bull riding practice instead. She had her first calf in the middle of a winter storm.

By flashlight, I thrust my arms into her wet and slippery uterus, attempting to straighten out the twisted calf as she strained in labor and Aunt Dot offered verbal instructions. After a difficult half hour delivery, we manually pulled the calf out of her belly.

The calf didn't survive more than two days after birth.

Without a calf to suckle, Aunt Dot then turned that heifer, now considered a cow, into a family milk cow.

I was a glutton for milk and easily consumed a half-gallon a day. No water for me. Not with unlimited supplies of ice-cold, rich, decadent, straight from the cow, milk. We stacked gallon-sized mayonnaise jars on the top shelf of the fridge, filled with rich milk. I shook the jars to redistribute the cream that floated to the top, then poured drinking glasses full, consciously observing the disparity between my old life and new. When I drank milk at Aunt Dot's, I took that awareness inside of me and squeezed it. Embraced it. Quietly felt gratitude pour through my bones.

By then, I was in the middle of my junior year of high school in Redding. No longer was I the kind of kid that school bullies picked on. I had changed. I had accepted a new calf rope as a Christmas present from Fred, and didn't feel guilty for it. I had helped Brenda decorate the Christmas tree, and my guilt for doing so didn't feel onerous. The power of religion had faded. The influence of Fluffy had diminished.

I was competing in weekend high school rodeos, and was hoping to acquire enough points to earn a qualifying spot in the state rodeo finals. That spring, during a practice session in Aunt Dot's roping arena, my rope horse Danny plowed over a steer and went down, bashing me in the head in the process. Fred let me lay in the dirt, unconscious, expecting me to come to on my own.

"Cowboy up!" he said.

Aunt Dot learned of it and drove Fred's beige Ford pickup into the arena where I was flopping around in spasms from a brain injury. She made Fred hold me down in the bed of his truck while she drove fifteen miles to the hospital. I arrived cussing and screaming, and fell into a coma shortly after.

She called my father to share the awful news. His primary concern was that I not have a blood transfusion, if it became necessary. Jehovah's Witnesses were adamantly opposed to blood transfusions, he told her.

Over the next two weeks, I slipped in and out of the coma and began referring to Aunt Dot as "Mom Dottie." After waking from the coma, I wanted out of that hospital. Badly. I was angry. I wanted a real pillow. I wanted home cooked food. I wanted to go back to Mom Dottie's. I remembered nothing of my recent horse wreck. I wanted to resume my bull-riding career. I wanted the fucking doctor to let me go home. I lay in my hospital bed for two weeks, consumed by fantasies of blowing up the doctor's house if he didn't comply with my wishes. After two weeks of listening to my complaints, the doctor sent me home with instructions for Aunt Dot to lock up all guns within reach. He warned her that my brain had been bruised and my head wasn't right yet.

My desire to burn his house quickly faded, and three months later, I entered the Red Bluff Junior Rodeo to resume my stalled bull-riding career and attempt to ride my 13th bull. On the 13th day of September, 1981. Slated for the 13th chute out of a row of fifteen. Everyone said I shouldn't expect much after my coma. No one expected me to ride.

What people don't know about bull-riding is that you can't talk yourself into it after the gate opens. Bull-riding isn't the physical sport that people imagine. Before you climb on top of the animal, you can have all the conversations you want in an attempt to build your confidence. You can play mind games all you like while stretching your legs down the narrow space between a bull's belly and the bucking chute. But once you strap your hand in place and ask for the gate to be opened, your subconscious takes over and you discover that you either want to be there, or you don't. There's no time to convince yourself that climbing on top of a thousand pound animal is not the stupidest thing you've ever done—once the ride starts. When the chute opens, bull-riding becomes a mental game first, a physical game second.

So no one thought I would actually complete my first post-coma ride, given that there was still some question as to whether or not my head was right. I counted the thirteens that had converged on that day, and grew so sick of hearing a "don't expect much" message that I allowed myself to get all worked up in a fit of anger. I convinced myself that unlucky numbers were bullshit. Screw that. For me, thirteen would be lucky. I would create my own destiny. I let that faux anger build into determination, twisted my mind into reversing a bad luck omen, and climbed on top of a white muley Brahma-cross bull for my thirteenth ride.

I strapped my hand into my bullrope…Fred stood on the gate and pulled the tail of my rope tight. Aunt Dot watched from the bleachers.

I nodded my head and grunted, "Let's go!"

The chute opened, and my brain decided that I really did want to be there.

It was a decent ride, all the way to eight seconds. Unlucky numbers are bullshit.

———◦◦◦◦———

That rodeo launched me into my senior year of high school. I was 6 foot tall and 155 pounds, built more like a bronc rider than a bull rider, so Fred added a third event, saddle bronc riding, to my list of high school rodeo competitions. The school rodeo club elected me president. I had acquired friends by then, all of whom were worldly. I no longer associated with Jehovah's Witnesses. Sara Collins was a beautiful little blonde that every other guy in the rodeo club dreamed of going out with. She was sweet and fun and built with all the right parts, and I happened to be the lucky guy she wanted to share it with. I did my best pretending not to notice, until friends began dropping comments about my being too stupid to get a clue that Sara had the hots for me.

That wasn't good. When you're in high school, you can't let your bull-riding buddies speculate on why you aren't interested in a cute blonde girl. I was close to graduation, and up to that point, I had evaded inquiries into my lack of dating by blaming it on the fact that Aunt Dot lived so far out of town that it just wasn't practical to have a girlfriend. It just wasn't. But under pressure, I asked Sara out. She suggested we go to the movies with her parents.

They drove us to the Art Deco Redding Fox Theatre.

I held Sara's hand in the backseat. We abandoned her mom and dad and found two seats at an opposite end of the theatre, our fingers entwined. I broke her grip often to wipe our mingled sweat from my palms.

Her parents drove me home after the movie, and I was so thankful for their companionship, not knowing what I would have done if left alone with their daughter. I had just turned eighteen.

Sara announced that she was my girlfriend, the definition of which requires a second date. My buddy Starsky offered to double date, so the four of us went to Whiskeytown Reservoir and sat on the beach doing nothing. Starsky wanted to hang out with his girlfriend Debbie, and Sara wanted to hang out with me, but I was bored out of my mind and had no desire to lay out in the sun while making small talk with the girlfriend I never wanted. I walked out to the water's edge and announced plans to swim all the way across the lake, with Starsky chasing after and yelling at me for being an idiot. I followed him back to the beach and spent the rest of the day talking to my new girlfriend, for hours, the whole damn day, doing absolutely nothing.

Darkness arrived, and we piled into Starsky's truck for the ride back home.

Sara was the first to get dropped off. I walked her up to the front door, knowing the appropriate behavior when on a date with a cute blonde girl while your friends are watching.

I bent down for my first kiss, under the porch light where everyone could see.

Sara stuck her tongue in my mouth. The stubble of my newly grown moustache chafed the sunburn on her lips. She pulled away, then drew me in for another wet kiss.

A week later, we held an end-of-year rodeo party at Wendy Meauchamp's house when her parents were away. We built a bonfire to huddle around, and Sara hopped into my lap with a blanket to cuddle under. I played the game, made cute jokes, and winked at friends who thought I was having an incredible time cuddling with Sara Collins.

Not so much. It turned into a two-way biology experiment. Sara unbuttoned her blouse under the cover of our blanket…a clear hint that I was supposed to do something about it.

I did. I was totally unprepared for breasts. They were soft, but not in a squishy way. That was interesting, and not what I expected. I was unclear on whether they were supposed to be kneaded or stroked. I couldn't imagine the possibilities on my own while surrounded by friends who clearly assumed something dirty was going on under our blanket, and I doubted that I was doing it right...until her nipples got hard.

I thought about all the locker room conversations when guys enviously assured me that having a girlfriend meant I would soon be "getting some"...and now that I was "getting some," I wondered what I was supposed to do with it. "Getting some" was the single most important focus of life amongst my friends, and I was profoundly disappointed once I had it. I had always been aware of my lack of sexual desire for girls, and while wrapping my arms around my first girlfriend and exploring her pointy nipples, I finally realized that the magic of puberty hadn't delivered an interest in the opposite sex, at all. And all my years of prayer hadn't delivered me from the sin of being a homo.

Sara was a sweetheart. She was cute and wonderful, affectionate and shapely, but that wasn't enough to generate physical urges for me. I cuddled under a blanket with my cute blonde girlfriend and her erect nipples, knowing I had no interest in being there. And somewhere along the task of nipple play, I abruptly realized that I was supposed to be enjoying an identical reaction with a body part of my own...but that wasn't happening. It occurred to me that Sara, given her weight on my lap, could recognize that my biological reciprocation didn't exist, and that's when I realized I better get out from under that blanket before she started asking questions I wasn't prepared to answer.

I graduated from high school a week later.

Armageddon still hadn't arrived.

COMING OUT

With six hundred dollars in scholarship money from Redding, I showed up in Glendive, Montana for the start of college. Two years prior, the men's rodeo team from Dawson Community College had been ranked number one in the national standings, and I wanted to be part of that team. After registering for classes on orientation day, I discovered that my six hundred dollars wouldn't cover the cost.

The closet-sized financial aid office introduced me to the concept of student loans. I completed the application and assured the financial aid officer that the loan proceeds were needed to pay tuition, then I spent half of it a week later to buy my first horse. I signed the promissory note, knowing I would never pay it back. My prior Armageddon indoctrination was still playing in my subconscious, inconspicuously, overriding plans for a future. That religious message had faded in volume, but I still had no plans for a career, or the repayment of student loan debt. My future was fuzzy, with no discernible end in sight, other than hopes that I might someday live forever in the New Order.

Armageddon would arrive soon, like a thief in the night, I still thought. There would be a tremendous rending of the heavens… thunder and lightning…a mind-blowing, ear-shattering torrent of sound as the heavens and earth were torn asunder…six-headed serpents…the Devil riding a red horse.

And there would be teeth gnashing...the Bible says so. I don't rightly know what that is, having never seen an actual demonstration of teeth gnashing, but there would be plenty of it. And tongue rotting, blood curdling, death and despair while God cast miserable sinners into the lake of fire and sulfur. That was my future, followed by a peaceful eternal life on earth in the New Order with a pet lion; everyone in The Truth would have a pet lion.

There was also, of course, the slight concern that Jehovah wouldn't allow me through the gates of the New Order, knowing I was a homo and all, but I couldn't see that admission as being a huge roadblock to entry, having suppressed my homosexual urges and believing He would cure me after Armageddon's arrival.

Having failed to attend any Kingdom Hall meetings in my two years at Aunt Dot's, I feared that Jehovah would not consider me to be a proper Witness. I hoped He would forgive my failure to adhere to our rigorous schedule of worship and maybe overlook all of my sinful desires while He yanked the eyeballs out of sinners before casting them into the fiery pit of the second death during Armageddon, but I wasn't really sure.

Virgil called to congratulate me on high school graduation.

He asked if I had attended any Kingdom Hall meetings in Redding. I confessed that I hadn't.

"You know, Armageddon is so close," he reminded me. "You might want to be concerned about that. The Bible says The End will arrive before the generation of 1914 passes away. There's not many of that generation left. The people of 1914 are almost gone."

His prediction hooked me—hard. It preyed on my unresolved guilt at abandoning The Truth, and weighed on my fear that the Witnesses could be right. I allowed Virgil's preaching to bring me very close to the edge of buying it. Enough to attend one more meeting in a Montana Kingdom Hall, shortly after I arrived in Glendive, giving it one more chance as an adult. One more opportunity to persuade me of their sole ownership of The Truth. One last occasion to resurrect the conviction I held as a child.

⸺ ⸺

I arrived in Montana under the delusion that I was a fabulous bull rider, and was shocked to discover that the skill level of the average intercollegiate competitor was astronomically higher than that of the average high school cowboy. My dream of becoming a world-class bull rider was shattered very quickly, and I didn't last beyond the first year of college rodeo.

But in my only year of competition, our team traveled from rodeo to rodeo on weekends, shacking up in hotels, four guys to a room, two in each bed. College cowboys have two extracurricular activities on their mind during rodeo road trips: getting drunk and chasing wool.

Teammates were speculating on why I wasn't chasing pussy, known as wool in cowboy terms. More than once I heard, "He's from California, and you know what that means!"

The perfect opportunity to prove my masculinity and assuage their concerns arrived by accident at the Crystal Bar in Bozeman.

The Crystal's claim to fame was "liquor up front and poker in the rear," a double entendre that is accurate and intended to be funny and has been claimed by many cowboy bars. The legal drinking age in Montana was nineteen at the time, but most cowboy bars were willing to overlook the specifics of how close you were to hitting that target, so I went to the Crystal to have a few beers with my buddies after the rodeo. Having a bull ride to complete the following day, I wanted to leave long before anyone else. Some sleep would be good, I thought, so I went back through the poker room and departed out the rear entrance.

I held the door for a young cowgirl who was also on her way home.

As I was being courteous and escorting her out, a couple of teammates came through. I held the door for them and latched on to the pretty cowgirl. We walked out to the alley together, and my pals assumed I was leaving with her. I disappeared into the darkness, accompanied by a hot cowgirl. In their minds, I was about to get some wool.

In the dark, I walked across town to the Best Western where we were holed up for the weekend, and I spent the night tossing and turning on a cold pile of lumber on the backside of the hotel parking lot. Around 8 am the next morning, I staggered back to the room to wake my buddies and fuel their conjecture with graphic lies of what I had done with that cute cowgirl.

"She was really wet," I told everyone. I had done it with her three times, I claimed.

The news spread quickly. By the end of the day, every guy on the team knew that Scott Terry had finally gotten some wool.

What they didn't know was that I had an enormous crush on another team member, a very handsome steer wrestler whom I will call Buck. Seems to me that, if I'm gonna tell a story about sexual tension between two cowboys, one of those cowboys should be named Buck.

I adored Buck, and I was really confused by the realization that he found frequent reasons to sleep with me. Choosing another cowboy to bunk with was generally a last-minute decision when we checked into a hotel, and you could never be certain that the person you originally thought you would sleep with was, in fact, the person you would actually wake up next to in the morning. It wasn't unusual to arrive back at the hotel after a night of drinking and find that your bed was occupied by two people—your original bunk mate whose body was wrapped around a girl whose name you did not need to know, and then you would be forced to go search for an empty bed in another room.

But that rarely happened to me, because Buck generally slept in my bed. I didn't know why. I went out of my way to keep my distance from everyone on the rodeo team, not wanting to put myself in the position of having to explain why I wasn't chasing wool. Social distance was imperative. Social distance prevented questions from being asked.

At the Missoula rodeo, Buck and I left the bar early—he was on his way to being drunk. I drove his truck back to our hotel, and we walked up to our room on the second floor.

Buck turned the TV on, then stripped down to his boxers and sprawled out over the bed, practically inviting me to look. We ordered a pizza to be delivered. He fell asleep, a hard beer-induced sleep, and I took long glances at his nipples, and his body hair, and the access hole gaping wide in the front of his baby blue boxers, wanting to touch him, wanting to explore what was passed out before me. Wondering if he shared my desires. Wondering why he often bunked with me. Wanting to run my hands over his body. Wondering if he would awake if I dared to touch him.

I didn't touch him.

Months later, we independently and unknown to each other signed up for a city-sponsored ski trip when the Glendive Park and Rec department crammed more than fifty people into the Red Lodge hostel for a weekend ski adventure.

Our chartered bus pulled into the hostel parking lot and I jumped off to stake out the farthest available vacant room.

Buck followed me. We would again share a room.

Minutes later, a third guy showed up—a dude who found every other room to be occupied and then got really bent out of shape when I quickly claimed the small twin bed in our shared room for myself and left the larger queen to be shared by the other two. Buck was visibly frustrated by my snub.

Our third-wheel roommate left for dinner, and I watched Buck step out of the shower moments later…thick, blond, furry, and uncircumcised.

He donned a pair of boxers and tackled me on the bed to wrestle in our underwear. He held me down, his hairy legs wrapped around mine, our lips only a slight shift away from touching, the full weight of his body on top of me.

My passivity killed Buck's enthusiasm, and he climbed off with a laugh that didn't seem necessary.

We had wrestled in our underwear before, but I didn't trust my instincts. When sexual thoughts of Buck crossed my mind, I just dismissed them as impossible. Buck wasn't effeminate. He didn't wear dresses. He often had sex with girls, or so the rumor was. In my mind, he wasn't gay. I couldn't think of him in any way other than being a handsome cowboy who gave mixed signals, and if he was interested in the way I hoped, I couldn't let myself do it in Montana because I'd never done it before and I didn't want to be a homo.

I would keep my desires a secret for eternity. I would never have sex, never fall in love, and would spend my entire life alone. All those thoughts and feelings got packed away in imaginary little boxes that could never be opened, even when I suspected that Buck was trying to pry them open.

———⊶⊷———

When you're away from family and starting life anew, nothing is more important than mail and phone calls from the people you care about. Grandma Terry faithfully sent letters to check up on me, loaded with grandmotherly advice to "Be a good boy" and recommendations to "Study hard." She often wrote to Sissy as well, but rarely heard back and complained to me that "Sissy's arm must be broke." I corresponded with Grams often, and she sent frequent and hefty packages of chocolate chip cookies with black walnuts around the holidays. And loaves of zucchini bread, also with black walnuts. And homemade fruitcake for Christmas, also with black walnuts, which I really loved. Not the black walnuts, I've never cared for black walnuts, but I loved her gifts, especially the fruitcake.

My college roommate, Charlie, saw the hand stitched quilt that Grams had given to me for my high school graduation, and he asked if she would sew one as a wedding present for his sister. Grams quoted him a price of a hundred-and-fifty dollars which appeared to be an enormous fortune to me but a bargain to him. Shortly after the quilt showed up in the mail, Grams sent me an electric blanket, purchased with a small portion of Charlie's money.

"Dear Grandson, I am so glad your roommate liked the quilt. The money really came to our rescue as we needed it. Gramps was really worried about you getting cold as I know as a child at home many times you didn't have enough covers to keep you warm. But we knew sending you covers would only go to Grant or Amber. Your Gramps always slept cold as a child as he was the only boy in seven and the girls all slept good as they slept together and after his mother remarried and got a stepdad he was very abused. When he was very young he left home and lived in some neighbor's chicken house."

I met my new college buddy, Rowdy, on the first day of school orientation, right after he had completed basic training for the National Guard. His name is honest-to-God Rowdy. For reals. His mom wouldn't budge from naming him Loren, so his dad demanded that his middle name be Rowdy. It was a compromise. Loren prefers to be addressed as "Rowdy." You would too, if your mom named you Loren and you were of the XY chromosome. His head was shaved, and I thought he was a farm boy. He wasn't. He was an in-town boy from Sheridan, Wyoming.

I spent an enormous amount of time with Rowdy, fishing and bow hunting and making up for fruitless years of hoping to stick an arrow in an Orland rabbit. We roamed the lower Yellowstone River bottom for weeks, searching for trophy whitetail and passing up countless opportunities that didn't measure up. I'd never killed a buck before, hell, I'd never even seen one killed. I had watched my father bring home many a dead deer, but I'd never witnessed the actual executions.

After three weeks of hunting excursions that were fruitless by choice, my patience ended. Frustrated, I announced to Rowdy, "Damn it. I'm gonna kill the next thing I see."

That prediction was filled moments later when a little antlerless whitetail jumped out of the wild rose bushes. I killed it with a single shot from my .270 Remington. My first deer was taken on an island in the middle of the Yellowstone River. Deer are so plentiful in Montana that you can shoot either sex, and can take more than one, most years. You can shoot just about anything, as long as it's old enough to have outgrown its spots. I shot that little Bambi right through the head, although that's not where I was aiming. It was an accidental kill, but I didn't tell Rowdy that.

I looked at my dead yearling buck, stretched out in the weeds, not old enough to have horns, realizing it had only been born a few months earlier and I would never hang it on the wall as a trophy.

I hadn't a clue what to do with it, but Rowdy did.

"Just run your knife up between his legs," he said. Don't cut the piss sack. That'll ruin the meat."

I nodded. "Yeah, I know." I'd seen many dead deer before, I told him.

"Now you gotta reach in and pull out the innards."

"Yeah, I know," I replied, unwilling to let him know I was a greenhorn.

We threw it in the back of my truck and I carried that little buck up the stairs to our second floor dorm apartment and hung it from the coat pegs in our front mudroom. It aged there for several days in the autumn cold, and looked like a dog, stripped of its skin, hanging from the wall. Probably weighed less than 50 pounds and was the best deer meat I ever ate.

——⊶——

Rowdy introduced me to my second girlfriend, Ingrid Frieschlander. Rowdy dated her first, but that didn't work out so well, given that he's an atheist. Ingrid was a local Baptist girl who came from solid German farm stock, and she completely pissed off her parents when she enrolled in college. Their only expectation was that she marry a local farm boy and produce kids. Ingrid was the smartest student in school, not to mention the most religious, which from my perspective meant she was "safe." Sex before marriage was not on her agenda, so we never found ourselves in an uncomfortable naked position. We did, however, find ourselves in religious debates over the conflict between her adherence to the Baptist ideology and my insistence that the JW's were the "true" religion, in spite of my no longer being a member. She challenged me often on that inconsistency, wondering why I no longer belonged to a church I still referred to as "The Truth." I couldn't answer her, at the time.

After two years of college, I graduated with an AA degree in Petroleum Technology. My father's influence led to that choice, I think. I had watched him climb out of the lower class and into a middle-American income bracket by working in the oil fields, and when Dawson College offered a certificate in that field, it seemed like a logical opportunity. It matched my background and my expectations for what I was capable of. After graduation, I went to work as a roustabout for Shell Oil for $9.60 an hour and no benefits. I was a contract employee with no health coverage, no retirement plan, no vacation, and no sick leave. I worked ten days on and four days off, driving around the oil fields in a two-ton winch truck, repairing equipment and patching leaks. My nose practically froze solid on Thanksgiving Day when I got called out for an oil spill in 40-below weather. Mid-day, I sat in the truck for a half hour to let my nose thaw before going back to work.

My father's oldest sister, Donnis, became a regular part of my Montana life. We talked often about my feeling stuck in the cold and desolate town of Glendive, and she convinced me to move to Chico to get a bachelor's degree.

After a year of working in the oil fields during the day and continuing the bartender job at night, I saved enough money, sold my rope horse for half of what I had paid for him, and returned to northern California.

———

For awhile, I lived in a studio apartment on 12th Street in Chico, a few blocks from the Peking Chinese restaurant on Main Street where my mom and dad had their first date. Each day as I walked to school, I passed the entrance and remembered that my parents had Chinese food on their first romantic evening, but not once did I set foot inside that establishment. You would think that I might have stepped inside, viewed the interior, and wondered which table was the site of my mom and dad's romance. You would think that I might have wondered what they talked about. It could have been really nostalgic to imagine the setting of the relationship that resulted in the birth of me, but I guess not, because it never occurred to me that I might want to know those things.

Aunt Donnis worked for the test office at Chico State and I saw her often. She was wonderfully aware of beautiful things, with the sense and desire to notice nature's glory wherever she went. She was in love with Celtic music, all things artistic, and awakening to the sound of birds singing the dawn of a beautiful new day. She got lost everywhere she went, but wasn't afraid to leave Chico via the maze of two-lane roads threading their way through the rice fields where wildlife and scenery overrode the well-known fact that she would most likely lose her way. Aunt Donnis was self-sufficient on a very tight bottom-tier university salary. She always had a pot of coffee and conversation to share, and could make terrific soup out of anything. That might not sound like much, but the ability to create great soup out of ordinary and inexpensive things is a wonderful and rare skill.

She was the first person I came out to as being gay.

It wasn't entirely by choice, but was truthfully the result of a lie. I had met another gay student—a short Italian guy with a big nose. Jerry Francone was handsome.

Prior to meeting Jerry, I thought I was about the only gay guy on the planet, not counting the hordes of homosexuals in Hollywood, of course. That's how things are when you grow up in rural places with a life like mine, particularly 30 years ago. Gay people were always tragic, were always from somewhere else, and had nothing in common with me. I assumed there were a few gay guys in Chico, the normal variety that have a delicate swish to their walk and more than one dress in their closet, but, in my mind, the chance of finding another rope-swinging, bull-riding, Wrangler-wearing, non-effeminate gay man within a thousand miles of me was practically nil.

But guys get horny. They just do. We're wired that way. So when I reached the breaking point at the age of 22 and couldn't bear to remain celibate or hold back sexual thoughts, I did what many men do. I went to the adult bookstore.

I sat in my truck late that night, parked in back of the porn shop, violently shaking with nerves, wanting to commit an unforgivable sin and buy some porn. Not just any porn, mind you. It couldn't be gay porn. I couldn't bear to let the bookstore clerk speculate that I might be a homosexual, so after a long mental battle in my truck, I quickly snuck in the back door and bought a swingers magazine. That was the closest I could get to male porn without going totally gay.

I spent months perusing the pages of heterosexual and bisexual couples who were looking to add a little spice to their relationships.

One particular ad caught my eye. A single man had posted a small listing without a photo that described him as a straight guy who enjoyed "going gay" on occasion. Dave lived in Cloverdale, exactly 3 hours and 150 miles from Chico if you drove the shortest route through the back roads. His posting made perfect sense to me. It confirmed my view of life. I imagined him as the only man of my kind within driving reach, and it seemed perfectly logical that he would be so far away. After months of wondering, I called him. He answered the phone on the second ring.

I shook to the point of being sick while talking to a man who, potentially, would be my sex partner. I shook so hard that I couldn't stand. My stomach squeezed itself into a stressed-out knot, on the verge of puking. I lay down on the floor, hoping to ease my nerves. My voice quavered. I stretched out across the carpet and shook so hard that I tried not to talk at all, letting him dominate the conversation with his deep voice, his undoubtedly masculine, blue-collar voice.

At his suggestion, I agreed to meet him halfway, an hour and a half for each of us to drive to the east side of Clearlake where he reserved a hotel room for our rendezvous. I drove to the lake the following weekend, fighting nerves and expecting to get all pissed about driving 75 miles for an ugly guy. I would get naked with him, regardless. He could have been ugly as fuck and it wouldn't have mattered. I was horny.

After two hours of driving, I pulled into the parking lot of a dumpy waterfront hotel on a Saturday morning. Dave's white pickup was parked in front, as he had promised. He stepped out of the cab.

The man I expected to be disappointingly ugly, wasn't. He was spectacularly handsome. One hairy chested, thirty-five year old building contractor, previously married, about six feet tall and built like a tank. He had a flawless moustache and an adorable black Lab in back of his truck. He was my fantasy come true.

We shook hands. He had a workingman's hands. They were larger than mine. His chest fur crawled out from the confines of his shirt.

I followed him into the lobby of the cheap hotel. He'd been there before.

The gayness of the accommodations jolted my senses. They didn't need to hang a sign out front, announcing the sexual identity of the place. It was obvious once you walked in. The whole world of unsuspecting vacationers who might have mistakenly entered the gay hotel to inquire about room rates were accosted by snapshots of men frolicking on the hotel grounds, splashing in the water, having fun. The wall behind the cash register was plastered with full color pictures of naked and semi-naked men, on public display in the hotel lobby. I averted my eyes at the overt and brazen exhibition of sexuality, not wanting to be caught staring. I wasn't gay. Not in public.

An old clerk at the counter leered and confirmed our reservation. He leered in a way that he intended to be complimentary. He knew our secret. Our secret wasn't a secret in that hotel. The gay hotel. The old man smiled a lot. Crooked teeth. Crooked old yellow teeth. He smiled more often than necessary. He needed a shower. He wasn't as old as he looked. He offered helpful tips about hot tub use and the hotel's clothing optional policy. He was more helpful than I wanted. He was entirely too friendly with Dave.

His familiarity offended the hell out of me. I wasn't prepared to be gay in public. Gay was a matter of private concern. I would not be gay in the outdoor hot tub, on display for the whole gay hotel to see. Gay is what I would do with handsome Dave behind the closed door of our gay hotel room.

The hotel proprietor smiled at me with his crooked old teeth, and I looked away. More than once I shielded my eyes from the sight of his flabby body, exposed by his scant tank top, too much naked time in the sun, I thought. I thought about his gay hotel and his gay hot tub that he practically sold to us with a wink and more smiles from his crooked old yellow teeth. I thought about his soft chest, tanned to leather. And I thought about kissing him and his crooked old teeth. The old flabby guy wanted to kiss me. I would not kiss him. I would kiss handsome Dave as soon as I got him behind the closed door of the gay room in the gay hotel where we would have gay sex. Gay sex had to include kissing.

Dave paid for the room and escorted me out. He knew what he was doing. He'd been there before.

He opened the door of our room, then took the far side of our bed and unbuttoned his shirt. I took the opposite side and left my clothes lying on the floor.

We met in the middle of the bed. We kissed.

I fondled his frontal parts, in awe of his masculinity, exploring what I dared, inhaling his scent, sucking his salty dick, wondering if I was doing it right. He tasted good. He had a perfectly beautiful and average dick. We had oral sex. Touching sex. Gentle sex. Clueless sex. Kissing sex. Fast sex.

He jerked off all over his belly. I didn't.

Spent from five minutes of play, Dave rolled over and turned his back to me. His semen dripped onto the sheets.

I curled up next to him, not ready to quit, craving something I hadn't finished.

"How much room do you have over there?" Dave asked.

"Oh there's plenty. It's a big bed."

"Great. Would you mind moving over to your side a little. I'm not really into the cuddling thing."

We lay in bed for ten minutes, not touching, while he came down from his orgasm. We took individual showers and dressed, then drove to Wendy's for lunch while avoiding a full discussion of what we would do with the rest of our time in the hotel. Our conversation was brutally simplistic. We had nothing to talk about.

I hadn't eaten all day, but I ordered a burger, knowing it would make me puke. My handsome sex partner thought that was stupid.

"Why did you order it, if you're not feeling good enough to eat it?" he asked.

"I don't know. Just thought I'd be able to get it down, once it was sittin' in front of me. But I don't think that's a good idea, now that I ordered it."

"Can I have it?" he asked.

"Sure." I pushed it across the table to Dave.

You've got to be wondering what the hell this has to do with Jerry Francone. I'm getting there.

We ended lunch and agreed there really wasn't any reason to stay the night. Our task was completed. I had no desire to spend time in the gay hotel. I gave Dave some money for half the hotel bill, then I drove back to Chico. I never saw him again. But before we split, Dave mentioned an out of the way park in Chico where men like us would occasionally meet up. A place where men could meet other men. Several months later, I was there.

That's where I met Al.

Al was not an attractive man. He was about half my height and twice my age, and he was uninterested in any sort of sex that did not include a gigantic dildo up his ass. The dildo was a painful toy with ridges that didn't have a place in my limited sexual repertoire. There was nothing good about that connection, other than the fact that, in my mind, he was the only game in town. A game when I would show up to his downtown apartment, unannounced, with hopes for sex that didn't involve a damn dildo. No kissing, either. He was too ugly to kiss.

Al insisted that I accompany him to the only gay bar in town.

"Why?" I asked.

"I just think you should go. It'll be fun."

"I don't think so. I'm not ready for that. What if someone sees me? I'm not going there."

"Oh come on…It'll be fun."

"How could it be fun? I'm not that kind of gay. Why is it so frickin' important to go to the damn gay bar?"

"I want my friends to meet you. You're cute. I'd like them to see you."

We argued for months. He got mad. I gave in.

We parked around the corner on 8th Street, and I walked in the front door of the Cherry Street bar with a short and ugly man named Al around midnight on a Saturday evening. That's where I met Jerry Francone.

I already knew Jerry. He was the operations officer for the Chico State Finance Club, and I was its president. By then, I was taking college seriously and I had hopes for the future. I thought I knew Jerry well, but clearly, not as well as I thought. I could have died when I found him standing in the bar talking to a group of lesbians he referred to as "dykes." It was too late to run back out. He had seen me.

Jerry couldn't have cared less. He was "out" to his family, and he couldn't imagine anyone being as uptight as I was. He'd grown up at a Catholic boarding school and was very comfortable with his identity. He took me on as his good deed project and began introducing me to other gay men, if not personally, at least by name. He knew a gay school counselor. Gay professors. Gym coaches. Firemen. Priests. Bartenders. Police officers. Oh my God, did he know things! Months later, frustrated with the painfully slow pace at which I was embracing my sexuality, Jerry insisted that I visit The Castro neighborhood in San Francisco. He said it would change my life and radically change my perspective on what it meant to be gay.

So I drove to the East Bay town of Hayward the following weekend, twenty-five miles outside of San Francisco. I'd been to Hayward before. My mother and sister had moved there a few years earlier, and I had driven down to visit several times. I didn't tell them I was in town that weekend.

I parked my truck in the Hayward BART Station parking lot and rode public transit into San Francisco, twenty-five miles away. Don't know why I didn't just park in San Francisco like normal people.

I disembarked at the first BART station across the bay, the Embarcadero, and walked halfway across the city to Castro Street with a folded map of San Francisco sticking out the back pocket of my Wranglers.

The Castro was swarming with weekend activity. I rounded the corner of the Twin Peaks bar, peering sideways through the glass windows. The bartender winked as I walked by. I looked away. He had a thick moustache like Dave's, a beautiful moustache. I thought he was probably gay. Maybe not. I wasn't sure. I wandered up and down three blocks of the Castro district twice, drawing attention in my cowboy clothes. A silver bull-riding trophy buckle decorated my waist. The thud of my boots on the pavement turned a few heads. I eyeballed men and mentally speculated on the odds of their being homosexual like me. When they boldly sized me up in return, I imagined they were merely fascinated by my tight Wranglers. The men who checked me out couldn't all be gay, I imagined. Especially the burly men with facial hair. They weren't gay. They couldn't possibly be gay. They were simply interested in the oddity of my clothes.

I leaned up against the Walgreens at 18th and Castro for an hour, staring at the Elephant Walk bar across the street, wondering if lunch might exist inside. In 1987, The Castro wasn't a dining destination. There were bars and hardware stores, but few places to eat. The Elephant Walk looked less like a bar and more like a lunch spot. Still, the windows were tinted dark.

My legs grew tired of standing. I squatted down in my cowboy boots, resting my back against Walgreens, working up the courage to explore the Elephant Walk, hoping they might serve something for lunch.

Hunger eventually drove me in.

I ordered a Budweiser, then spent five minutes peeling the wet label off of the amber glass. I laid it wet and intact on the wooden bar, a perfect rectangle, while avoiding the gaze of other bar occupants.

A man left his window seat and walked over to occupy the empty barstool next to me. I ignored him.

I ordered a burger from the bartender.

The guy next to me said, "Hello."

I turned my head to acknowledge him for the first time. Thirty-something. Short. Friendly. Blue eyes. A handsome little guy who looked like he played rugby.

"First time here?" he asked.

"Yeah." Discomfort registered on my face. "It's the first time I've been to San Francisco."

"Really? Me too. I'm from Kansas City. Been here for a few days. My sister lives here.

He stuck his hand out. "My name is George."

George ordered a Tanqueray and Tonic. George only drank Tank and Tonics. After a brief conversation and eye contact that relayed mutual interest, he asked, "Are you gay?"

"Yeah," I answered. "That's why I'm here. It's my first time."

We talked for another half hour at the bar, then George walked me up and down The Castro as my tour guide. Virtually everyone we met was gay, he said. I didn't believe him.

He drove me over to his sister's Geary Street apartment in her Mercedes. She took us out for Italian dinner in North Beach and then dessert at the Opera Plaza Café, and I spent the night with George in her spare bedroom on the second floor, having sex in San Francisco with a handsome little guy from Kansas. Sex that suited me. Sex that included kissing. No dildos.

I rode BART back to Hayward the next morning, half expecting my truck to have been stolen. It wasn't. I drove back to Chico, perfectly happy. Not once did I think about Jehovah. Not once did I think about Armageddon. Not once did I pray for forgiveness.

When I arrived in Chico that evening, Jerry came over to my apartment to share some news.

He had crossed paths with Aunt Donnis over the weekend. They knew each other from work on campus, and he bumped into her outside of the library. I had earlier told Aunt Donnis of some fictitious plans to spend the weekend with Jerry, somewhere that sure as heck wasn't The Castro in San Francisco, so she quizzed him about our plans for the weekend, wondering why he wasn't out of town with me.

Her questions caught him off-guard, unaware of the lie I had given her.

I had been caught.

But Jerry was brighter than average. He made up a quick story for why he was still in Chico and where I had disappeared to, and he was reasonably certain that she believed him.

The guilt I felt for lying, or getting caught, was enormous. The weight was burdensome, and I couldn't bear it. I couldn't lie any longer. It was time to tell the truth.

Seven years had passed since I'd left the Jehovah's Witnesses, and while I occasionally noticed shadows of guilt cross my conscience, I had for the most part rejected their teachings. I no longer had random moments when I gazed up into the sky and wondered if the death and destruction of Armageddon would arrive that day. I no longer felt doomed for abandoning The Truth. I no longer believed that The Truth was the truth. I no longer hoped that God would cure me of my homosexual problem. I was 23, and the time had come to unload my secret.

Circumstances and lies convinced me to tell the truth. I drove over to Aunt Donnis's apartment to confess to something no one knew or would approve of.

She cut an apple into bite-sized pieces in the kitchen while I occupied an easy chair in her living room, ten feet away.

We talked about school. We talked about her favorite yogurt shops in Chico. She chewed on bites of apple. We talked about where I had gone for the weekend.

"I'm gay," I blurted.

She stopped chewing for a few seconds.

"And how are you doing with that?" she asked.

We talked for hours afterwards. She was fantastic and supportive, and from that moment on, Aunt Donnis and I could talk about anything.

LOTS OF GOOD THINGS

I don't know how you know when you've found the place where enough is enough, or when it's time to turn the spigot of memories to the "off" position, but I think I'm there.

When I reached the end of what I wanted to write, I began doubting some of my memories. Did John Denver really oust the Jehovah's Witnesses from one of his concerts? Was my 13th bull ride really out of the 13th chute? How could Grams have possibly remembered that it cost $16 to send us home on PSA airlines? I scribbled a long note of various facts to check.

Two days later, I found myself in the TV lounge at the health club, watching a basketball game, something I never do. I've never watched an entire sporting event on television in my life, unless you count the National Finals Rodeo. Or my teenage years of Professional Wrestling for the porn factor. Or the single Super Bowl game ten years ago at a party, but that doesn't really count because I spent most of the visit relieving boredom by standing guard over the chips and guacamole. Spectator sports aren't my passion, and I don't ever sit in the TV lounge at the gym either, being that it's full of men throwing miscellaneous sports trivia in a struggle to impress one another. I don't speak that language or find it interesting, so I've never hung out in that room when finished with my workout.

But for some unexplainable reason, I found myself there two days after jotting a note to research old PSA airfare prices, minding my own business, watching the Stanford women play basketball, bored out of my mind, ignoring the constant banter of sports trivia. An older Indian gentleman relentlessly tried to draw me into conversation, sharing statistics of the Stanford women's basketball team, something I know nothing about.

I ignored him. Rudely, in fact.

He shared opinions of television commercials as they appeared.

I continued to ignore him, still not interested, and still not very nice about it.

A United Airlines spot showed up, prompting him to share his thoughts about the unlikelihood of United successfully emerging from bankruptcy.

"The whole airline industry is fucked up," he said. I ignored him.

"I used to fly on PSA 30 years ago," he added.

I stopped ignoring him.

"Really?" I asked. "Me too."

"Oh yeah? I used to fly down to LA on PSA to see my family, about 30 years ago. It cost $16 to fly to Southern California back then…"

I about fell out of my chair. I practically ran out of the health club, carrying an odd sense of validation with me, but in slight shock over the oddity and timing of that conversation.

For weeks after, I looked for him during my workouts, wanting to validate our conversation. I wanted to know his name. I wanted to have that conversation again.

I envisioned a scene where I would find him and cleverly bring up the PSA discussion, only to have him subsequently accuse me of being a lunatic. Maybe he wouldn't remember our conversation. Maybe it didn't mean as much to him as it did to me. Maybe his name was something ordinary, like John, which wouldn't do much to give our odd conversation any credence.

But his name isn't John. It's Sunny. Not Sonny like Cher. Or Sunni like I would have guessed a man of Indian descent would spell it. It's Sunny, like a warm sunny day on Road FF in the middle of August when you fly away from Orland for $16. I know this is true because I finally asked, needing proof that our conversation wasn't fiction.

That opportunity arrived several months later on a Saturday evening. People don't flock to the gym on Saturday nights, but I finally bumped into him again, late at night in a deserted locker room, only the two of us, me tying my shoe laces while he blow-dried his hair. He doesn't have enough hair to require a blow dryer, he's as bald as I am, but I don't think anyone should tell him about that. If he's got the self-confidence to blow-dry his hairs in public when he's seriously bald, the more power to him.

I sat on a stool, very slowly tying shoelaces, thinking this was my opportunity to confirm the details of our conversation and ask for his name. I laced up my shoes, very slowly, cinched them tight, untied them, started all over again, very slowly, thinking, "Jeeezuz, how long does it take for a bald guy to blow-dry his hair?"

But he eventually turned off the blow dryer and checked himself out in the mirror, then turned around and caught my eye.

I said, "Hey, I was thinking of you the other day."

Sunny cocked his head and gave me one of those, "WatchootalkinboutWillis" looks.

I laughed and explained, "I was talking to my grandmother last week"—which isn't true because she's dead but he doesn't need to know about that—"and she was telling me about how it cost $16 to fly me down to southern California on PSA 30 years ago. I told her you recently said the same thing. That was a funny coincidence."

His eyes lit up. "Oh yeah, that's right! We talked about that a ways back, didn't we. In fact, I still have one of those tickets. From thirty years ago. It cost $16. I can prove it."

I still bump into Sunny every now and then and, unbeknownst to him, I feel a tiny connection between us, like he's my friend but he doesn't know about that. It makes me feel good to see him, but wouldn't make any sense to tell him so. Someday, Sunny might read this book and recognize his role in my story. That would be a nice thing.

—∞—

In 1987, while enrolled at Chico State, I flew back to Missouri for a visit with Grams and Gramps.

Grams cooked ground venison spaghetti in a cast iron skillet for supper, being unaware that people generally mix up spaghetti in something other than a skillet. The venison was killed by Gramps earlier that winter, but not on purpose. It was road kill. An unfortunate doe had wandered into the road about halfway down the hill between their house and the doughnut shop and got plastered by Grandpa's car, so he called the local game warden and asked for permission to haul it home, which he did, then he cut and wrapped it in the kitchen with Grandma's help.

Grams pulled a few squirrels out of the freezer for dinner the next day…critters that Gramps had shot the previous October. She fried them in the spaghetti skillet with a bit of water to "tender 'em up a little bit."

In 1989, just before I graduated from college, my grandparents flew back to California for their 50th wedding anniversary celebration in the Orland Grange Hall, a location that turned out to be too small, given what seemed like about five hundred folks who showed up to participate. Gramps was pushing 70 and rode back and forth from Chico to the Orland festivities in my truck, refusing to wear his seatbelt, stretching it over his shoulder instead, manually holding it in place, just to reduce the risk of a ticket from a passing cop who might notice my elderly passenger who refused to buckle-up.

Gramps was consumed by fears of burning to death if I wrecked the truck and trapped him inside, held against his will by a seatbelt that wouldn't let loose after a fiery accident. And he was terribly concerned about the ability of the human race to survive upcoming years, the difficult ones, another Depression, just say. He feared that the proficiency to hitch mules to a plow was lacking in modern society. Mule-plowing men such as himself were disappearing, and that concerned him, immensely, as I discovered on our drive from Chico to Orland while he stubbornly held a seatbelt across his chest and lamented the fate of a world bereft of men with the knowledge necessary to plow a field.

Over the ensuing years, I had many conversations with my grandparents about our childhoods, Gramps' and mine, good and bad. We bonded over memories of my summer adventures in Orland, and they often cried over reflections. They filled me in on the frustration and helplessness they felt during those years. More than once, Grams said, "We should have just kept you kids when they sent you up to Orland on one-way tickets. It's terrible, how Fluffy did you kids," an amazing statement, given how little my grandparents actually knew.

Grams mentioned the electric blanket that she had sent to me in Montana, and the recognition that I was cold as a child, but I don't know where she got that idea from. It did not come from me. I never shared specifics with them. I never told anyone about my chilly nights in the Wyoming trailer when I wanted to ask for the extra yellow blanket in the hall closet, but didn't because blankets, transistor radios and Kool-Aid belonged to Fluffy. Nor did I tell anyone of the occasional times when I slept in my clothes in the Evanston basement to ward off the cold.

My grandparents had nothing more than vague suspicions because Sissy and I rarely talked. That's not what children do. It's the crux of child abuse, banking on the fact that children rarely tell. The certainty of the intimidator. The impotence of the powerless.

Grandpa died in 1991, and shortly after, Grams flew into San Francisco for a visit. I drove her down to Aunt Dot's new house in Santa Cruz.

We sat at the window of a Monterey wharf-side restaurant for dinner that night, boats bobbing up and down in the harbor, waves lapping against wooden pillars of the pier, a slow sun setting on the horizon. It was a stunning location but an unfortunate choice, because Grams didn't do seafood. Or oceans. Or house cats, either, but that's irrelevant. We could just as well have hauled her to Mozambique, as far as she was concerned. Monterey was a completely foreign world at her age of 70-something, and she couldn't rightly eat dinner, what with the pervasive stench of sea salt, rotting fish parts, and other oddities that made her proclaim an inability to understand how anyone could possibly enjoy a meal in such a dreadful place.

"Why, I've never smelt such a terrible thang in all my life!" That's what Grams said.

As an adult, I hid my homosexuality from my grandparents. I didn't want to tell them the truth. To me, it seemed an enormous hurdle for them to overcome. Aunt Donnis thought they had figured it out on their own, but I wasn't willing to risk their rejection by confirming it.

I was forced to tell the truth when Grams flew out to California in 1999 for what turned out to be her final visit. Being that I am the only relative who lives in the Bay Area, I was the logical choice to pick her up in San Francisco and drive her to the family gathering in Chico the next morning, which meant she would stay the night in my home for the first time. The problem was that my home wasn't just my home. I owned it with my partner. Grams knew of his existence and had invented her own explanation for his inclusion in my life as a classic result of the high cost of California housing, but I drove from the airport with my grandmother, wondering if I had a disaster waiting ahead when she was confronted by the truth.

Our drive was uncomfortable and tense. The closer we got to my Oakland home, the more uptight she became and the more I realized that Grams understood the significance of my "roommate." I dreaded their introduction.

We pulled my truck into the driveway…I unloaded her luggage from the back…she met my roommate…and the tension vanished. We gave her a tour of the house and garden, showed her the master bedroom with the king-sized bed where her grandson slept with his roommate, and all of her trepidation melted away. It was unbelievable. At dinnertime, Grams quietly disappeared into the living room. She returned, dragging a rocking chair behind her, and sat in the kitchen and rocked back and forth and laughed and chatted honestly and lovingly while I fried chicken. I couldn't have asked for anything more beautiful than that.

In 1990, Sissy got pregnant for the first time. She soon married the father and I walked her down the aisle on her wedding day because that made much more sense than asking our father to do so. (He wasn't invited, in case you're wondering.) Tragically, she lost that child soon after birth, then moved to a trailer park south of Seattle and had three more children. Shortly after becoming a mother for the second time, she returned to The Truth and took her husband with her.

I told Grams about it.

"I don't know why they want to get mixed up with that cult!"

That's what Grams said, not much liking Jehovah's Witnesses. She was disappointed when I shared the news of Sissy's return, but even though I don't share Sissy's beliefs, in many ways I think The Truth is good for her. She is very certain that her religion is the only road to God and I am equally certain that it isn't, but some people need answers to problems, and when Sissy got to that point, I think she found it very easy to re-embrace her old religion.

She's happy being a Witness and I'm happy for her. As odd as that sounds, I still feel my responsibility as her protective brother. I have seen her living conditions in a singlewide trailer while holding down a part-time job at Wal-Mart. I have listened to her struggles with enormous health problems, and I've seen her tears over the stresses of marriage and financial inadequacies, and at those moments, I am glad that she's a Witness. It doesn't matter that I don't share her conviction for The Truth. It doesn't matter that I see so much of her life as a mirror image of our father's. The Witnesses give her a hope for a better existence after Armageddon. They give her the same gift they gave our father—an explanation for why life isn't easy and a belief that hers will get better when God "brings this wicked system to an end." They provide simple answers for people who have found rock bottom. That's a good thing and I'm glad she has it, in spite of my belief that the main ingredient behind religion is often a pile of horseshit.

⎯⎯ ⎯⎯

My mother and I are alike in so many ways, a surprising fact, given that we had no contact as I grew up. We're both stubborn and strong willed, traits I didn't know about as a child but are clearly big pieces of who I am as an adult. It's confirmation to me that nature has more influence over your identity than nurture.

Interestingly enough, Mom doesn't know much about our history with Fluffy, but she is aware of Sissy's struggle to reveal or bury it. Mom caught her first glimpse on my twelfth birthday, April 4, 1976. The day Sissy escaped. Their Sunday afternoon drive out of Fillmore was filled with depression and elation. A Sunday afternoon battle between Sissy's guilt for leaving me behind and the conflict she found at the joy of her own departure.

Sissy and I had one unintentional discussion with Mom on that topic when she found herself in the middle of the ritual-bonding-reliving-the-old-days conversation that Sissy and I often have. It was painful to hear and I think it gave her a tremendously heavy sense of guilt, but it shouldn't have, because it wasn't her fault. Young and immature mothers often give their children up for adoption, and that is essentially what mine did. I can't fault her for that. There is no connection, in my mind, to her inability to embrace her responsibility as a mother and the inability of my father to protect us from Fluffy. I'm not certain if Mom is aware of my feelings or understands how I've resolved the lack of her presence as I grew up, but my father's choices are completely unrelated to those made by her. His choices aren't her fault. But it's upsetting to hear details, so we've never had that conversation again. Our relationship isn't a typical mother/son interaction, but that's okay. We're content with what we have, and that's a good thing.

──🙘🙙🙚──

I have imagined that, if Grant and Amber ever read this story, they won't believe it. I think they have acquired a trait from our father in that they are completely incapable of wondering why Sissy and I left their home. They can't possibly know why their older siblings disappeared and they have never asked since. They were too young to recognize the disparity in our lives, and besides, things that aren't normal can sometimes become normal when you don't know any different.

They've had almost no contact with my father's side of the family throughout their lives, but my cousin Sheri hosted a family gathering when her mother, my Aunt Donnis, was dying from cancer. We about fell over in shock when Amber walked in the door with Virgil and Fluffy. Amber hugged me without first introducing herself, but I didn't recognize her, not having seen her in almost twenty years. I couldn't deal with the unexpected appearance of her mother, so I left the party when Amber was done with her hug—a snub which Amber took personally. That's too bad, because I didn't mean it personally. It wasn't her fault.

As Aunt Donnis's death got closer, Virgil and Fluffy called a few times, offering to visit her in those final days. She didn't understand why.

"I don't hardly know those people," she told me.

In one of her phone calls with my father, the topic apparently shifted to some disparaging comments about my being gay. He quoted scriptures and Aunt Donnis essentially told him to go to hell. That was the last time he offered to see her.

The following year, Grant left a message on my office voicemail. He only lives an hour away, so I returned his call and invited him and his new wife to my house for dinner, just to get acquainted. His wife was really nice, and I thought we had a very pleasant evening. I braised tuna steaks with green olives for our meal, served over polenta, but in hindsight, that wasn't a good choice. I really like that dish, but I don't think Grant's wife was a fan. Regardless, I enjoyed their company and thought Grant had grown into a likable adult. It felt good to reconnect with him, with the exception of two rough spots.

We had a brief mention of my unwillingness to associate with his mother, and a very small comment about my no longer believing in The Truth. Out loud, I speculated that my being gay would conflict with their religion and restrict their ability to have anything more than a shallow relationship with me, but Grant assured me that he would overlook that problem. He also said that, as an adult, he had proven to himself that The Truth was the truth. I commented on how that was a good thing because, let's face it, if you belong to a church that calls itself "The Truth," you might as well believe you do, in fact, have the truth. So we swapped email addresses after dinner, and a week later I sent them a note, thanking them for having dinner with me. I included a list of addresses and phone numbers for all the family members that Grant doesn't know.

I've never heard from him again. I don't know why, but I think he was probably so freaked out over being in the home of two homosexuals who were perfectly normal guys with a perfectly normal life in a perfectly normal house with no dresses in their closet, that he couldn't imagine ever having a meaningful connection with me. I have even imagined that he might have concocted a fantasy similar to mine as a teenager. A fantasy of how I would save Sissy from Satan and fulfill my obligation to Jehovah—to save my sister from this wicked system and bring her back to The Truth. I've often wondered if Grant had formed an identical fantasy in his own teenage years, only to have it burst when he got to know me as an adult, realizing I would never again share his religion.

<hr />

My buddy Rowdy got married in Montana a few years ago, and I was best man at his wedding. Since then, Rowdy has had two sons. He named the first Xzavier and the second Zyggmund. That's right. Zyggmund. With two 'g's. My spellchecker doesn't know what to do with either of those names, which is understandable. Rowdy refers to his boys as X and Z. Swear to God.

Our friend Ingrid attended Rowdy's wedding. It was the first time we had seen each other since I practically fled Montana and showed no interest in marrying her. We had a falling out several years after I left, brought on by my thinking that it was time to tell her I was gay. So I confessed to being gay in a long phone call, after which she sent a letter filled with Bible quotes and what she referred to as "Christian love." We didn't talk for several years after that. That whole "love the sinner, hate the sin" mentality doesn't sound very nice when accompanied by scriptures that recommend putting me to death.

But we reconciled several years later, and it was really nice to catch up with her at Rowdy's wedding. Ingrid married a farm boy after I left Montana, just to please her parents, and after two children and 20 years of an abusive marriage, she is on the verge of divorcing him. Her parents have practically disowned her for that. Their preacher insists that Ingrid's only role in life is to submit to the will of her husband, the Bible says so, and she has committed an unforgivable sin by seeking a divorce.

Ingrid no longer adheres so strongly to the Baptist faith. That's understandable.

—∞—

As an adult, I've been back to Orland a few times and have found that things generally look the same, albeit poorer. The whole town has dried up and is no longer a destination for poor immigrant Okies. It is now a struggling community of Hispanic farm workers, fighting to overcome their own poverty. It's déjà vu in a different color. Unfortunately for Orland, practically every downtown building is now vacant. Nobody parks in the middle of the street, anymore. There are plenty of empty slots along the curb and most residents drive twenty-five miles to shop at the Wal-Mart in Chico.

The Orland Frosty Cone shop has disappeared and the old movie theatre has been converted into a part-time fundamentalist church where mostly-poor and mostly-white people go to sing Hallelujah and praise the Lord on weekends. The auction yard was torn down and a cheap strip-mall now stands in its place.

I've also been back to Redding a few times in the last twenty years and have driven out to Aunt Dot's old house twice, just to see it again. She doesn't live there anymore and you can't actually see more than a section of the roof from the end of the dirt road, but I've parked by the corral where we kept the rope cattle and sat there and cried. Not the bad kind of cry, but the good kind. The kind when you're so engulfed in emotion from old events that you can't help but cry. I quietly whispered "Thank you" under my breath, even though there was no one around to hear me say it. I'll go back there again someday…I'll again murmur "thank you"…and again I'll cry…but that's okay. It's the good kind.

Aunt Jan took me on a drive to visit the non-existent town of Newville awhile back, just to wrap ourselves in family history. There's not much of anything to see in the town of Newville except for a pretty little creek with thick stands of cottonwood trees that I remember being much smaller thirty years ago. There isn't even a place to stop for a Coke. Most of the old site is now covered by corrals and loading pens, and cowboys on horseback marking and branding calves.

We slowly drove by to watch present-day cowboys from the Drew Ranch sort cattle. They drove calves across the creek, perhaps the very same spot where my young father went skinny-dipping in hot summer months. I felt a tremendous urge to stop my truck and have a brief chat with them. I wanted to point out where, fifty years earlier, my grandfather had built a smokehouse to cure bear hams. I wanted to tell them that, up on the hill overlooking town, old bachelor Byron Milsap's house had once stood and my aunts were still telling stories of their lovely visits with him.

Byron Milsap has long since died and his house burned to the ground. Aunt Donnis speculated that Byron might have been gay. She wondered if he had lived a lonely existence in Newville simply because he had few choices, being gay at that time. Aunt Jan said the only original building still in existence in town is the gas station booth, but it is unidentifiable as such and in danger of falling over and erasing all that is left to mark the memory of Newville. Cattle now lean against that decrepit shack, and it is on the brink of collapsing into a pile of rotten lumber.

Grandpa's ashes were scattered at the lonely Newville cemetery, per his request, but don't tell anyone about that. He's not supposed to be there. That burial ground is reserved for original Newville families who built the town and ranches that sustained it, albeit for a short time. My grandfather doesn't qualify for inclusion, being only a poor immigrant Okie, but that cemetery is the most appropriate place for him to rest. It's beautiful and he will be happy there...mostly under a magnificent old oak tree, overlooking the creekside meadow in back. I say "mostly" because he got scattered in parts. Some parts went over by the barbed wire fence on the east side, a few parts elsewhere. But, if you want to hang out proper with Gramps when you go visit, he's for the most part killing time under the oak tree. When I go, I think I might join him. Perhaps my ashes will be scattered there as well. Hopefully under the same oak, and hopefully a long, long time from now. I'm not in a hurry to spend eternity in Newville, but you gotta put these requests in early, you know.

————∞∞∞————

My father still isolates himself from family. His contact is infrequent, his phone calls are rare and superficial, and he is still waiting for Armageddon to change his life. The generation of 1914 is as dead as can be and Armageddon still hasn't arrived, but he continues to preach that "the end is near." In my mind, his religion has allowed him to check out of reality for most of his adult life—certainly during my childhood when the blinders of faith obscured his chance of having realistic hopes for the future.

Over the last couple of decades, relatives and old family friends have occasionally asked dumb questions of me...like, "How's your dad?" and "Have you talked to him recently?" It irritates the snot out of me when people ask those questions. I struggle at those moments, wondering why they would ask something so ridiculous. Why would they ask? What should I tell them? Don't they know?

Generally, I just force a smile and mumble something along the lines of, "No, we haven't talked in awhile" and leave it at that, because the truth is, no one knows. Sissy didn't tell. I didn't tell. People have only known that we left home early—she went to Mom's and I wound up at Aunt Dot's, and as the years have gone by, I've always thought it was too late to explain.

I've had a few occasions over the last twenty-five years to talk with my dad, none initiated by me.

We had a telephone conversation in 1997 when I shared a small piece of my pent-up anger. I asked why I struggled to find enough to eat in Fluffy's home. I asked if he knew how underweight I was when I showed up on Aunt Dot's doorstep.

"Why did you treat me that way?" I asked him.

He answered, "When you were a baby, you got sick if you ate too much, and that's why we didn't let you eat much when you were growing up."

I mentioned my crawling into the horse trailer in the middle of Wyoming winters.

"Why did I have to do that?" I asked. "And how could you not feel my pain when I told you about it?"

"Well, I didn't think you needed to do that very often," he answered. This is my father.

I asked why we didn't get Kool-Aid. That was a mistake. He laughed off the stupidity of that complaint. It sounded silly to complain about not getting Kool-Aid.

He did invite me over for a barbecue. I declined. Armageddon still hasn't arrived, but if I attend his barbecue, I know what will happen. Any discussion of my childhood will be off limits, but he will slide in a few comments of how near Armageddon must be. We are in the last days, he will remind me. The end is near, he will say. The New Order will solve our problems, he believes.

Sissy attempted to rebuild her relationship with Virgil and Fluffy after she returned to the Jehovah's Witnesses. As a Christian, she decided that she must forgive and forget what they had done to her. They attended some Kingdom Hall meetings together and commiserated about the evil forces in this wicked system of things. They shared some prayers to Jehovah. Craving closure, Sissy attempted to open verbal dialogue of her years of abuse at their hands, but her attempts were rebuffed.

In frustration, she eventually gave them an ultimatum. Take some responsibility for her miserable childhood, she said, or abandon their newly established relationship. They chose the latter.

Sissy and I don't associate with Virgil and Fluffy anymore. We know how it feels to wake each morning, desperately hoping for a shred of approval for existence…very aware of the mess it makes when childhood messages get inside your head and play hell with all that seems right. I spent at least ten years after getting out of their control, waking with sweaty and angry nightmares. Jolted from sleep by visions of my childhood, pounding the pillow in anger and wanting retribution. Awakened by tears for not understanding why. Those awful memories came back to visit on many nights, frequently haunting me, and didn't dwindle away until my first romantic relationship when my first boyfriend taught me that I could love myself and others would, too.

THE POINT OF THIS STORY

Religion still invades my life today. When Sissy returned to the Jehovah's Witnesses, our relationship died. Sissy fears that, if she accepts a homosexual into her present life, she will forfeit her future life when Armageddon arrives. Not only that, but I am an "apostate," which is the pejorative phrase for someone who voluntarily abandons The Truth. For Jehovah's Witnesses, one can't be anything worse than an apostate, except perhaps, for being gay. I am gay. I am a worldly homosexual apostate. In my sister's eyes, I can't get any closer to being bound to the Devil. Her religion tells her so.

It's a shame that religion can come between people who love each other. It's always a struggle. For both of us. I wish it wasn't. I like to hope that religion will someday loosen its grip on her, but I have no faith that will ever happen. I have very little faith at all, in fact, when it comes to religion. I no longer believe in religion.

I feel immensely fortunate to no longer belong to the Jehovah's Witnesses, but it wasn't an intentional desertion. My journey out of that faith didn't come overnight. It only came through subsequent years of viewing the world without the distortion of religious sunglasses. Over time, my belief that The Truth is the truth faded into nothing, and today, I no longer have a scrap of religious dogma in my body. Theological absolutes no longer ring my bell.

In spite of the fact that I have an enormous distaste for organized religion, I do believe there is a higher purpose to the universe and perhaps an afterlife. Spiritual, but not religious, people say. That's what I am. It's something I don't feel a need to fully understand or explain, but it no longer seems possible to me that any organized religion could own the toll road to God. In my mind, if a Creator exists, He can't possibly care what faith you claim, or what building you attend on Sundays, or which holy book you believe in, or who you love or what religion you're born into or how many times a day you pray, or if you buy a toothpick holder for your stepmother on her birthday. People who believe that God approves of them as they scour the Bible for selected and antiquated rules on daily living, are mistaken. If there is a Creator, I'm convinced He will judge everyone on how they treated others, because the only thing that could possible matter to Him is that you treat people, especially children, like you love them…even if you don't.

—⚯—

It's been almost two months since Grams' passing and her ashes have already been scattered at the Newville cemetery with Grandpa's. We held a family gathering to remember her yesterday. Most of her family met at Aunt Jan's house where her son Jason pan-fried venison and elk steaks for lunch—the most appropriate meal we could have in memory of Grams.

The Virgil and Fluffy and Grant and Amber contingent didn't attend. Amber was giving birth to her second baby that week, which provided a convenient excuse for Dad to miss his mother's service, just as he missed his father's service.

I understand that when we held Grandpa's funeral many years ago, Dad was parked in his truck around the corner from the Baptist church. I wonder what thoughts were with him while he sat alone. Did he shed tears? Did he feel lonely? Did he reminisce about life and family, dreaming about "what-ifs" and "do-overs?" Did he wonder why he drove two hundred miles to the memorial service, only to isolate himself in the solitude of an empty truck? Did he believe his God would abandon him if he entered a church of differing beliefs? I don't know how he felt while refusing to show up to the celebration of his father's life, but I think he couldn't join us, even if he wanted to, because he doesn't approve of entering churches other than a Kingdom Hall, even for a memorial to honor his father. That's truly sad.

I drove home last night after the celebration, a long and ponderous ride with thoughts of Grams and her descendants and conclusions that everything had come full circle and life was good and everything was right. I am so thankful for the ripples that my grandparents cast into my life. And my wonderful aunts, and the minor acts of kindness from all those people I hardly knew.

And that's the point of this story…to say thank you.

Thank You.

I love you, Grams.